Worlds at the End

In the series *Critical Race, Indigeneity, and Relationality*,
edited by Antonio T. Tiongson Jr., Danika Medak-Saltzman, Iyko Day,
and Shanté Paradigm Smalls

ALSO IN THIS SERIES:

Wendi Yamashita, *Carceral Entanglements: Gendered Public Memories of Japanese American World War II Incarceration*
Joo Ok Kim, *Warring Genealogies: Race, Kinship, and the Korean War*
Maryam S. Griffin, *Vehicles of Decolonization: Public Transit in the Palestinian West Bank*
Erin Suzuki, *Ocean Passages: Navigating Pacific Islander and Asian American Literatures*
Quynh Nhu Le, *Unsettled Solidarities: Asian and Indigenous Cross-Representations in the Américas*

Pacharee Sudhinaraset

Worlds at the End

Los Angeles, Infrastructure, and the Apocalyptic Imagination

TEMPLE UNIVERSITY PRESS
Philadelphia • *Rome* • *Tokyo*

TEMPLE UNIVERSITY PRESS
Philadelphia, Pennsylvania 19122
tupress.temple.edu

Copyright © 2024 by Pacharee Sudhinaraset
All rights reserved
Published 2024

Cover and information graphic design by Once–Future Office

Library of Congress Cataloging-in-Publication Data

Names: Sudhinaraset, Pacharee, 1980– author.
Title: Worlds at the end : Los Angeles, infrastructure, and the apocalyptic imagination / Pacharee Sudhinaraset.
Other titles: Critical race, indigeneity, and relationality.
Description: Philadelphia : Temple University Press, 2024. | Series: Critical race, indigeneity, and relationality | Includes bibliographical references and index. | Summary: "This book mobilizes a women of color feminist reading practice to examine the role of Los Angeles's infrastructure in literary works by Indigenous, Black, Asian American, and Latinx writers for whom the catastrophic breakdown of the U.S. settler state is the moment of resurgent possibility"— Provided by publisher.
Identifiers: LCCN 2024016416 (print) | LCCN 2024016417 (ebook) | ISBN 9781439925508 (cloth) | ISBN 9781439925515 (paperback) | ISBN 9781439925522 (pdf)
Subjects: LCSH: American literature—Minority authors—History and criticism. | End of the world in literature. | Colonization in literature. | Built environment—California—Los Angeles. | Los Angeles (Calif.)—In literature, | LCGFT: Literary criticism.
Classification: LCC PS153.M56 S83 2024 (print) | LCC PS153.M56 (ebook) | DDC 810.9/3279494—dc23/eng/20240725
LC record available at https://lccn.loc.gov/2024016416
LC ebook record available at https://lccn.loc.gov/2024016417

9 8 7 6 5 4 3 2 1

For my Mama, Papa, Belén, and Nara

Contents

	Acknowledgments	ix
	Introduction: Writing for the End of the World	1
1.	Los Angeles's Infrastructural Palimpsest: An Apocalyptic Origin Story	21
2.	Archipelagos of Refugee Worlding: Survival under Cold War Military Infrastructures	67
3.	Infrastructures of Termination and Esther Belin's Imagination of Decolonial Mobility	99
4.	Infrastructures of Flight: Life on the Roads of a Disintegrating World	127
	Coda: The Dark Century, or The Century of Light	149
	Notes	155
	Bibliography	183
	Index	197

Acknowledgments

This book is an outgrowth from the labors, visions, support, and hopes from a collective of family, teachers, mentors, friends, and coconspirators. I could never adequately thank everyone, but I will try my best to do so here.

To my parents, Jitlada and Sirivat Sudhinaraset, who worked themselves to the bone raising my sisters and me. Thank you, mama, for your fire and spirit, and for always reminding me to speak to our ancestors, even to those I have never met. Thank you to my papa, for his steadfastness, patience, and calm. Even though I know my parents might never read my book, I hope it makes them feel proud. My parents also gave me a cheerleading squad and the best set of friends that a person could ever ask for. My eldest sister, Vacharee Sudhinaraset Oberbeck, taught me how to be brave and loyal as she chased away schoolyard bullies; my little sister May Sudhinaraset continues to show me that anything is possible with her unending optimism and hard work; and my youngest sister Amy Sudhinaraset teaches me to seek beauty and adventure in all things every single day. All three of them model for me how to be a good sister, daughter, mother, and friend.

Growing up in Long Beach, California, I was lucky to be one of many who were raised by a network of aunties and uncles: Nitaya Pungauthaikan, Sujitra Natipadab, Suvimol Natipadab, Doungporn Panichpakdee, Thaveesub Pungauthaikan, Prayuth Panichpakdee, Soropong Natipadab, Somsak Nateepadab, Kunlaya Natipadab, Suvad and Carol Natipadab. Some are still with us and some aren't, but they all remain. They in turn gave me brilliant cousins who have rounded out my cheer squad: Tanya Panichpakdee, Mina Panichpakdee, Dungjai Pungauthaikan, Niyada Pungauthaikan, Parichart Pungauthaikan, Suvad Anthony Natipadab, Ryan Panichpakdee, Robert Panichpakdee, and Michael Natipadab. Thank you to my brothers Mike Tsui, Kenny Kong, Michael Oberbeck, Miah Cook, and Chris Lee for your love and care throughout the years. My sweethearts Elizabeth, Paul, Emily, Samantha, Amali, Miles, and Amaya have brought me such joy.

My thanks to my teachers at University of California, Irvine (UCI), Lindon W. Barrett, Jason Denman, Beheroze F. Shroff, and Victoria Silver. Lindon played a pivotal role in my pursuit of graduate studies and he is deeply missed. At the University of Washington (UW) I was able to develop the political questions that were only beginning to emerge when I was an undergraduate at UCI. At UW, I encountered faculty, students, and other community members who introduced me to decolonial feminist pedagogies that continue to influence me. My dissertation advisors Chandan Reddy and Tom Foster were ideal mentors. Tom Foster's intellectual depth of knowledge astounded all of us. Chandan Reddy's generosity, care, brilliance, and political commitments are unceasing, and I hope I grow up to be just like him some day. I will always value Moon-Ho Jung's grounded life advice and intellectual guidance. I remain grateful to Eva Cherniavsky for her wisdom and friendship, and to Caroline Simpson, Anis Bawarshi, Juan Guerra, John Webster, Rick Bonus, Stephen H. Sumida, Gail Nomura, and Elizabeth Simmons-O'Neill for modeling how to be a teacher and a mentor.

During my studies at UW, a cohort of graduate students helped me understand the stakes of our work and at the same time they made Seattle home. I will always be grateful to Kate Boyd, Sydney Fonteyn Lewis, Sooja Kelsey, Jason Morse, Jed Murr, Christian Ravela, Suzanne Schmidt, and Simón V. Trujillo for the cultural organizing work we did together through the Race/Knowledge Project. I learned so much from each and every one of them. Thank you also to Mike Viola, Andrew Rose, Curtis Hisayasu, Jane Lee, Raj Chetty, Melanie Hernandez, and Angela Rounsaville for their friendship. My dear friends Kate Boyd, Suzanne Schmidt, Christian Ravela, and Sergio Casillas were the best mix of fun, intense, and brilliant writing buddies. What would I have done without you all?

My friends and colleagues at New York University have given me vital support and encouragement in developing and finishing this book. The English Department has been a great source of inspiration for me and I am grateful to Elizabeth McHenry, Crystal Parikh, Sonya Posmentier, Haruko (Hal) Momma, John M. Archer, Patrick Deer, Lennie Hanson, Nicholas Boggs, Elaine Freedgood, Jini Kim Watson, Honey Crawford, Dara Regaignon,

Sonali Thakkar, Zachary Samalin, Urayoán Noel, Greg Vargo, Phillip Brian Harper, Toral Gajarawala, Thomas Augst, Wendy Lee, Jennifer Baker, Julia Jarcho, Patricia Crain, Juliet Fleming, Maureen McClane, Lytle Shaw, Christopher Cannon, Una Chauduri, Rajeswari Sunder Rajan, Andrea Adomako, Carolyn Dinshaw, Paul Edwards, Lisa Gitelman, Ernest Gilman, Misho Ishikawa, Jenny Mann, Paula McDowell, Cyrus Patell, Jess Row, Martha Rust, John Waters, Sukhdev Sandhu, John Guillory, Bryan Waterman, Brandon Woolf, and Robert Young. Hal has been an exceptional mentor and Crystal must have read my entire book manuscript at least three times. Thank you to Alyssa Leál, Lissette Florez, Patricia Okoh-Esene, Mary Mezzano, and Jaysen Henderson-Greenbey for being such wizards at keeping everything running and for the important role they play in maintaining our community. Seeing Hancil Celestine each morning when I entered my office at 244 Greene Street to write reminded me that everything would be all right.

I am grateful to S. Heijin Lee, Dean Itsuji Saranillio, Paula Chakravartty, Feng-Mei Heberer, Hentyle Yapp, Chris Barker, Valerie Forman, Kimberly Phillips-Fein, Cecilia Marquez, Liz Ellis, Tao Leigh Goffe, Amita Manghanani, and Laura Chen-Schultz for their inspiring political and intellectual commitment. I am incredibly thankful for the invigorating conversations with colleagues through my fellowship at the NYU Center for the Humanities from 2021 to 2022: Ulrich Baer, Molly Rogers, Alia Ayman, Derek Baron, Paula Chakravartty, Terrence Cullen, Karen Elizabeth Finley, Isaac Hand, Feng-Mei Heberer, S. Heijin Lee, Melissa Lefkowitz, Wendy Lotterman, Pamela Newkirk, Cristina Vatulescu, and Matthew Zundel. I want to further thank the NYU Center for Humanities for awarding me a Book Subvention Grant during the final stages of this book's completion. I would also like to thank the students I have had the privilege of encountering and working alongside: Miriam Juarez, Mariana Romero, Estefany Lopez, Heba Jehama, Nicholas Silcox, Corey Risinger, Yuxin Zheng, Zohal Karimy, Nicholas Caldwell, Dan Truong, Sarah Shea, Justin Aoba, Ya-Yun Ko, Samuel Teets, Sheyuan Wang, Ellen Tagtmeier, Smaran Dayal, Alex Ramos, Mercedes Trigos, Nicole Eitzen Delgado, Xavier Fitzsimmons Cruz, Nicholas M. Duron, and Jake Gianaris. You've all made this job all the more worthwhile. Thank you to Bret Beaufeaux, Danielle Berkman, Adam Spanenberg, Abdul Wasay Majumder, Cecil Louden, and Albaro for cultivating community at Coral Tower for my family. Thank you to Kate Baier, Kerri Smith, Ashley Richardson, and all of the Faculty Fellows in Residence for your steady presence over the past few years. The Global Asias Summer Institute writing group with Heijin, Mei, and Hentyle fostered a support system that sustains me still. To my cosmic twin, Heijin, your commitment to friendship, family, motherhood, and intellectual labor is moving. I am grateful for my conversations and inspiring exchanges with Hee-Jung Serenity Joo, Stephen Sohn, Victor Mendoza, Lisa Lowe, Helen Zia, Karen Tei Yamashita, Maxine Hong Kingston, Katy Xiong, and Betsy Huang. Min Song and Laura Kang provided invaluable feedback at a crucial time during my manuscript workshop.

    I am honored to publish my book with Temple University Press, which has made significant contributions in U.S. Ethnic Studies. Shaun Vigil has been an ideal editor and supporter of the project. Thank you to the entire team at Temple who have helped see this through to the end: William Forest, Gary Kramer, Irene Imperio Kull, Ashley Petrucci, and Jamie Armstrong. My thanks to the two anonymous readers for their thoughtful and insightful feedback, and the coeditors of the Critical Race, Indigeneity, and Relationality series, Antonio T. Tiongson Jr., Danika Medak-Saltzman, Iyko Day, and Shanté Paradigm Smalls. I am particularly indebted to Iyko Day, who generously gave me feedback on draft after draft of the entire manuscript throughout 2023 as I was wrapping up my revisions. I thank her for pushing me to make bolder claims, for her unending encouragement, and for her invaluable feedback. Many thanks to Kali Handelman for being an exemplary developmental editor, for helping me build the book up, and for sifting through a great deal of feedback. Thank you to Josh Rutner for working on the index in the final stage. I am honored to have Rob Sato's beautiful watercolor painting serve as my book cover. For a long time, it has been the only way I could picture the book in my hands, so thank you Rob for your magical vision. To the geniuses at Once–Future Office—Taylor Hale, Dungjai Pungauthaikan, and Gilda Gross—thank you for being able to visualize the "maps" and openings for every chapter, and for designing the cover of my book. What a wonderful process we shared.

    Thank you to my friends and family who have nourished me over the years. Gail B. Fox, Robert Fox, Ventura and Cruzita Chávez, and Michelle Trujillo have modeled regeneration, endurance, and love, and I will be forever grateful for their kinship and support. Thank you, Pedro Trujillo and Margie Trujillo, for your warmth and kindness. Salumeh Eslamieh, Jyotswaroop Bawa, Marie Antoinette Antonio, María Del Mar Hernandez Mercado, Andrés Aceves, Sean Tollison, and Kathy Fletcher-Tollison have always kept my spirits up and given me plenty of encouragement. When I arrived in New York in 2014 with a four-month-old, in a new city, with a new job, Lornette Lewis, Myen Zablan, and Lamarana Bah took care of Belén and eventually Nara. We are so lucky to have them in our lives. Thank you to my New York family, Dungjai Pungauthaikan, Christopher Lee, Milana, Elle, Mina Panichpakdee, Niti Poosomboon, Nikki Chung, Doug Daniels, Nomi, Théa, Nicholas Chan, and María Alejandra (Male) Sandoval Avila, for the care, celebrations, food, good times, and for grounding life over here on the East Coast.

Finally, thank you to my three loves. Simón V. Trujillo, words are wholly insufficient in describing how important you are. With you there is everything. Thank you for reading my manuscript more than anyone else has ever read anything, and for loving me and our babies so well. Belén and Nara, thank you for your spirit, your wisdom, and your kindness as your dad and I continually learn how to be your parents. You teach us so much and I cannot wait to see what other wonders you will bring.

Worlds at the End

WRITING FOR THE END OF THE WORLD

- Uruguay • San Salvador • Cuba • Haiti • Dominican Republic • Jamaica • Trinidad
- Venezuela • Brazil • Patagonia • Argentina • North Carolina • New York • Canada
- Pacific Ocean • Catalina Island • San Clemente Island • Bay of San Diego • Bay of Santa Monica • Bay of Smoke of San Pedro • Bay of Monterey • Hudson Bay • Plymouth Rock
- Los Angeles • El Pueblo de Nuestra Señora la Reina de Los Ángeles de Porciúncula
- Tovaangar • Arroyo Seco Parkway • 110 Pasadena Freeway • LA River • Manzanar Concentration Camp • Yaangna • LA Aqueduct • Owens Valley • Freeway System
- LA bridges • East Los Angeles • Mexico • Tijuana • Koreatown • Chinatown • 110 Harbor Freeway • Pacific Rim • Mazatlan • Downtown LA • Pimu • San Clemente Islands • Kinkipar
- Hollywood • Vietnam • San Diego • Camp Pendleton • Guam • Philippines • Wake Island
- Hong Kong • Thailand • Malaysia • Indonesia • Okinawa • Samoa • Hawaii • Singapore
- South China Sea • Institute of American Indian Arts • Sherman Institute • Riverside
- The Four Corners • Dinétah • Perris • UC Berkeley • Robledo • Acorn • Milky Way

Introduction

> Lord, I confess I want the clarity of
> catastrophe but not the catastrophe.
> Like everyone else,
> I want a storm I can dance in.
> I want an excuse to change my life.
> —"Catastrophe Is Next to Godliness," Franny Choi

> Write the things which thou hast seen, and the things
> which are, and the things which shall be hereafter . . .
> and what is past and passing and to come.
> —Revelation 1:19

This book begins at the End. A vexing concept usually marking the closure of time, an epoch, or an event, the end may also signal the unveiling, a remainder, or the emergence of something new, even if we do not yet know what it is. A revelation, the apocalypticist would call it, or perhaps, in poet Franny Choi's terms, a "clarity of catastrophe" where the "world keeps ending, and the world goes on."[1] Toward the end of the twentieth century, in her 1997 novel *Tropic of Orange*, Japanese American writer Karen Tei Yamashita irreverently pondered the moment that initiated the end of the world. Arcangel, the novel's performance artist and prophet of doom, is first introduced on the steps of an opera house in Montevideo, Uruguay. He proclaims: "*The end of the world as we know it is coming!*" Taking on the character name Chilam Quetzal, he gesticulates wildly, and air-clicks away on an imaginary calculator, assessing when we should expect subsequent doomsdays based on the ancient Mayan fifty-two-year calendrical cycle. Following Christopher Columbus's journey across the ocean and into the Caribbean, Arcangel declares that the "discovery" of San Salvador, Cuba, Haiti, and the Dominican Republic in 1492 initiated a cycle of catastrophe that would place the end of the world in 2012. The year 1492, "the great discovery" and "the great curse," could be the "last greatest moment of doom." Arcangel then quickly disrupts the idea of 1492 as *the* moment of doom as he pauses to consider how the first doom could be marked by Columbus's "discovery" of Jamaica in 1494, or Trinidad and Venezuela in 1498, even as "others might place the first doom in 1502 when Columbus discovered Martinique." Restructuring the space-time coordinates of 1492 as the originary moment of the cataclysm of conquest,[2] doomsdays unfold across the "New World" and its newly christened harbors, bays, oceans, and rivers in the expansion of Western European empires. In every instance, the end is marked in the "discovery" and paradoxical beginning of a new world order, reflecting the eschatological time of apocalypse wherein the *eschata* (the last things) are already laid in the *prota* (the first things). Tracking the pathways of colonization to remap a landscape of apocalypse, Yamashita makes immanent the temporal relationship between the end and beginning *in place* where—and not only *when*—the end/beginning are always already present in each other.[3] Eschewing the notion of a singular catastrophe, Yamashita reveals how the world has ended in many places only to continue, over and over again, elsewhere. With these recalculations in mind, doomsday is far-reaching, happening anywhere and all the time, and yet also never comes.

In its common usage, the apocalyptic has become synonymous with destruction and catastrophe itself and is a phenomenon that has secular and eschatological significance. In its origin, apocalypse is a narrative about transformation. Before 1500 B.C.E., Egyptians, Sumerians, Babylonians, and Indo-Iranians believed that the world was created and protected by the gods. While there was instability and chaos in the world, they believed that the world could never be destroyed, would remain unchanged, and would exist endlessly. Sometime between 1400 and 1000 B.C.E., the Iranian prophet Zarathustra (Avestan in his native language, Zartosht in modern Persian, and Zoroastra in Greek) disrupted this static worldview and promised a total transformation and perfecting of the world through the destruction of life. This presented a radically new perception in which time and history and human responsibility disrupted the fixity of the known world, which now stood on the verge of destruction and paradise (from the Old Persian word *paira-daêza*).[4] In this way, apocalypse is connected to a new and "better" world (ushering in a paradise for some—presumably the righteous—and destruction for others). In the centuries that followed, Judaic, Christian, and Islamic eschatological beliefs developed from Zoroastrian apocalyptic notions of monotheistic worship, Paradise, Heaven and Hell, Judgment Day, the final revelation, Satan, angels, and demons.[5] At its root, the apocalyptic is about an unveiling, from the Greek word *Apokalypsis*, meaning "something uncovered." It signifies a revealing of the mysterious divine, a reading, or the uncovering of a series of events leading up to the end of the world; it is located, significantly, in the word. In its religious mandate, the apocalyptic is an imperative to write God's message to uncover visions for the future. The book of Revelation is John's response to God's call to "write the things which though has seen, the things which are, and the things which shall be hereafter . . . and what is past and passing and to come" (Revelation 1:19).[6] If apocalypse is at its core about an errand to write presciently, then literary scholars have much to offer in the understanding of the end of the world and the work of revelation.

The literary texts I study work in the breakdown of secular and religious genealogies of apocalypse and seize upon this errand to write things anew amid a world ablaze. In this account, the apocalyptic is not only an imminent moment of doom but also a narrative of regeneration that differs from religious apocalypse. Within late-twentieth-century Christian millenarianism, human intervention is cast aside through faith in a preordained history where God will save the righteous. It establishes a preordained fate, where the ending has already been crafted, and the beginning and middle are orderly, destined, leaving no room for historical intervention.[7] Although Christian millenarianism provided the U.S. state with a justifying language of good and evil that was fundamental to the emergence of neoliberalism, there remains a deep and abiding tension between an immanent theological hope for the "end times" and the teleological secularism around which liberal institutions and neoliberal governmentality are organized. For neoliberal conservative intellectual Francis Fukuyama, History is not understood as a progression of events; rather, History (with a capital "H") is a coherent, evolutionary process that has been fully formulated through the supposed triumph of capitalism and its ideological struggle against the breakdown of Eastern European communism, and through political shifts in South Asia, Latin America, and Southern Europe toward liberal democratic systems of government.[8]

Notably, *Tropic of Orange* roots its apocalyptic cycles of colonial destruction in 1990s Los Angeles, California, a place that represents an ideal allegory of "worlds at the end," with its well-known roadway and highway infrastructures, its culture industry, and its disaster narratives of racial uprisings, earthquakes, floods, and conflagration. *Worlds at the End* intervenes in critical studies of apocalypse by approaching LA's infrastructure as a palimpsest of colonial pasts and decolonial futures. Rooting the collision of apocalyptic worldings in the very materiality of LA's built environment, Yamashita disrupts the unilinear temporality of colonial modernity. Along with a caravan of Southern migrants and a motley cast of characters, Arcangel literally pulls five hundred years of destructive imperial worldmaking into Southern California's freeway system in his northern migration to fight a wrestling match with SUPERNAFTA, the Lucha Libre embodiment of the North American Free Trade Agreement (NAFTA). Yamashita refuses the disembodiment of neoliberal ideology as the violence of Latin America transects Los Angeles's past and present histories of racial uprisings, genocide, segregation, incarceration, urbanization, and dislocation—for many, clear signs of doom in our modern capitalist world.[9] Refusing to capitulate to a singular catastrophic time, the very structure of the novel is assembled through an overwhelming geographic palimpsest marked by the novel's various characters such that LA emerges as a multinarrative system. Rafaela Cortes is one of the laboring migrants who travels back up to LA with Arcangel. She is married to Bobby Ngu, who is described as "Chinese from Singapore with a Vietnam name speaking like a Mexican living in Koreatown"; he hustles and works multiple menial jobs to achieve the "American dream" (15). Following the paths of crisscrossing freeways, their stories overlap with that of Gabriel, a Chicano investigative reporter who is dating news reporter Emi, the granddaughter of Manzanar Murakami, a *sansei*, unhoused, exsurgeon, exmodel minority. Named after the Japanese concentration camp where he was once detained, he now conducts the sounds and movements of Los Angeles from the freeway overpass. Buzzworm rounds out the geographic mapping of characters as a "walking social services," roaming the "hoods" of downtown LA to reconfigure gentrification as *gentefication,* through and for *"el gente,"* or the people. This dizzying cast of characters moves across and through LA, and together they remap visible and invisible infrastructures of transportation and spatial organizational systems in a dialectical stream of destruction and regeneration. When read through *Tropic of Orange,* LA is rendered a place of doom through which the revelation of racialized gendered material conditions appears through the failures of basic maintenance systems for sustaining life.

Worlds at the End attends to a particular body of literature that renders LA's infrastructure, or the material foundation, as being central to the rise and consolidation of the apocalypticisms that constitute, sustain, and disintegrate colonial life. While we tend to mainly conceive of infrastructure as the literal built elements of the environment, in my study, the freeway, roads, waterways, schools, energy grids, and prisons are the material representations of practices that govern human life through dispossession, coercion, and subjugation—all of which are erased by LA's triumphalist teleological narratives. As such, "infrastructure" references the inextricable nexus of the materiality of the built environment, the ideological apparatuses of state bureaucracy, human and nonhuman fields of sociality, as well as the cultural production and reading practices that help make sense of the spatiotemporal politics of the region. My engagement with apocalypse uniquely resonates in the place of LA to understand infrastructure as, to borrow from Deborah Cowen, an "object and method of inquiry" where the "extraordinary power of cities both in and as infrastructure systems" are illuminated to understand the afterlife of colonization and the life of decolonial imagination.[10] As a method of inquiry, infrastructure offers a reading practice for apprehending the teleological temporality of apocalypse to also propose alternative heterogeneous racialized and gendered worldings.

Materialized as infrastructure, modernity's notion of progress is linked to fears of decline, doom, and apocalypse, which in a linear temporality is solely apprehended as destruction and catastrophe—the end of time or the end of history. In this interpretation, apocalypse is concurrently the consequence and limit of liberal modernity's linear progressive temporality that understands the end of the world singularly within a unidirectional axis, with a beginning, middle, and end. Worlding in this logic is configured in a secular, capitalist temporality through a sequential and unbroken "empty homogeneous time" underwritten by a colonial spatiality of *res nullius* and *terra nullius* (nobody's thing and nobody's land) crucial to the notion of modernity's progress.[11] This notion of time and space is created through an apocalyptic trajectory marked by far too many European colonial "discoveries" within an epochal transformation of "disenchantment"—or "degodding," as Sylvia Wynter occasionally calls it.[12] In contemplating an ethics for imagining an end to this world for Black emancipation, Denise Ferreira da Silva argues that if we do not "*expose how Time works*" and how it is grounded in a universalist notion of "Thought" and "Truth," the racial dialectic will continue.[13] Though obscured and elided by both the triumphal temporality of liberal modernity and the despondent concession to a definitive cataclysmic finality, there is an abundance of temporal and spatial alignments that can, as da Silva proposes, "[end] the grip of Time" to "restor[e] the World anew."[14] This is a demand for a different notion of revelation and reworlding.

Rebuking the universalisms of religious, colonial, and nationalist temporalities, *Worlds at the End* highlights the subjugated imaginaries of racialized and colonized subjects for whom modern progress signaled manifold forms of death, dispossession, destitution, and erasure. Invoking apocalypse as stories of the end times that name acts of destruction and rupture, continuance and renewal, I build upon Yamashita's work, and the works of a collection of Los Angeles writers at the turn of the twenty-first century, whose apocalyptic insights arrest the linear and singular temporality of the region, and its racialized population, as a place and object of doom. In doing so, I return to the revelatory dimensions of apocalypse and intervene in LA's "disaster" reputation to track the dialectic between destruction and regeneration. As the quintessential city of modernity's so-called triumph, LA also consequently signals its failures within a national apocalyptic imagination, making it a paradigmatic site for this study. A place of Indigenous continuance layered over by Spanish and Anglo colonial conquest and utopian dreams of empire and multiculturalism, LA has been habitually represented as "doom city," the "disaster capital of the universe," a place of "nightmares" overrun by racial conflict and ecological ruin. LA in the twentieth century has been popularly constructed as the prototypical city of our collective apocalyptic future.[15] Such is the peculiarity of LA. The city's association with literary, intellectual, and filmic disaster is a refraction of the infrastructural, environmental, and racial instabilities that have made doom synonymous with the city.

In *Worlds at the End*, writers of color engage with LA's infrastructure as a marker of capitalist violence and as material structures revitalized by subjugated people for whom the collapse of the settler state also reveals moments of possibility and regeneration. As such, infrastructure is not intrinsically good or bad, but a site of layered and ongoing contestation. Reckoning with LA's apocalyptic infrastructure through the literary works of Esther Belin, Octavia E. Butler, Cynthia Kadohata, lê thi diem thúy, Alejandro Morales, Helena María Viramontes, and Karen Tei Yamashita provides a certain apocalyptic imagination grounded in its built material environment. This heterogeneous group of Asian American, Latinx, Indigenous, and Black authors work with an insight that grows from their positionalities and proximity to the failures of state governance. Within their imaginaries, apocalypse is not only catastrophe but an opening for the instantiation of heterogeneous temporalities that do not demand the enclosure of linear progressive time.

I follow the literary pathways of travelers, refugees, migrants, and Indigenous people moving through the apocalyptic infrastructural landscape of Los Angeles, a city crumbling under the very pressures of modernity, to explore how many have long lived and survived at the end of the world so that "the end" is never really a bounded *finality*. These revelatory worlds gesture toward the destructive specters of Los Angeles in the long twentieth century—racial uprisings, drought, conflagration, earthquakes, Indigenous genocide, gentrification, incarceration, and the destruction of Indigenous, Black, Asian, and *Mexicano* communities—but they do not remain in modern or postmodern nihilism. Theirs is a refusal to submit to the apocalyptic temporality, or the worlding, of white, heterosexual, patriarchal colonial infrastructure. As such, I index the apocalyptic valences that operate through capitalist systems of abandonment as well as alternative forms of emancipatory revelation. I pay particular attention to how they disparately imagine material and transitory landscapes in order to create sites for analyzing antagonistic and intersecting racialized histories in the region. Together, their roads and pathways interweave LA's freeways with its river and aqueduct, Manzanar Concentration Camp, Paiute territories, the Owens Valley, Vietnam, San Diego, the Pacific Ocean, the Sherman Institute, an Indian boarding school in Riverside, the Diné reservation in Arizona and New Mexico, Northern California, and the stars. Their landed, oceanic, and aerial routes and passages illuminate nonteleological Indigenous, Asian American, Latinx, and Black epistemologies. As such, Los Angeles and infrastructure arise as sites of relationality grounded in incommensurable but related and interconnected histories and formations to imagine what affinities can be forged at the end of the modern colonial world.

Los Angeles at the End

> The best place to view Los Angeles of the next millennium is from the ruins of its alternative future.
> —MIKE DAVIS, *CITY OF QUARTZ*

> A good part of any day in Los Angeles is spent driving, alone, through streets devoid of meaning to the driver, which is one reason the place exhilarates some people, and floods others with an amorphous unease.
> —JOAN DIDION, "PACIFIC DISTANCES"

The distinctive manifest destiny of Los Angeles is its triumph of infrastructure to manipulate the region's unpredictable natural environment over vast landscapes. Roads and freeways mark what Mike Davis calls the "ruins" and the "future" of LA while they also are, in Joan Didion's words, "devoid of meaning" and exhilarate and flood "others with an amorphous unease." Beginning with the Arroyo Seco Parkway, now more commonly referred to as the 110 or the Pasadena Freeway, the freeway network was constructed in 1939. Touted as "creating an environment of beauty over their locale, as witnessed by a flower-lined section of Los Angeles' Arroyo Seco Parkway," the freeways were also cast as "spectacular fortresses" reminiscent of the medieval times, serving as an icon of development, and one of the "wonders of the modern world."[16] Reyner Banham's seminal 1971 study on LA, *Los Angeles: The Architecture of Four Ecologies*, viewed LA's freeway networks optimistically as part of a broader world-historical evolution, as "work[s] of art," an "autopia," and "monument[s] against the sky," placing them within the "canonical and monumental form" of the "great streets of Sixtus V" in baroque Rome and the *Grands Travaux* of Baron Haussmann in Paris during *la belle époque*.[17] The freeway system, for Banham and LA's boosters in the early to mid-twentieth century, was positioned as the definitive structure for the future of urban design and the prototypical city, echoing earlier Anglo settler progressive narratives of Los Angeles. LA's infrastructural departments, such as the Department of Water and Energy, promoted LA as a city that emerged from a Mexican township: once a pueblo and now a boomtown; once a mission and now a metropolis; once composed of ranchos, now filled with high-rises.[18]

Los Angeles's freeway system is part of a much broader infrastructural narrative of progress key to the expansion and rise of global capitalism and U.S. empire that involved hydrology, oil, and the concretization of the LA

River, as well as systems of Indigenous reeducation and elimination, incarceration, and the growth of the U.S. military complex. Deeply embedded within "promises" of twentieth-century "modernity, development, progress, and freedom," this late period of infrastructure is conceptually rooted in Enlightenment temporal notions of a world in progress, moving linearly through the dissemination of knowledge, people, and matter.[19] In the twentieth century, LA carries a unique position as an infrastructural region in the production of U.S. nationalist ideologies of freedom and progress. Ever since the Korean War, Los Angeles has been the primary U.S. city for defense contracting and for weapons research and development. This aerospace industry grew into a high-technology industrial complex that manufactured both civilian aircraft and advanced space exploration, weapons, and national defense that by the 1960s transformed LA into the largest technopolis in the United States.[20]

My chapters move through the transitory landscapes of Southern California, through the broader megalopolis of LA, the counties of Riverside, Orange, and San Diego, across the Pacific Ocean to Vietnam, and into the cosmos, following the region's imperial footprints through LA's racial colonial infrastructure. The "borders" of Los Angeles ebb and flow as LA signals a city, at times a county or an entire region, and at other times a cultural dream or nightmare, blurring the signifier of "Los Angeles" for its inhabitants and tourists alike. With the ports of Los Angeles and Long Beach, the militarized port city of San Diego, the cultural center of Hollywood, music, and filmic production, tourist and entertainment industries, financial corporations, aviation and aerospace technology, the region is a significant economic center and postmodern icon. As such, Los Angeles serves as a metonym for the entire region of Southern California, an imperial megalopolis stretching from the militarized outposts of San Diego, to Riverside, through downtown LA in a far-reaching infrastructural network moving into its hinterlands of the Owens Valley, the Asia-Pacific region, and throughout the U.S. Southwest in ways that shape contemporary thinking about the global emergence and breakdown of colonial modernity.

Spanish and Anglo colonizers were inheritors of Indigenous systems of roadways, erasing some, and keeping others as ancient prehistoric trails became foot trails, then concrete roads and freeways. Preceding the arrival of humans, transportation passageways were spread across the natural landscape of shoreline, wetlands, arroyos, mountains, and rivers by mammoths, mastodons, and other migrating life that flattened the terrain with their bodies, creating a prehistoric highway system through the mountains to the coast. Arriving thirteen thousand years ago, the big-game hunters of the Clovis culture might have followed and extended these trails, as did the Milling Stone Horizon people. By the time the confederation of tribes (Tongva, Gabrieleño,

Shoshoneans, Mission Indians, Moompetem) arrived, between 3,000 and 1,500 years ago, there was an established infrastructure for habitation. Tongva people called the LA of their world Tovaangar, a region ranging from Palos Verdes, to San Bernardino, from the LA Basin southward to Orange County and westward into the ocean to Catalina (Pimu) and the San Clemente Islands (Kinkipar). Almost three hundred years after the "discovery" of *Alta California* in 1542 by Juan Rodriguez Cabrillo and his crew by sea. Sixteenth-century Spanish crown rules of colonization and settler town planning, consolidated through the Laws of the Indies, marked a square just under five miles across in 1781 when the area was christened "El Pueblo de Nuestra Señora la Reina de Los Ángeles de Porciúncula" ("the town of Our Lady of the Angels of the Little Portion"), and officially would be called El Pueblo de la Reina de Los Ángeles. This small beginning square of Los Angeles would increase by eighteen times across nearly 469 square miles. Located far away from the *Californio* Spanish mission society of the eighteenth century, the presidios and pueblos that spread through much of what is now the state of California between 1769 and 1832 mainly expanded across the coast. In the 1850s Anglo white miners settled in the Eastern Sierras. The mines around the town of Cerro Gordo in the Inyo Mountains of the Owens Valley were pillaged for their silver bullion, which was shipped into Los Angeles. This enriching plunder sparked an unprecedented surge in capital that transformed LA from a quiet, remote town to a central location for capital-intensive ventures in the 1860s and onward. In the aftermath, the population of LA exploded. In 1868, LA's population stood at just 4,500; by 1930, the population had increased to more than 1.2 million people.

More recently, Kelly Lytle Hernández has demonstrated the way Anglo settler society was distinct from the Spanish colonial era of occupation of Los Angeles. While the Spanish sought to subjugate Native peoples for their labor under a new social order within the territory of the Tongva, elimination was not their goal. In 1848, with the end of the U.S.-Mexico War, the basin shifted into an Anglo settler capitalist society, inaugurating a new era of colonization founded upon the elimination of Native sovereignty. For two centuries, the end of slavery and the growth of policing, criminalization, and incarceration, according to Hernández, served as the eliminatory foundation for these very ends, turning LA into the "city of inmates," and the carceral capital of the United States, if not the world.[21] The political economies of incarceration, prison, U.S. militarization, and highways converge throughout the twentieth century and are foundational to the emergence of the growth of LA as an imperial metropole. The new social hierarchy of U.S. white settler society geographically shifted the terrain of the region through the dislocation of Indigenous and migrant communities of color, creating new forms of racialization, containment, and colonial territoriality.

Apocalypse in my study becomes a concomitant narrative to the teleological success story of liberal capitalist development, marking the spectacular possibilities and failures of its infrastructural capacity. LA poses as a uniquely apocalyptic site precisely because of its singular infrastructural growth as a region nestled between mountain ranges and the Pacific Ocean. Los Angeles is an alluvial plain with underlying fault lines—with the 800-mile San Andreas fault marking the biggest in the world—that threaten the surface with landslides, floods, and earthquakes. The area of Malibu represents the wildfire capital of North America, if not of the world.[22] A place cut through and paved over by concrete freeways, LA has often been studied as a decentralized region bordered by mountains, desert, farmland, tract housing, and wildlife habitat. In mainstream, popular, and cultural discourse, Los Angeles is a region that has been rendered through its continual destruction and its attendant narrative of the good life. At the turn of the early twentieth century, Southern California was envisioned as the promised land for Anglo-Saxon racial fantasies for a particular set of writers and boosters who ordained LA as the capital for Aryan supremacy.[23] While the mythmaking and literary invention of Southern California in the "booster era" (1885–1925) was dominated by images of a hospitable and healing climate, a picturesque landscape, a mission myth that described "grateful Indians, happy as peasants," and the "ideal Protestant city,"[24] these seemingly idyllic images of Manifest Destiny were also accompanied by disaster fiction filled with threats of the Yellow Peril via images of "hordes" of invading Japanese and Chinese, and later the overwhelming presence of migrants from the global south.[25] In 1915, Los Angeles burned for the first time in literature.[26] During the Great Depression, LA's Edenic image was dismantled by a gathering of American novelists and antifascist European exiles who drew upon the crisis of the middle class and shifted the dream of the city into a nightmare through noir.[27] The peripeteia of LA, from an image of New Jerusalem to New Babylon, continued in the ensuing decades in literature and film.[28] As *Battle: Los Angeles* director Jonathan Liebesman has said, "People love watching Los Angeles get destroyed."[29] Writers, filmmakers, and artists alike have delighted in the fiery death of Los Angeles through ecological and environmental catastrophe, alien invasion (both human and otherworldly), racial unrest, decay and ruin, and financial disaster.

LA scholars within the fields of urban geography, sociology, and architectural history importantly study the emergence of Los Angeles through questions of global capitalism in the moment of the 1990s and early 2000s. In his 1998 book *Ecology of Fear*, Mike Davis finds at least 139 novels and films since 1909 where the destruction of Los Angeles is the central theme. The idiosyncratic emergence of Los Angeles, as both heaven and hell, as Bertolt Brecht characterized it,[30] has long preoccupied LA scholars. LA scholars such as Norman Klein and Mike Davis have importantly studied the ways Los Angeles emerged as noir fantasy in the twentieth century, tracking how Los Angeles has served as an exceptional metropolitan region that encapsulates broader U.S. politics of immigration, incarceration, globalization, industrialization, postindustrial capitalism, and neoliberalism.[31] Both Davis and Klein have examined the crime fiction of noir as a distinctly LA genre that from the 1930s to the 1990s expanded the image of Los Angeles as the dark underbelly of tourism, consumerism, Hollywood, and glamour.[32] By 1992, after the Rodney King uprisings, Klein argues that LA represented the "most dangerous city in the country" for a collective imaginary that was oversaturated by media coverage of the insurrection.[33] While Davis and Klein's studies of LA uncover important historical and cultural dynamics that foreground the materiality of Los Angeles within broader global formations and move through and beyond national and hemispheric borders, their projects at times view LA heavily within narratives of decline and through a linear time frame of liberal capitalism.

Materialist Feminist Methodologies, Infrastructure, and Relationality

My analysis of apocalyptic epistemes and infrastructural placemaking draws from decolonial and women of color feminist genealogies that emerge as a radical feminist critique in the late twentieth century struggles for social justice. These struggles include Black, Brown, Asian, and Indigenous radical movements, the women's movement, gay liberation, and new left movements.[34] Women of color feminism's explicit intervention into these formations underscored the essentialist logics of racial, gendered, classed, or sexual identities. Scholars such as Kimberlé Crenshaw, Chandra Talpade Mohanty, and Roderick Ferguson advance the intellectual work of women of color feminism and queer of color critique through the "intersectionality" of race, gender, class, and sexuality, which makes untenable fixed and singular identity categories such as "woman," "Black," "worker," and "gay."[35] Chandan Reddy brings women of color feminism to critique the violence of liberal modernity while Grace Hong uses the relational framework to analyze capitalism's progressive temporalities of the possessive individual subject.[36] In my readings I mobilize a women of color feminist analysis to elaborate upon liberalism's progressive temporalities as the reverse of apocalyptic decline. This approach is grounded in relational politics that recognize incommensurate but interrelated histories that cannot be reduced to singular identities, temporalities, embodiments, or geographies. More specifically, my readings enact the framework as an alternative mode of comparative-race analysis and revelation of solidarity that does not situate Asian, Latinx, Indigenous, and Black racialization under universal regimes of similarity or commensurability. Stressing the unviability of totalizing knowledge for antiracist and decolonial worldmaking, I build with women of color feminism and queer of color critique to theorize alongside what remains and challenge liberal modernity's disavowal of its own violence and epistemological erasure.[37]

By bringing women of color feminist critique to the apocalyptic politics of infrastructure, *Worlds at the End* draws upon and broadens the historical scope and analytic possibilities in feminist intellectual practice. Approaching LA's infrastructure through a women of color feminist analytic opens up how we can think about the relational politics of built environments, which has been a perennial question of women of color feminist critique. Although infrastructure has not been a significant analytic in literary studies, Grace Hong's reading of Cherríe Moraga's movement through Boston's transportation system illuminates otherwise obscured interconnected racial and gender formations that are revealed through the sociality of the train.[38] My authors, I argue, mobilize literature to help me grapple with questions of infrastructure for women of color feminist politics, offering a reading practice for what is absented, cannot be seen, and excised by hegemonic discourse.[39] In the works I examine, landscapes literally expand and shift the panorama of what can be perceived, offering new visions of the dialectics of capital accumulation and the formulation of cross-racial political configurations. These overlapping forces, particularly conspicuous in 1990s and 2000s Los Angeles, amount to an apocalyptic space-time that these writers appropriate and redeploy. This politically transformative mode of apocalypse reframes imaginations of decline and disintegration. Stretching the analysis and politics of women of color feminisms, the literature I study envision radical and new socialities across racial difference, illuminate histories of ecological disfigurement otherwise obscured by the built environment, and adumbrate lifechances for surplus populations that, to evoke Audre Lorde, were never meant to survive.[40]

The growth of Los Angeles imagined through progress for some, and the end of the world for others, emerges through its infrastructural underpinnings and lends itself to understanding infrastructure as a relational concept. As Daniel Nemser highlights, infrastructure disappears certain things from view as it makes other things appear, and contradictorily it facilitates progress and destruction where global capitalism and primitive accumulation is, building upon Karl Marx, "'written in the annals of mankind in letters of blood and fire,' . . . but also in bricks and paving stones."[41] Studying the question of infrastructure through the literary work of Esther Belin, Octavia Butler, Cynthia Kadohata, Alejandro Morales, lê thi diém thúy, Helena María Viramontes, and Karen Tei Yamashita enlivens the subterranean and palimpsestic worlds of Los Angeles, offering stories that move against a teleological and singular worldmaking of apocalypse. If apocalypse is a narrative about transformation, infrastructure provides colonial and decolonial modalities in which to create and transform the material world. From the nineteenth century, infrastructure was tethered to the work of government and allowed states to separate the political sphere from nature, the human from the nonhuman, producing states and subjects, and corporations and capitalist networks.[42] Infrastructure, according to Patrick Joyce in *The Rule of Freedom*, must be understood as an integral technology of liberal governance that guaranteed freedom and progress through the subjugation and racialization of others.[43] Opening onto incommensurate imaginaries of various possible worlds, Los Angeles is transformed through a pluriversal practice of, in Arturo Escobar's words, a "collective weaving of *a place*" for coexistence, for a place where "many worlds fit" against a "one-world" imagination of a single universal container that subsumes other worlds and excises multiple and fractured universes.[44] This form of place-based politics builds out from women of color feminist insight on racialized and gendered embodiment and how different communities move and are mediated in social, human, and other-than-human structures and relationships. Infrastructure—as spatial and temporal, material, and symbolic—provides the conditions for the production and movement of "people, things, and knowledge" and structures all of my chapters to reveal and rupture the linear time of capitalist modernity.[45]

According to Daniel Nemser, recent scholarship on infrastructure in the fields of science and technology studies, anthropology, history, and geography has studied the mediating work of infrastructure in facilitating the exchange of people, objects, and spaces across distances; reconfigured urban space; and bundled seemingly disparate substrata of life (water, people, streets, energy) into networks that "form," "reform," and "perform" modern life, "governance and politics," "accumulation and dispossession," and "institutions and aspirations."[46] The distinct nature of infrastructure lies in its invisible operations: "operating 'beneath' (*infra*) the surface of the phenomenal world while facilitating the operations on which the world depends," the system of pipes, wires, tunnels, the flow of water, energy, waste, and data that regulate modern life becomes "visible only when it fails," making itself known only through its breakdown.[47] While infrastructure typically signals the material built environment, the geo-extensive system of infrastructure, Deborah Cowen has illuminated, serves as a "vehicle of domination" that builds, reproduces, and orders human life and is also "a means of transformation."[48] Within the field of disability studies, Jina B. Kim reveals how infrastructure references both the systems that maintain human life and the uneven dissemination of resources that "optimize life for some while conscripting others to death and disablement."[49] The substrata of infrastructure, in its material forms, are rich sites of historical inquiry precisely because of its accretion, or "archaeologies of differential provisioning that predate neoliberalism" that disparately manage human life and implement dispossession and violence and its effects of "containment, premature death and division"—all of which are disavowed in the name of progress.[50] In one sense, the monumental presence of freeways is so hypervisible in its ever-presence that its histories of destruction and segregation are rendered invisible. Ever-present, infrastructure is taken for granted in such a way that obscures its own historicity. This is where the apocalyptic comes into play, not as a moment of judgment, but as a mode of diagnosing, revealing, uncovering obscured worldbreaking and worldmaking histories that are bound up within the infrastructural creation of LA's pluriverse. What lies below, beneath, or within—"infra"—reveals LA's infrastructural layers as entire worlds that overlap, exist in tension and elision, for the exploration of historical transitions and bonds between the past, present, and future. A women of color feminist approach to LA unearths accounts alternative to world-ending projects of white heteropatriarchal supremacy and makes the durability of infrastructure ephemeral. LA's roads, energy networks, water systems, subterranean, waterway, pathways, and concrete landscapes in the literature I study enliven infrastructure as ever-transforming, never fixed or lifeless.

An Apocalyptic Imagination

Diverging from the singular world of liberal capitalist apocalypse, I conceptualize apocalypse as offering ruptures and breaks within linear narratives of modernity in order to disrupt the overtemporalization of liberalism's racial order. Moving backward, forward, imagining alternative presents, and diving into the subterranean substrates of Los Angeles, the literature I focus on reenters the constructed world of LA to dwell on what grows out of LA's habitual representation as an apocalyptic landscape based off of the failure of its basic support system. Though the narrative of modernity's infrastructure is often invoked to tell the story of the region's progress and decline, infrastructure is less frequently engaged with in terms of apocalypse and as sites of rupture by and for communities of color.

The post-1990s literary works I study echo the sense that LA is supposed to die by fire, earthquake, and ecological destruction, yet these worlds do not remain within the fatalism and cynicism of LA noir. As such, catastrophe is recast as opportunities for materializing alternative geographies and lifeworlds. For example, one literary function of the freeway is for it to serve as a distancing, voyeuristic writing device that facilitates movement through the city. During the 1965 Watts Rebellion, LA was underscored as a place through which race war would break out, shifting the way literary culture engaged with disaster and the city. Writers such as Joan Didion described the death of LA in 1965 from a distance: "The city burning is Los Angeles' deepest image of itself.... For days one could drive the Harbor Freeway and see the city on fire, just as we had always known it would be in the end. Los Angeles weather is the weather of catastrophe, of apocalypse."[51] Didion's disembodied experience of viewing the city from driving on the freeway empties LA of its inhabitants and insurgent racialized gendered communities. In Didion's apocalyptic imagination of LA, communities and alternative possible worlds are rendered invisible, and Didion's distanced driving experience forecloses heterogenous notions of time and incommensurable spaces that can emerge from the burning landscape.

I use the term apocalyptic imagination to name the convergent and ever-shifting geographical and human collisions drawn from a set of fin de siècle writers—Belin, Butler, Kadohata, lê, Morales, Viramontes, and Yamashita. Together, they reveal an apocalyptic imagination grounded in the differential politics in LA's built environment that gives shape to disparate and simultaneous ideas of the end of the world, the future, the past, hope, abandonment, violence, and regeneration. Regeneration within Indigenous feminist terms, according to scholars such as Leanne Simpson and Maile Arvin, is concerned with new growth and life cultivated after destruction and through a vast network of kinship that does not center biological reproduction or genetics. It is a commitment to people and places that refuse settler colonial notions of time and place, giving way to a notion of Indigeneity as a condition in which people are in deep genealogy with lands and oceans, where a sense of place is understood through ancestral terms.[52]

Unlike the voyeurism of LA's boosters and freeway enthusiasts, Belin, Butler, Kadohata, lê, Morales, Viramontes, and Yamashita offer counter-archaeologies of Los Angeles. They inspire alternative discourse that is informed by an awareness of the ways that various communities of racialized and gendered subjects have been dislocated and redefined through the building and deterritorialization of the city. They traffic in the residual in the sense that Raymond Williams conceives of it, as being formed in the past but still active in present cultural processes and expressions of experiences, meanings, and values that cannot be verified in terms of dominant culture.[53] These writers come from communities across Southern California, the Western Hemisphere, and the Pacific Rim and have been affected by the manifest destiny of a broader global economic system. Even through destruction, they remain attached, not detached, from the place of LA as they imagine Indigenous and migrant networks and movement.[54] These writers and poets are also very much informal scholars of the region's history. Octavia Butler's rich archives at the Huntington Library, for instance, attest to the research she conducted to write her science fictional works, just as Esther Belin's engagement with the Indian boarding school system provides a way to grapple with the interrelationship between Southern California's capitalist expansion, Native American labor, and the extinction of Diné modes of living.

Throughout my chapters, I deploy the work of fiction to dwell in a fluid and nondogmatic space of apocalypse that requires speculation. Literature is unlike social scientific discourse, which is, in many ways, belated, retrospective, confined to empirical fact and representation, and unable to break out of linear temporalities that organize the past, present, and future. Karen Tei Yamashita herself initially studied Japanese immigration to Brazil through the disciplines of history and anthropology, but found that in order to adequately capture Japanese Brazilian life, "it had to be fiction." Within fiction she "began to see an entire world." Through literature, she "could create complex characters out of the many people" she met, and she came to "know" her subjects in a "very different way."[55] Literature exists within a dialectic with social scientific discourse to break through the confines of empirical fact and representation to simultaneously retell the unfolding of the world, where we have been, and where things might lead. Both historical and speculative, literature offers the imaginative capacity to deconstruct and reconstruct our apocalyptic imagination. At the same time, the authors I study use the cultural forms of the novel and poetry to upend conventional definitions of literary production as part of an elite literary culture in the developmental narrative of the nation-state. In these works, I find social, spatial, and political universes that are unbeholden to a linear temporality of documentation and are uniquely positioned because they are not bound to representing an empirical narrative of the past, and can gesture back and forward to different imaginings of destruction and regeneration through a place-based politics. This field of literary production articulates worldmaking as a radically multivalent labor of historical retrieval, unraveling, and speculation, one that reframes the concept of worlding into a practice of discerning heterogeneous lifeways and epistemological fields. This is a play with the temporal and spatial thickness of the apocalyptic that gives insight into how a particular modern epochal "structure of feeling" of abandonment, dissolution, and disintegration can offer an emancipatory imagination at the turn of the twenty-first century.[56]

Chapters: The Pathways of the Book

Just as infrastructure is part of longer processes of accretion, my chapters build upon each other, moving through acts of destruction and regeneration found within waterways, pathways, roadways, and airways. Beginning in the Tongva Basin, Chapter 1, "Los Angeles's Infrastructural Palimpsest: An Apocalyptic Origin Story," argues that LA's deep settler colonial infrastructures of removal and dispossession entailed intertwined narratives of the channelization of the LA River, the construction of the LA Aqueduct that siphoned water from Paiute territories in the Owens Valley, and the construction of the world's first modern freeway system through the destruction of Black and Mexican American communities. I bring together Alejandro Morales's historical romance *River of Angels* (2014), Karen Tei Yamashita's magical realist novel *Tropic of Orange* (1997), and Helena María Viramontes's *Their Dogs Came with Them* (2007) to develop a palimpsestic method of reading to offer a recursive vision of infrastructural apocalypse. In doing so, I illuminate the colonial precedents informing militarized removal, displacement, and dispossession of Black, Latinx, Indigenous and Asian American people in the contemporary era. This methodological approach offers a layered and entangled narrative that persistently rewrites the apocalyptic terrains of Los Angeles. Settler colonial infrastructures may be contiguous, and their narratives of durability might appear everlasting, but they do not remain intact. Together, these three texts offer accounts of the region's capitalist transformation, and its shifting infrastructural regimes and cartographies across the Western Hemisphere and deep into LA's subterranean waters.

Chapter 2, "Archipelagos of Refugee Worlding: Survival under Cold War Military Infrastructures," expands the imperial metropole of Los Angeles southward to San Diego and across the Pacific Ocean to Vietnam to position LA as part of an archipelagic cartography of U.S. militarized infrastructure. Counterintuitively, I claim lê thi diem thúy's 2003 novel *The Gangster We Are All Looking For* as an archipelagic LA text. I do so to offer an understanding of LA as an imperial metropole through its military-oceanic infrastructural connection to San Diego, California. While LA's Hollywood constructs the Vietnam spectacle and liberal narrative of freedom and progress, LA is also the repressed site of massive defense industrial production. San Diego, on the other hand, is the unglamorous militarized hinterlands of LA, the material site of human armaments, and is the port for Vietnamese refugee arrivance. In other words, if LA is the fantasy of war, San Diego is the militarized real. *Gangster* lays bare an oceanic symbiosis and underlying contiguity between the fantasy and materiality of war. Lê's use of ekphrastic language pulls away at the screen that conceals LA's military-industrial infrastructure and its extension throughout Southern California and across the ocean.

Continuing with the exploration of the U.S. military's foundational role in the expansion of U.S. empire, Chapter 3, "Infrastructures of Termination and Esther Belin's Imagination of Decolonial Mobility," considers conquest in relationship to Los Angeles's nascent role in U.S. infrastructures of Indian termination. Diné poet Esther Belin's collections of poetry *From the Belly of My Beauty* (1999) and *Of Cartography* (2017) illuminate how Indian boarding schools, energy extraction, and the roadways connecting the Indian reservation and LA are all part of a broader infrastructural network of termination. Exploring violent assimilationist practices, Belin's poetry does not understand U.S. settler colonialism as linear and simply repeating, but as a "whirl" in which U.S. termination policy and practices fortify and magnify colonial technologies in disorienting and unpredictable ways. Against the spatial capture of Native people on and off the reservation and Indian boarding schools, and against fixed romanticized ideas of a return to a precolonial homeland, Belin draws upon California and the U.S. Southwest as a zone of decolonial mobility. Challenging static ideas of Native termination that confine Native Americans to the past, as being from a bygone era, as immobile, and as nonurban, Belin offers a poetics of traveling on the road for a practice of Diné worldmaking within and beyond LA's association with urbanism, automobility, and infrastructural "modernity." In this way, Belin shifts dominant narratives of LA's roadways and offers a unique poetic practice to imagine what it means to be mobile and "on the road" as a Native person.

Chapter 4, "Infrastructures of Flight: Life on the Roads of a Disintegrating World," continues on LA's freeways, this time through Octavia Butler's postapocalyptic novel *Parable of the Sower* (1993). In Butler's 2024–2027, LA's freeways and roadways are routes of forced migration, colonization, and flight. In Butler's not-so-distant future, freeways no longer assert the dominance of modern automobility, but exist in a state of disintegration where the nomadic characters use the collapsed pathways for their own ends. Travelling northward and up to the stars, this novel, I argue, emphasizes the generative nature of entropy for building transits of flight. The malleability and ever-changing infrastructures of LA is how Butler imagines building after the end. This is a reimagination of end-of-the-world narratives from the Bible, the scientific death theory of entropy, Black radicalism, and popular culture to realign the histories of the Middle Passage, histories of Black migration, and mobility for a twenty-first-century crossing.

Finally, my Coda, "The Dark Century, or The Century of Light," brings together the threads of *Worlds at the End* through a meditation on Cynthia Kadohata's 1992 LA novel, *In the Heart of the Valley of Love*. The literature I study reveals that the end has come many times, that the single-model world has been built upon the destruction of others, but that different worlds exist abundantly and are made continuously. Their worldings are neither isolated nor equivalent; nor are they incorporated into a universal and homogeneous protocol. Rather, they name profoundly linked histories of violence that create disparate racialized and gendered communities and imaginaries of the world. Apocalypse is both an ancient and a contemporary anxiety about life on the brink of an end time. Disaster is part of the apocalyptic narrative but apocalypse is not disaster alone. An account of the revelation, or unveiling, apocalypse marks moments of transition and offers stories of doomsdays that will give rise to a resurgence and regeneration. As Frank Kermode writes, everyone thinks their moment is really the last, but "crisis is a way of thinking about one's moment, and not inherent in the moment itself."[57] The specters of inevitable and irreversible climate disaster and extinction, racial uprisings, a global pandemic, and the proliferation of genocide and warfare have haunted the completion of this book. Every generation thinks it is the last. So, how can we build in such a way that imagines the end differently?

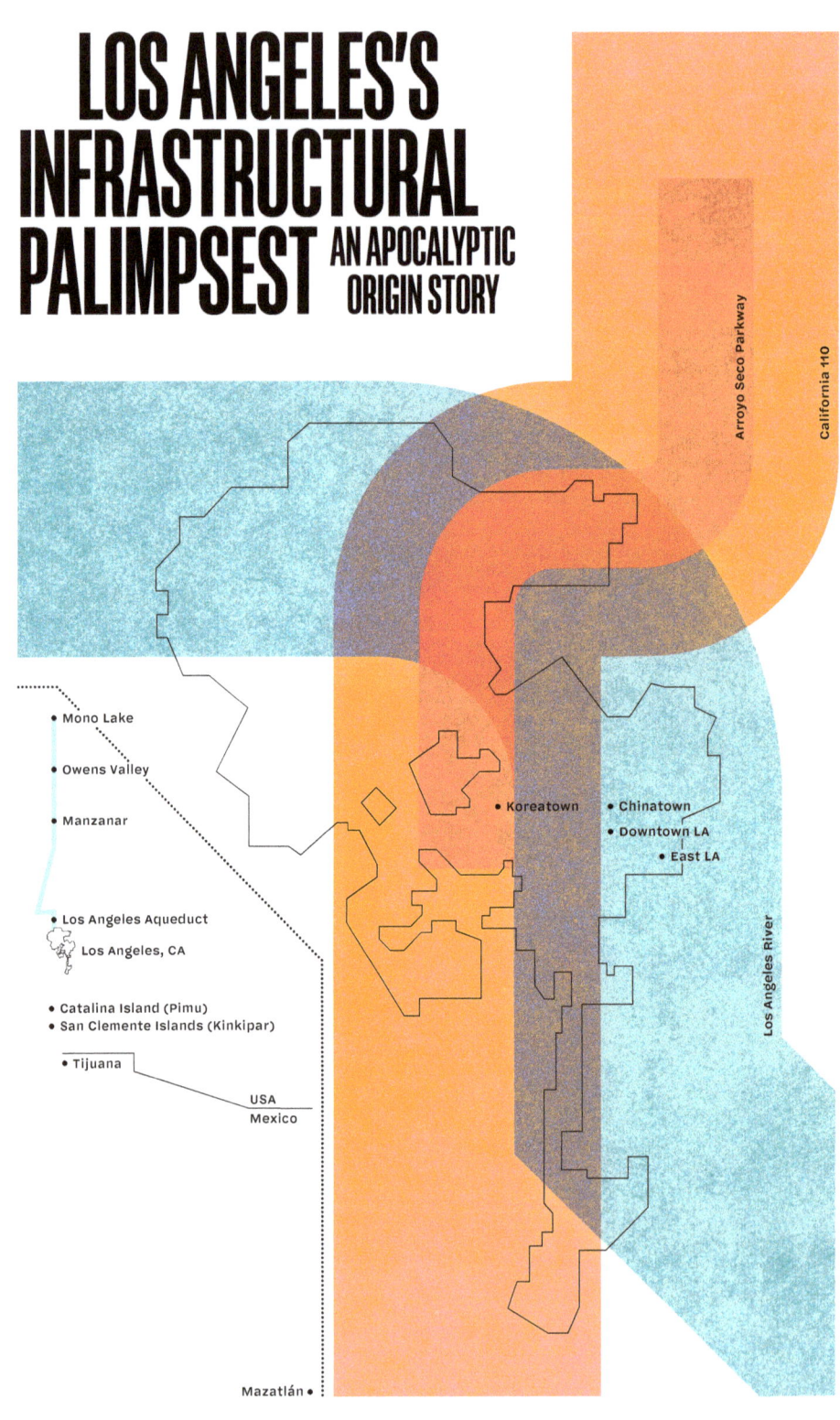

LOS ANGELES'S INFRASTRUCTURAL PALIMPSEST AN APOCALYPTIC ORIGIN STORY

1

> In time to come, the lakes will melt the foundations of the world, and the rivers will cut the world loose. Then it will float as the island did many suns and snows ago. That will be the end of the world.
> —Okanagan Traditional,
> "The Beginning and the End of the World"

Just three hundred years ago the Los Angeles River sustained the entire ancient Los Angeles Basin with its marshlands, woodlands, and forests of oak, willow, sycamore, elderberry, and wild grape. Once called the Porciúncula River by Spanish explorers beginning in 1769, "Wanüt" or "Orít" by the Tataviam, and "Paayme Paxaayt" (West River) by the Tongva, the river provided an abundant habitat for trees and wildlife, and supported one of the largest communities of Indigenous people in North America. Before the river was diverted by Spanish and Anglo settlers for irrigation and domestic use, its waters freely flowed anywhere it wanted, meandering, and traveling across Southern California, connecting with other rivers, marshes, small ponds, flowing west, shifting course in unpredictable and destructive ways. Sometimes called an "upside-down river," because its flow mostly comes from a subterranean source, not mountain runoff, the LA River contributed to the alluvial plain and the rich soil deposits of the Los Angeles area. The river was so central to the emergence of Los Angeles in the nineteenth century that it is safe to say the city would not exist if not for the river. As one of a few reliable year-round sources of water, the LA River provided the growing Spanish, Mexicano, and Anglo population of Los Angeles with water for drinking, and for agricultural irrigation that made Southern California a major agricultural site and transformed a semiarid landscape into the city's booster image of an Edenic garden. So central was the river to Los Angeles that the original name the Spanish settlers gave Los Angeles was "El Pueblo de

Nuestra Senora la Reina de Los Angeles del Río Porciúncula," Town of Our Lady the Queen of Angels of the River Porciúncula (meaning "small portion").

But now, in the early twenty-first century, it is easy to drive past or over the once great river without a second glance, as sewage and street runoff trickle down its channels. As Los Angeles expanded into a dreamscape for Anglo Americans in the early twentieth century, the city gained the rights to the river's waters, diverted its surface stream for domestic use, pumped its underground flow for the city's growing water needs, cleared the floodplain forest for cultivation, cut down trees for fuel and fences, and replaced the marshlands with roads and industry. Between 1938 and 1940, the city "armored" the river to wash out storm runoff, permitting industrial development in the floodplain. In the end, the Los Angeles River, which was so central to pre-nineteenth-century life in the basin, was forced into a "concrete straitjacket" by the U.S. Army Corps of Engineers, destroying the riparian ecology of the city for the promise of industrial land values and temporary flood abatement.[1] Now, after raging for tens of thousands of years as a sustaining force for the basin, the river empties into San Pedro Bay at Long Beach and is one of the most polluted urban rivers in the country. The life, suppression, and destruction of the river is part of a longer apocalyptic story tethered to the transformation of Los Angeles from the late nineteenth century from a quiet pueblo, built of adobe, to a major metropolitan city in the mid-twentieth century.

This chapter follows LA's story of water and concrete by linking the channelization of the LA River to the construction of the LA Aqueduct, its water theft from Paiute territory in the Owens Valley, and the construction of the freeway system that razed Black and Mexican American communities in Alejandro Morales's novel *River of Angels*, Karen Tei Yamashita's *Tropic of Orange* (1997), and Helena María Viramontes's *Their Dogs Came with Them* (2007). Written by a cohort of fin de siècle Los Angeles writers, *River of Angels*, *Tropic*, and *Their Dogs* help name and counter the world-ending consequences of patriarchal white supremacist grids of colonial infrastructure that was central to the worldbreaking and worldmaking of Los Angeles in the twentieth century. Infrastructures of settler colonial capitalist destruction do not remain intact for long in these stories but are continuously remade as sites of regeneration from the margins. Infrastructure in this sense serves as a palimpsest, defined by Daniel Cooper Alarcón as a document or manuscript of "competing yet interwoven narratives that [change] the way we think of cultural identity and its representation, as well as enabling an examination of history, cultural identity, ethnicity, literature, and politics in relationship to each other, providing a new vantage point."[2] Approaching LA's infrastructure as palimpsest, infrastructure becomes a layering of entangled narratives and archives of destruction and revelation for a decolonial perspective. As palimpsest, apocalypse is a genre of contradictory spatial and temporal transformation that is constantly being written, rewritten, and overwritten. In this way, their narratives of LA become layered with historical, political, and social meaning. With this understanding of apocalypse, the cataclysm of white settler modernity, dispossession, and the U.S. state is not a totalizing world-ending event. By reading these texts alongside each other, I trace the terrains of the Tongva Basin, the LA River, the manmade river of the Los Angeles Aqueduct, and LA's freeways as contiguous logics of settler colonialism that built the seemingly durable foundations of the city. In particular, these texts grapple with the aftermath of the Progressive Era (1890s–1920s) as a key moment of modern building during Los Angeles's rapid growth as the "capital of capital" for the Pacific Rim.[3] Their narratives offer accounts of Los Angeles's capitalist transformation through an exploration of its shifting infrastructural regimes and geographies. Within this transformation, the erasure of Indigenous, Latinx, Black, and Asian American worlds open onto alternative epistemologies of the geographical landscapes upon which LA is built.

Morales's, Yamashita's, and Viramontes's disparate palimpsests signal contradictory spatial and temporal lifeworlds in which the end and the beginning overlap and eschew the linear temporality of inevitable extinction. Moreover, these three writers embed their characters into LA's landscape in such a way that reveals how infrastructure is physical object and material form, but also sees, in line with infrastructural scholars, "people as infrastructure," connecting the notion of infrastructure to a system of social relations.[4] In *River of Angels* (2014), Alejandro Morales treats the site of Los Angeles as a palimpsest and archive of contemporary and ancient topographies and people of the region. The novel explores the development of Los Angeles across three generations of two families of bridgebuilders: the Ríos and the Kellers. *River of Angels* is set in a transitional period between a precapitalist Mexican landholding class, which depended upon Indian slavery and peonage, and an emerging capitalist free wage society at the end of the nineteenth century.[5] The Ríos family are Mexicanos living at the edges of the Los Angeles River as Anglo families begin to move into the area from the late nineteenth century to the earlier half of the twentieth century. Morales's historical romance unfolds across a series of crises marked by the transitional period in the capitalist development of LA, beginning in 1842 with the arrival of Mexican and Chilean miners, two years before the start of the U.S.-Mexico War (1846–1848), in the Pueblo of Los Angeles, and moves into World War I, into the Great Influenza Pandemic of 1918, and into the mid-twentieth century. This novel brilliantly imagines how Los Angeles's Anglo American colonial infrastructural foundations mark the incursion of a new capitalist mode of life and its attendant patriarchal masculinist white vision of LA that breaks with the river and shifts the region's racial hierarchies. At the same time, the novel does not nostalgically look back for a Mexicano mode of living but instead calls upon Indigenous epistemologies as a critique of both Spanish colonization and Anglo American occupation to signify new forms of surrounding life beyond official archives. Layering a new mode of capitalist world-building across and through the LA River, this novel draws upon Indigenous mythology and stories of the region, and it finds in the city's subterranean waters a narrative of continual returns of vanished human and other-than-human life.

I follow Morales's pathways of water and concrete with an exploration of Yamashita's *Tropic of Orange* (1996), which offers an elaborate narrative structure that intersects the lives of a motley crew of laborers, performers, and unhoused characters traversing Mazatlán, Mexico, Singapore, China, and Vietnam, who literally move with them the boundaries of the Western Hemisphere and global Asia, colliding in a confrontation between the military forces of the state on the freeways of Los Angeles. In Yamashita's novel the freeway performs a crucial narrative function that pulls together the novel's multiple storylines. Following the structure and cycles of colonization of Arcangel's journey discussed in my Introduction, *Tropic* brings the hinterlands of the city and the Owens Valley—the location of Manzanar Japanese concentration camp, the homeland of the dislocated Paiute Indians, and the beginning point of the LA Aqueduct—along with the Southern Hemisphere onto the freeways to reimagine the interlocking histories of immigration, incarceration, colonization, and imperialism that converge in LA.

Finally, representations of LA freeways in Helena María Viramontes's 2007 novel *Their Dogs Came with Them* confront the material history of the construction of LA's freeways that would come to conspicuously dominate the region. Treating the freeway as part of a longer colonial infrastructural regime, Viramontes moves the reader back to the 1960s and 1970s to narrate the seemingly quotidian lives of a multiracial community in East Los Angeles in a period of intense freeway construction. The freeway, in Viramontes's novel, is turned into a tablet to be rewritten upon and transformed, advancing a different way of keeping record. All the while, there is an acknowledgment of the impermanence of the function of writing and the freeway. Infrastructure provides Viramontes with a formal narrative structure for her novel where LA freeways offer generative cultural sites for the emergence of disparate communities. As a layered world, Los Angeles emerges as a live archival field in *River of Angels*, *Tropic of Orange*, and *Their Dogs Came with Them* to account for epistemological erasure and to theorize alongside what can and cannot be written over.

The palimpsestic register of infrastructure lets me come to a different relational analysis that invokes what it means to think about Indigeneity through various modes of Chicano writing. Although Yamashita is not Chicana, *Tropic* is in many ways a Chicanx narrative, taking on the cultural consciousness of chicanismo. The same is true of Morales's novel, because women of color feminist politics, closely aligned to queer feminist critique, unhinges feminism from the notion of fixed bodily female identities. Queer theorists such as Jack Halberstam and Juana María Rodríguez have argued that queer subjects do not just mean queer-identified, lesbian, bisexual, gay, two-spirited people, and transsexuals. To think of queer politics is to think about the challenge to heteronormativity, about those who live without financial safety nets and live outside of an order of time and space that has been created for a dominant few at the expense of many others.[6] Women of color feminist methodologies do not reserve feminist critique only for easily identifiable female bodies, nor are Chicanx-Indigenous politics reserved solely for Latinx and Indigenous peoples; rather, feminist and racialized politics are boundless. Chicanx texts in form are palimpsestic, recursive, extratextual, border-crossing, about subjectivity and space, for the interrogation of multiple forms of colonialism. If the texts were read through a conventional ontological mode of comparative racialization, the focus would emphasize the similarity and/or difference between Japanese American writing and Chicanx writers. Shifting to an inquiry around palimpsestic infrastructural narrative modes reveals how these writings differently come to understand the urgency and impossibility of Indigenous ways of knowing. Working within the field of Chicana feminist narrative, these texts are connected to movement, and to the rejection of patrilineal storytelling practices, the reclamation of a version of patriarchal authority, or coherent territory. Rejecting the solidity of the present, they open onto a different politics of Indigeneity, and imagines alternative relationships that migrants, settlers, and Native people can have in the space of LA. As such, these writers offer a way to theorize the built environment as an archive to reconstruct alternative epistemologies of time and place. This chapter argues that the palimpsestic forms of the novels open onto understanding infrastructure as an archival practice to grasp the contemporary apocalyptic landscape of Los Angeles. The palimpsest understood in this way dialectically reveals how infrastructures serve as archives while archives themselves are forms of infrastructure. In their literary texts, infrastructures as palimpsest serve as forms of recordkeeping—workers' bodies are cast into concrete, concrete roads are built over foot trails—and offer a method to peer through the veneer and access simultaneous layers in order to construct an archive for the present.

I put these particular three texts together to trace how the living entity of the LA River is trapped by steel and concrete but lives on and is liberated in unexpected ways. The Indigenous divine of the LA River breaks through Morales's matrilinear narrative that centers the river as a sustaining force against historical erasure; the ecstatic breaks through Yamashita's magical realist novel and channels up subjugated geographies of the Owens Valley through her conductor/shaman figure Manzanar and the force of the freeway; radical acts of prayer, meditation, and levitation power Viramontes's naturalist text and serve as reminders that the foundations of LA can crack and freeways can be repurposed. Suturing *Tropic* with *River of Angels* and *Their Dogs,* Chicanx histories of LA are put into conversation with U.S. infrastructures of Japanese incarceration, Indigenous annihilation, Black and Mexicano erasure. Their texts offer a recursive vision of infrastructural apocalypse by illuminating precedents that inform militarized removal, displacement, and dispossession in the contemporary era where history is not simply repeated but fortified and expanded. Their palimpsestic writing practices are not, in Robert Nichols's words, "simple tautology." Recursion in this sense is not a "completely closed circuit" but a "loop back" to different starting points that "builds upon or augments its original postulate."[7] Their palimpsestic registers help theorize the relationship between the infrastructural production of LA in a dialectical relationship with multiple forms of elimination and dispossession that includes but is not limited to Native tribes of California. A study of infrastructure across these three texts reveals how the practices of removal and dispossession are rooted in a longer history of Indigenous dispossession and elimination. Capitalism in their imaginations is a structure that has innovated world-ending acts; yet, these world-ending acts are not, as these texts reveal, a singular event or end time. They are part of a longer process of colonization that has erased alternative epistemologies of LA from official records. These writers, then, are part of a broader decolonial imaginary that seeks to upend white settler colonial logics of capitalism. Their works materialize and animate the LA River, the freeway, East LA, and those who have been rendered dead, buried, or nonexistent. They teach us that as long as there are relational and shared practices, apocalypse is a condition in which living and struggle occur.

Subterranean Returns in Alejandro Morales's *River of Angels*

Alejandro Morales's *River of Angels* begins with an autobiographical prologue narrating the author's drive northbound on the I-5 freeway on his way to a book event at the downtown LA library. Lost in thought, Morales looks out at the skyline and offers a layered mode of perceiving the city. He sees the bridges and the LA River and contemplates how the city is "a palimpsest with archives layered one on top of the other by human beings crossing into this vortex since the ancient people settled here near the river" (xi). He sees people and archives that are no longer visible to the eye. At the crowded event, Morales is pushed into the hallway, where he discovers historical photographs of LA covering the walls. As he peers at them, "their world and time peers back." The photos reveal different stages of bridge construction over the Los

Angeles River circa 1931. He identifies workers with their sleeves rolled up, wearing heavy rubber boots, smiling back at him as they congregate around a cement mixer. The images beg him for recognition as he attempts to "make them live again and again" through his gaze. He touches the images and prays, asks for help, and speaks to the men in the pictures. Staring at them, he begins, "naturally . . . [to] start looking for Mexicans" but it was difficult to "distinguish between a Mexican and an Anglo. [He] find[s] one Asian," who could also "be Mexican. [He] see[s] two black men, but they also could be Mexican" (xvi). The photographs reveal that they work for the "Sun Construction Company," the same name as the construction company in *River of Angels*. Finally identifying Mexican workers Morales, the son of Mexican immigrants born in East LA, sees in them the Zapata mustache, eyes, and sensibility of his grandfather and father.[8] Morales longs to hear them speak or make a sound, to "tell" him something, to "communicate a feeling," or a "memory to [him] now here in this place" (xvi).

In an interview, Morales shares that he was inspired to write *River of Angels* by these old photographs of the crews that built the downtown bridges across the river. As he began to research he was unable to find any significant information about the workers, wishing he "had found payroll sheets, ledgers identifying the workers who built the Los Angeles bridges."[9] *River of Angels* speaks back to the archival erasure of Mexican presence in the construction of Los Angeles. While Jacques Derrida has proclaimed that the final apocalyptic annihilation is "the total and remainderless destruction of the archive," Morales reveals how the archive itself performs a destructive function.[10] According to Saidiya Hartman, in the context of Black enslavement, the archive "dictates what can be said about the past and the kind of stories that can be told about the persons cataloged, embalmed, and sealed away in box files and folios. To read the archive is to enter a mortuary; it permits one final viewing and allows for a last glimpse of persons about to disappear into the slavehold."[11] Morales illuminates how official archives have enacted the destruction and erasure of human and nonhuman life in Los Angeles and turns to the novel form to materialize the sounds and utterances from a precapitalist LA. Morales reveals how the archive serves as an informational infrastructure that disseminates, regulates, and organizes historical knowledge for the present and the future. At the same time, the built infrastructure of freeways and bridges serves an archival function. Although Morales is unable to find information that would identify the workers, they are ever-present throughout the novel. Even though they do not carry a main storyline, they carry the storyline of labor that lay the bricks in the Simons Brickyard of Southern California and built the bridges over the LA River. The men are buried in concrete while building the infrastructure for the bridges while the women perform the domestic work that supports the elite Mexicano and Anglo families. In this sense, *River of Angels* offers an alternative archival practice grounded in a literary infrastructural imagination. In the absence of official historical records of Mexican workers, Morales turns to fiction to build a world that the official archives cannot recognize. Morales treats the site of Los Angeles as a palimpsest and archival layering of contemporary and ancient topographies of human and other-than-human entities.

The novel's third person omniscient narrative voice provides access to multiple characters in the novel, including the river, to narrate an apocalypse marked by the destruction of precapitalist infrastructures that worked alongside the wildness of the river, and the creation of new colonial forms of infrastructure. At the opening of the novel, the river is an unruly living entity with a voice, thoughts, and feeling, not a passive resource to be extracted or controlled. The narrator describes how the first gold miners from Mexico and Chile were drawn into the ancient basin with stories of striking it rich in California's rivers and streams, but

> the Río de la Porciúncula did not give up its stones easily. The Indians believed that the river spirit considered all that existed in its waters living precious objects, sending out its river energy to bring them back. The native people knew that in some way, some time, all things from the river would return to the river. The river's spirit would never be controlled; it was unpredictable; it was greater than man (3).

The pilfering of the river's gold stones is part of a longer story of extraction that persists through capitalist infrastructural world-building. Capitalist infrastructure projects become a vessel for the continuous extractive masculine settler colonial project that imagined Los Angeles as a modern city for Anglo Americans. Resource extraction and the proliferation of a monetized economy imbues the river's stones with value. Mining and panning for gold fuels the growth of capitalism and changes the value and significance of the river's stones, but here Morales reframes extraction as a form of gift-giving that must be reciprocated. The miner is not figured as the primary actor, but is the receiver of the river's stones, which are part of a larger lifeworld in which everything that exists in the water is precious, a gift that must be returned. The river here is not figured as belonging to anyone, but belongs to itself. To understand that the river is "greater than man" means to understand that the Euro-American will to dominate nature, to control the river—itself part of LA's early precapitalist infrastructure—cannot last. The novel demonstrates how this imagination can be enacted only through the death and dispossession of the LA River and its shifting relationship with the Ríos family.

Morales forefronts the survival of the Ríos family through a Tongva cosmology that centers the river as part of a regenerative palimpsest generatively tied to Indigenous epistemologies, notions of place, and returns. A palimpsest in many ways is a framed narrative that concedes its premise on the narratives that came before, and is activated by surrounding stories that cannot clearly be discerned. The story begins with the patriarch and matriarch of the family, Abelardo and Toypurina Ríos, in the late nineteenth century when they begin a transportation business that carry newly arrived homesteaders, farmers, settlers, and travelers across the LA River on a barge. Without Abelardo's help and his knowledge of the region, the newly arrived Anglos could not cross or build along the river's edge, as it would sweep them all away. Abelardo's familiarity with the river comes from the ancient people, the Indian fisherman who talked to the steelhead trout, asking the trout permission to catch and eat them, he listened to the animals, the vegetation, the wind and rain, to "understand the river's voice, to sing the river's cycles, to know the river's space and to sense the river's movement" (6). Described as "excitable, like a child, [where] every year the Los Angeles river played with its banks like toys. Every year the river carved out new toys, and as time progressed the river created its story. Abelardo learned how to detect the river's feelings by sitting for hours, sometimes for days, listening to the Indian elders, the wise men, the wise women, whose culture, stories and language had survived thousands of years, enduring even the brutal invasion and conquest by Spanish soldiers and Spanish priests" (6). The perceived destructive forces of the river are reframed by the narrator as a mischievous being, playing with what lies on its banks, and as time passes the river enacts new terrains and narratives. The river's stories and feelings are to be understood over time, just as the Indian elders are able to extract the river's mood—not its commodities—through a reciprocal relationship of listening and not taking in ways that teach them how to navigate the river to ensure their own survival.

The omniscient narrator enables Morales to recount from the perspective of the river and Abelardo, describing an account of Spanish colonization, as a brutalizing world-ending event for the people of Yaanga ("place of the poison oak tree"). By many accounts, the village Yaanga was the largest Tongva village; located slightly west of the LA River, Yaanga now rests beneath a nexus of freeways and carceral structures: the 101 freeway, the 10 freeway, slightly south of the Los Angeles County Sheriff's Department Men's Central Jail and the Twin Towers Correctional Facility, and just north of the Metropolitan Detention Center and the LAPD Metropolitan Detention Center. According to the novel's narrator, Spanish Franciscan missionaries and soldiers traveled north from Baja California in 1796, converting the Indian population to Catholicism, and also then into a dependent labor source "to be exploited to the limits of human decency" (6). The Spanish soldiers "took all their European hands could grab, but mostly they demanded women, who became permanent slaves at the military posts" (6). The Spanish raided the villages, forced women to clean, wash, and cook, and "the younger women were raped and made to understand that at any time they had to acquiesce" (7). Once released, these young women returned to their villages and families, carrying with them infectious diseases from the Spanish soldiers, devastating the ancient tribe of Yaanga. These violent histories and memories, of the transformation of Indian men and women from freedom to slavery, of intruders arriving on the banks of the Los Angeles River, of sexualized submission, are embedded into Abelardo's memory and the terrain. With their lives disrupted, and having lost "control of their land, language, religion, and bodies," Native people, Abelardo recalls, ran away to the chaparral, they lived in open fields, in the forest, and beside the river in treacherous conditions (7).

The destruction of Spanish domination becomes part of the narrative structure of the river finding within its system of knowledge modes of survival under Anglo colonization. At times, the river flash floods, overflows from snow runoff, or its treacherous currents pulls settlers and travelers under. Rather than trying to constrain it, Abelardo understands that he has to love, respect, and listen to the "voice of the river, the language of the river, living next to the river, possessing the secrets of the river" in order to survive the Spanish conquest, Anglo settlers, priests, and the "fickle river itself" (8). The river is depicted as a live archival entity with a record of stories filled with sound, language, and capriciousness and connected to an ancient belief system. The Ríos family is linked to the region's worship of Chengiichngech, the Tongva's creator god, a shamanlike figure whose teachings revolved around the preservation of life on the land and the mediation between the natural and supernatural worlds. Chengiichngech's teachings pervade everyday life, and instill laws and rituals between human and other than human entities. Those who disobeyed, or did not heed, Chengiichngech's teachings were punished with starvation, disease, or attacks by bears and serpents. Later, those who believed in Chengiichngech were seen by the *gente de razon* (people with reason) as *gente sin razón* (people without reason) for worshipping a heathen god, and as such, part of a primitive past that should be left behind.[12]

The shift in the Indigenous belief systems of the river is part of a new structure of racial formation in the region. Race seen in this way operates, as Daniel Nemser emphasizes, "a sort of infrastructure, a sociotechnical relation that enables the ongoing functioning of specific machineries of extraction and accumulation."[13] Historically, Tomás Almaguer explains, Mexicans were part of the "gente de razon," with their Spanish ancestry, romance language, and Catholic beliefs; they were seen as being in closer proximity to Anglo Americans; and they were designated as "white" against the definition of the "nonwhite" California Indians, Chinese, Japanese, Black, and dark-skinned mestizos, or "greasers," who were seen as "gente sin razon."[14] *River of Angels* highlights the tension of racialized landholding Mexicans like the Ríos family who were on occasion able to pass as white in contrast to the darker-complexioned non-landholding working-class mestizo population. As Tomás Almaguer illuminates, "Gendered and classed values of uplift and respectability rendered non-elite Mexican and Indians abject."[15] While the Ríos family could pass as ambiguously white, California Indians were never given the option to integrate into Anglo American society, due to their "'savage' culture and 'heathen' traditions and rituals."[16] California Indians were emphatically regarded as "nonwhite," politically disenfranchised and segregated. Their very existence on coveted land made them out to be obstacles to Anglo American progress and civilization, extensions of the wilderness that needed to be tamed and transmuted.[17] While this white narrative of progress depends on the excision of early Mexican and Native bodies and their epistemologies, *River of Angels* explicitly reveals the interconnection between human and other-than-human modes of survival.

The novel's title itself intertwines the name of the city and their family name, as the stories of the Rivers (Ríos) family, a mestizo Latino family descended from Native Americans, and the Kellers family, a competing Anglo family who moves into the area in search of building wealth through the development of Los Angeles, are interwoven. Abelardo and Toypurina's sons Otchoo and Sol continue to build their family's construction company while navigating an intensified transitional period of urban development. When Sol mysteriously disappears for a number of years into the depths of the LA River, Otchoo and his wife Agatha expand the family's construction business, named after Sol, the Sun Construction Company. In one of the novel's most poignant scenes, Otchoo Ríos breaks from his familial relationship to the river when he is pressured by the bank to anglicize his name to Oakley Rivers. In an effort to avoid any problems that might arise while establishing the family's construction company, the bank's lawyers push Otchoo to adopt a "strong," memorable, and easily pronounceable name. Mourning this break, Otchoo says, "It's a sacred name. It has to do with trees and the river. . . . It's a name the elders pronounced when my mother gave me birth" (26). A blessed appellation given to him by the elders upon his birth, *Otchoo* means "oak tree" and it references the meeting of the land and the river, and the towering trees that lined the river's stream. The riparian lifeworld of the river's oak trees provided acorns, a staple food source since 2500 B.C.[18] Women of the Tongva Basin crushed, washed, and transformed the acorns from seeds to nutritious soups, mashes, and breads, fueling a great population growth along the coast of what we now call California.[19] While Otchoo's name is erased from official papers, the loss of his name also signals the waning of a mode of subsistence life that is destroyed through the rise of capitalist infrastructure over the region's riparian spaces.

In the novel, the local transitions of LA, and the anglicization of the Ríos family, are set within a series of broader catastrophic global transformation. At the same time that Oakley changes his name, the narrator tells the reader, "many people believed that the world was coming to an end" (27). Horrible riots broke out across Europe that would ultimately lead to war; the monarchies and dictatorships in Russia and Mexico were threatened with revolution; borders were threatened with invasion; new forms of disease and plague broke out in global pandemics killing millions. Large populations in Europe, Asian, Africa, and Latin America migrated, in search of safer places to live; and Mexicans, who had "been present in the northern territories of the North American continent for thousands of years," migrated north to their ancestral homelands, marking an "exodus that would last more than one hundred years" (27). A particular world was "coming to an end," as a new notion of whiteness came to organize a new racial hierarchy in the growth of Los Angeles as a suburban model for the nation in the twentieth century, a model that promoted and enabled white flight from downtown LA through racially divided neighborhoods, restrictive covenants, and a segregated busing system.

This racialized transformation of place is captured through Albert and Louise's spatial perception of a developing LA as they walk along the highest point of the viaduct's pedestrian sidewalk. The reader is given a panoramic view of LA below from Albert and Louise's perspective. The river, the reader is told, flows into the ocean and becomes a landmark for segregation. To the north and west were the homes of Hancock Park, Hollywood, Brentwood, and Beverly Hills, homes built as investments in "middle-class residential ventures for Anglo-American families" (103). Along the river to the Eastside, Albert and Louise see zoned areas for industrial development and working-class Anglo families. Dislocating, relocating, and evicting the original Mexican *colonias* in Los Angeles, Mexican houses were torn down and pushed to the edges of these newly developed areas, against the river banks, railroad yard, and abandoned farm-worker camps, company towns, outside the peripheries of the city's Anglo-only sections in what was thought of as "Mexican reservations" (103–104). As Raúl Homero Villa has argued, LA is a paradigmatic site of urban Chicano history where Mexicano workers were essential to the construction of the city's restructuring, but as residents they were also in its path.[20]

White dominance in Los Angeles required not only the suppression of precapitalist modes of production and the subordination of "nonwhites" but also the eradication of precapitalist modes of perceiving the landscape. Eventually, Otchoo's son Albert falls in love with Louise Kellers, the daughter of a competing Anglo American family of builders. Albert and Louise's relationship reflects the conflicting investments in LA's topography and visions for the future.[21] As an engineering student at USC, Abelardo tells Louise that USC's engineering professors and students are studying the river, asking "old timers" and the "oldest Mexicans" questions about the river, because they know its oldest history. This new project, Abelardo discloses, wants to cement the river; by "finding out where the river ran and flooded in the past, they can map its future courses and floods" (102). Louise believes this study to be "good for history," and that the cement and concrete will help stabilize the river, to help Los Angeles grow, and she tells him, "That's what my family's investing in, Albert" (102). This academic project reveals an instrumentality of collecting knowledge and archival building for capitalist forms of investment and possession through dispossession. In one sense, as David Scott has argued, the archive is "a domain of positivity, of pure materiality" with an "impulse to collect, to order, and classify" (vi). At the same time, the archive's "meta-dimension" must be understood at the level of "a discursive condition of *possible* statements of knowledge, at the level of a *generative* discursive system that governs and regulates the production and appearance of statements—what can and cannot be said. An archive therefore is an implicit and constitutive part of the epistemic background of *any* knowledge, the dense network of allusions, events, concepts, images, stories, figures, personalities, that inhabit the *sub-terrain* of statements, animating them, giving them a sense as well as force."[22] Albert and Louise's relationship marks the tension between these competing dominant modes in envisioning the "modernization" of LA. Debating with Albert, Louise claims that there are "benefits" to laying concrete into the foundations of the river, echoing a capitalist logic of destruction for investment in the future. Albert is ambivalent about the idea. He tells her, "Cement will take the river's freedom away. I don't think that's right, cementing something that's natural. The river is part of the natural geography of Los Angeles, and by burying it under tons of concrete, they're trying to turn it into something that it's not. If they do it, imprison it, attempt to smother its natural flow, the river will have its revenge by carrying a great flood that will tear away the tons of cement, forcing its way to wherever it wants to flow. The river will rise and create its own course—cement or no cement" (102). Morales's twenty-first-century readers know that straightjacketing the river does come to pass, but Albert offers a prophecy, still, that the earth, no matter how much the Kellers family wants to restrain it, will follow its own course. Rooted in generational knowledge, the river is transfigured as a palimpsest with a refusal to be entirely written over by concrete. In my conception of palimpsest, human subjects who write are not the only ones who can leave a record. The river is an entity that provides its own archival account. The river has the ability, according to Albert, to exact revenge, to break through the concrete, and disrupt the foundations of the city.

Morales's infrastructural account of LA demonstrates a palimpsest of colonial worldmaking in Los Angeles that begins with Spanish colonization onto which Anglo American capitalist worldmaking writes over. Part of the future of LA is embodied in Louise's Uncle Philip, the head of the Kellers family and a white supremacist who is the founder and president of Kellers Lumber in Los Angeles. Uncle Philip envisions Los Angeles as a "city of an Aryan future," a "European city, a new Germanic center of wealth and culture in America," with only Aryan entrepreneurs settling in the heart of Los Angeles. His white supremacist ideologies develop throughout the story as he attends meetings of the Aryan Club of Southern California at the University of Southern California and grows to admire German obsession with racial purity and the Aryan race.[23] Members of his club believed that their wealth could control the "growth, social order and racial development of Los Angeles" (137). As a figuration of a white supremacist masculinist ideology of the time, Uncle Philip embodies the Anglo American psyche of westward expansion, and of "manifest destiny," that saw as its mission, and divine right, to occupy and conquer the entirety of North America for white settlement.

In *River of Angels,* white futurity, and its infrastructural worlding project, is built upon the domination over women's bodies and nature, a fear of miscegenation, and the supplanting of matrilinearity that becomes configured through the suppression of the LA River.[24] The tension between the two families increases as Uncle Philip violently contests their relationship. Louise and Albert's love prevails but is cut short when Philip murders Albert. Historically, white men gained political and economic opportunities, and were the inheritors of thousands of acres of land, through the trafficking of Mexican women between old Mexican families and the emerging Anglo ruling class.[25] *River of Angels* overturns this narrative by breaching white men's unrestricted claims to white American women, and so breaching their exclusive access to California land. Central to white supremacist logic is the reproduction of white bodies, and the control of white women's bodies in particular, against the threat of miscegenation. Uncle Philip becomes obsessed with Louise as he watches her throughout the novel, staring at her body, praying that she has not become "polluted" with Albert's blood. Philip believes that Louise, as an Aryan woman, had to "marry right . . . to produce Aryan progeny . . . for the sake of the family and, most importantly, the master race" in order to protect the "purity and the sanctity of his bloodline" (182). Philip believes he has to protect the family's women by making sure they marry Aryan men, and not the genetically inferior "subhuman races" of "brown and . . . yellow-skinned people" arriving in Chinese, Japanese, and Mexican "hoards," or the "filthy, syphilitic drunks—the so-called American Indians" (182). These races, Uncle Philip believes, have to be sterilized and eliminated to "maintain America as a country of racial purity" (182).[26] Discourse of racial purity was tethered to nineteenth-century discourse of the LA River in the expansion of LA. In the late 1800s, the Los Angeles River was seen as offensive, undrinkable, nauseating, with tales of corpses of animals, "Chinamen," and Indians floating in the water. The "foul" river is rerouted to "N****r Alley," the term used for Native Americans, Italians, Basques, Jews, and Slavs. As Los Angeles expanded toward the end of the nineteenth century and the LA River became more polluted and further associated with Mexicans and Indigenous people, the river was perceived as a primitive water system, leaving Los Angeles in need of the Los Angeles Aqueduct to help fulfill a forward-looking "vision" of LA, filled with pure drinking water, neat lawns, gardens, fountains, and pools modeled after Anglo European "gentleman's" estates. Whereas the disorderly and "dirty" Los Angeles River was aligned with racialized people and backwardness, the LA Aqueduct and its "purity," and ability to extract and control nature's resources, was seen as moving Los Angeles along into the future. Euro-American Manifest Destiny and westward expansion become inscribed upon white women's bodies, as pure vessels that need to reproduce for the superior race, as well as onto the bodies of Indian, Chinese, and Mexican women. At the same time, in California in the nineteenth century it was deemed permissible to marry Mexicans as European Americans saw the advantages of marrying wealthy upperclass Mexican women, who were considered "chaste, beautiful, and charming," from ranchero families, even as Anglo American visions of LA's future move Mexican labor to the periphery.

In many ways, *River of Angels* is a story about the "nonwhite" workers who built the bridges, worked for the construction company, and took care of the Rivers and Kellers families. Throughout the novel they go unnamed, but they appear as the mass that holds up the two differentially elite families. The omniscient third person narrator resuscitates the bodies of Mexican builders entombed in the very concrete of LA's foundations against the absence of Mexican builders in official records and accounts. Louise's father, Ernest Kellers, heads up the Kellers's construction company, and hires groups of "mixed-race workers, mostly Mexican" in his lumberyard and construction sites. He finds that the only way he can make a considerable profit is to hire "Mexicans eager to work for him in dangerous working conditions and for substandard wages" (86). Early one morning, Ernest, his foreman, and twenty-five workers, all Mexican, go to the edges of Griffith Park to pour cement into a fifteen-foot-deep by ten-foot-wide foundation for a water tank facility to be used to maintain the park and railroad tycoon Samuel P. Huntington's herd of cattle.[27] As Ernest motions the crane operator to pour the cement, against the screams of the workers to stop, Ernest sees one of the workers, trapped in the latch release lock, fall to the bottom of the foundation as five hundred pounds of fast-drying Portland cement "entombs" him (87).[28]

The worker's body is buried in a cement graveyard in the process of urban development. Interred within the concrete structures they build, they materially become part of the structures that hold up the city. Within this building site, the class hierarchy is clear, with Huntington on top, whose absence automatically puts him out of harm's way. Ernest is somewhere in the middle, then the foreman, and last the workers, whose warnings could not be comprehended by Ernest because he did not understand Spanish. Coupled with the changing forms of labor extraction, the five hundred pounds of concrete weighs down heavily in this scene, as it starts, stops, is poured, and ultimately fills up the empty space of the pit and the worker's body. LA is literally built upon dead Mexican laboring bodies.

Against the domination of concrete, Morales draws on Indigenous stories for a historical narrative that contests colonial infrastructures and its modality of archiving. It is significant that Morales names the matriarch of *River of Angels* Toypurina, instilling from the beginning a legendary spirit and presence of female Indigenous revolution, willpower, and survival. Toypurina evokes the legend of Toypurina, a Gabrielino medicine woman and religious leader of the Hapchi-vitam who helped lead a rebellion with two chiefs and warriors from six villages against the San Gabriel Mission in 1785, fourteen years after Spanish missionaries and soldiers claimed Tongva land upon which the mission was built. This rebellion was ultimately crushed by the Spaniards.[29] According to Spanish reports, Toypurina was a witch who used her powers of seduction to convince local Gabrielinos to rebel against the mission. But according to Indigenous legend, Toypurina was a powerful shaman who was able to control the Catholic priests during the revolt so that others could attack the Spanish soldiers. Once Toypurina was captured, a sham trial was held where she entered the interrogation chamber, kicking away a stool, and declared, "I hate the padres and all of you, for living here on my native soil, for trespassing upon the land of my forefathers and despoiling our tribal domains."[30] Instead of centering the legend of Toypurina, the rebellion against the San Gabriel Mission, exoticizing Mexican women as "spoils of war," the river is the center of this matrilineal narrative. Morales presents a love story that does not continue Euro-American nor Chicano patrilineage. Instead, the matrilinear story ends with the survival and leadership of the women in the family, overturning Anglo and Mexican claims to patrilineal heritage. As the son of a prominent Mexican Indigenous Californio family, Albert eventually marries Louise, an elite European American woman. Eventually, Otchoo, Albert, and Sol all die, leaving Louise and Agatha in charge of the construction company. Uncle Philip moves to Mexico to atone, where he is cared for and is rehabilitated by Mexican Catholic priests. At the end of the novel, he returns home to Los Angeles to make amends with the remaining women in his family. Yet, the story is not matrilineal merely because the men die and all the women survive.

The story is matrilineal because it goes against the white settler patriarchal linear logic of progress and development that seeks to dominate racialized and gendered subjects and to dominate the river. *River of Angels* is matrilineal because it centers the cyclical temporality of the river, its revolutionary logic of returns, and the multiplicity of worlds that the river inhabits. The river tells the apocalyptic stories of genocide, of remains, and of people who carried with them a hope and a reckoning, encouraged by shamans, that the disappeared Indians were not dead but were "taken to another place by brothers and sisters who had existed for thousands of years. These ancestors were the earth spirits, so powerful that they could move mountains and transfigure their bodies to trick the evil invaders. They could be as minute as the smallest particle, as big as the tallest human and as imposing as a mountain. The earth spirits transformed their physical human likeness into reptiles: the lizard people" (7). Taking different forms—from mountains, to tiny particles, to humans, to reptiles—to fight off the invaders, their ancestors' transfiguration dwells in and exceeds human forms, and reaches for broader networks of kinship.

As such, colonizers are not the only source of infrastructural imagination. The River Lady, a "withered old Indian woman" whom some call curandera and healer and others call "witch," describes Abelardo and Toypurina's son Sol as "a child the river brought to [her] by the Lizard people and the kindness of the river" (36). Vanished Indian nations had not perished but lived, transformed, and survived through their adaptability underground with the Lizard people. The ability to build and imagine infrastructure in the novel dives deep into Hopi legend. According to Hopi legend, the ancient and advanced race known as the Lizard people lives in underground cities, along the Pacific coast, with its capital city beneath what is now Downtown Los Angeles. Using "magical" chemicals, the Lizard people formed a massive network of underground tunnels to escape a cataclysmic meteor shower, a "huge tongue of fire" that threatened to destroy all life in its path, and future fires.[31] Their subterranean shelters, with their stockpiles of food, were meant to keep the Lizard people safe from future disasters. Underground, they kept safe the tribe's archive and history, the origins of humans, and creation stories in a collection of golden tablets. These stories and disappearing Indians remain submerged, underground, and reemerge when those on land most need them. According to the narrator, the lizard people would send humans who sent them "back to the surface to save humans who were in trouble" (8). Although he was aged in years between a boy and a man, Sol could not speak or walk; like a newborn baby, he dragged "himself on the floor like a lizard" (37). The

Lizard people, according to one of the elders, had saved Sol at the moment of his drowning. Sol adapts to the Lizard people's underground city, breathing like an amphibian with less oxygen. Back on land, Sol possesses a special amphibious gift of breathing and sees the world with a lizard-human sense of perceiving multiple worlds, times, and spaces. The river takes Sol, but his life underwater initiates a rebirth. His return is the river's offering that helps the family navigate a white patriarchal relationship to the landscape (38). The reckoning of returning ancestral earth spirits recurs throughout the book, and potently appears through Sol and the generative subterranean world. Believing that Sol drowned in the river, the family moves on, but years later the River Mother finds Sol half-buried in the river's debris, and raises him in preparation to be reunited with, and to save, his family. Throughout the novel, Sol is a kind figure who has a "magical" touch with plants, animals, and people. Toward the end of the novel, a large lizard visits Sol and declares, "I come from the river" (224). Peering into the eyes of the upright lizard, Sol is reunited in kinship with *el lagarto*, one of the lizards who saved him from drowning in the river. Embracing *el lagarto*, there is a recognition of Sol's subterranean transformation in the reptilian underworld beneath the city and in the river's waters (224). The novel's subterranean politics and dwellings reimagine a palimpsestic landscape that is not easily seen, reminding us that there is no such thing as a final annihilation, that the disappeared are not gone forever and will eventually return.

Karen Tei Yamashita's LA Soundscapes

The story of the LA River is indelibly linked to the story of the building of the LA Aqueduct. The channelization of the LA River cut off the region's water supply, and in response to a growing water-hungry city its leaders constructed the Los Angeles Aqueduct, a two-hundred-mile concrete channel that siphoned water out of the Owens Valley. Overlapping with the Progressive Era, LA's expansion can be placed within an intense period characterized by political and social activism, reform, scientific discovery, industrialization, urbanization, rising standards of living, the development of new technologies, and a drop in death rates.[32] As the "dawn of the 'concrete age'" the Progressive Era announced a period of construction for the expansion of the U.S. empire. This period signals a revolutionized shift from older colonial settlement patterns and raw material extraction toward modes of capitalist infrastructural and economic development.[33] LA's expansion into a global city made abstract declarations of U.S. greatness concrete, formulating a progressive masculinist vision of urban development. The building and celebration of the Los Angeles Aqueduct was rooted in a masculinist logic of conquest that financially benefited wealthy white men such as water commissioner

Moses Sherman, railroad baron Henry Huntington, and *Los Angeles Times* publisher Harrison Gray Otis, who, knowing of the plans for the aqueduct, purchased soon-to-be-lucrative land around the aqueduct's terminus in the San Fernando Valley.[34] Urbanization, President Roosevelt believed, would force Native Americans, "mere savages, whose type of life was so primitive as to be absolutely incompatible with the existence of civilization," to inevitably "die out" as the West was settled with densely populated urban areas.[35] With this understanding of the Progressive Era's notion of progress, cities were seen as symbols of colonial power and development against rural areas. Los Angeles was positioned as the apex of Anglo American conquest in the Americas, the city of the future that came to "define the future of cities to come."[36]

The U.S. national narrative expanded through global imperial projects of dam-building and large-scale irrigation projects led by international cadres of hydraulic engineers. The aqueduct was hailed as a great achievement and triumph of "superengineers" like William Mulholland. The City of Los Angeles now owns most of the valley, having "purchased" Owens Valley land to transport its water southward to Los Angeles, leaving in its wake few resources for local populations.[37] Boyle Workman, a leading pioneer of Los Angeles's real estate development in the early twentieth century, declared that "every tree, every lawn, every blade of grass in this section as it exists today, is a forced growth, made possible by man's ingenuity in bringing water to what otherwise would be a treeless waste."[38] Indeed, this attests to "man's ingenuity," but it also serves as a reminder that there is water and life in LA because it has been taken away from elsewhere. Against Morales's logic of giving back, when the water arrived over San Fernando's Newhall Pass on November 5, 1913, the aqueduct's chief engineer, William Mulholland, surrounded by U.S. flags, declared to the euphoric crowds lining the aqueduct, "There it is, take it!" The idea that water is something that can be taken, without giving anything back to the lakes, rivers, and streams from which it was taken, is part of a patriarchal capitalist endeavor upon which modern day Los Angeles was built. As Michael Rogers, an elder from the Bishop tribe, has illuminated, "In the Native American culture, if you take, you must give something back and we have yet to see that, in order to keep in balance with the environment. We cannot have balance if there is only take."[39] To understand the surrounds—the river, the freeway, the aqueduct, the water—as alive also means there needs to be a reciprocal relationship in which something must be returned and given back.

By 1926, thirteen years after the building of the Los Angeles Aqueduct, after one million years of existence, the Owens Valley Lake, which in 1878 extended 110 square miles across and 50 miles deep, disappeared.[40] A brine pool remained in the center of the lakebed, creating dust so fine that once breathed in, it cannot be exhaled because the diameter of the dust particles is less than ten micrograms. Called "particulate matter-10," or PM-10, the powdery dust is composed of a toxic mixture of arsenic, nickel, selenium, and cadmium. This poisonous cocktail of dust moved asbestoslike through the Owens Valley and its neighboring towns in Inyo County, absorbing into the blood, causing allergies, fibrosis, cancer, lung scarring, decreased lung capacity, and lung diseases such as pulmonary fibrosis. Affecting not only the delicate ecosystem in the surrounding wilderness area, it reached the twenty-two hundred Paiutes living in Inyo County. The largest remaining Paiute population in the United States, the Paiute in this region have long suffered from dust-related health problems. The official "beginnings" of Los Angeles have indeed marked the erasure and the end of multiple forms of life.

The drama of the LA Aqueduct and water theft has been culturally memorialized through Roman Polanski's award-winning 1974 film noir *Chinatown*. In the crime thriller the water wars at the turn of the twentieth century are cast primarily through the actions and consequences of white bureaucrats and actors. I turn to Karen Tei Yamashita's *Tropic of Orange* and the innovative narrative strategies that open up a simultaneity of palimpsestic infrastructural imaginaries. *Tropic of Orange* blends the narrative strategies of film noir with magical realism, boosterism, and the apocalyptic—genres that have all contributed to the contradictory cultural representations of Los Angeles as a land of health and sunshine, and as a place of "disaster," climatic change, uprising, fires, earthquakes, and drought. Yamashita has stated that she pays no reverence to these forms, satirizing and parodying the genres as it is useful, but that she is incredibly reverent about what she writes about.[41] I find this to be absolutely true.

Published in a post-1992 LA uprising, post-NAFTA period, *Tropic of Orange* has been importantly and widely studied within the context of liberal multiculturalism, neoliberal economic transformation, ecocriticism, and globalization, and it constitutes a significant text for the hemispheric, borderlands, and transnational turn in Asian American literature.[42] Born in Oakland, California, on January 8, 1951, Yamashita spent most of her childhood growing up in Gardena, California, to parents who had spent World War II incarcerated at the Topaz War Relocation Center in Millard County, Utah. *Tropic* captures LA in a particular time and place when, according to an interview with Yamashita, LA "itself seems to be changing; [she] had written the book in response to a very narrow vision of Los Angeles as Hollywood and a racially divided city between blacks and whites, but maybe the current response to the book is precisely this changing recognition of LA as Latino and a crossroads for global migrations."[43] The characters represent "folks who have not in the past been necessarily represented in the literature about LA: Latin American and Asian immigrants, African Americans, and homeless."

Yamashita emplaces these groups through a "layered geography ... [that] ... may merge or be distinct yet also represent the city," which, Yamashita describes, is "forever changing, but it is home, and this also means that home is also not fixed but changing."[44] Hers is a fictional account of constantly transforming communities and geographies.

While Morales delves into a subterranean world to contest Indigenous and Mexicano elisions from official LA archives, Yamashita creates a frenetic text structured by LA's intersecting and overlapping infrastructural grid of freeways, waterways, and carceral and labor apparatuses. Yamashita's novel deploys a palimpsestic textual aesthetics beyond what "official" accounts or maps of LA might reveal, by establishing "hypertextuality" from the beginning of the novel. When the reader first opens the book, the traditional "Contents" page is followed by a "HyperContexts" feature that maps out the characters' distinct yet interrelated storylines over the duration of the novel, which is just seven days. The novel opens with the Contents of the plot, moving linearly, beginning on "monday: summer solstice" and ending with the final chapter, "sunday: pacific rim." Placed at the beginning of the book, the Contents acts as a typical "Table of Contents" that provides a sequential list of the novel's chapters, including page numbers, topics, and locations. The chapters are grouped according to the day of the week with each corresponding to an overarching topic, such as "tuesday/diamond lane" referencing the freeway's carpool lane. Each chapter centers a specific character's experience of the day under that topic heading. This Contents page offers a standard chronological practice of reading a novel.

Following the Contents is a HyperContexts grid that offers the reader an experimental mode of navigating the novel. This different map of the book prepares us for the dizzying narrative plotlines, alerting the reader to the possible overlapping narratives that cannot be contained in a singular linear narrative. While Contents focuses on containing the novel and its storylines in a singular sense, the "hyper" or "excessive" "context" emphasizes the formal interventions of the text. Context performs the work of establishing what immediately precedes or follows a passage, or it is text that helps determine meaning. Context emphasizes literary composition, construction, or the infrastructure of writing itself, weaving together words, sentences, and ideas. On the very top, the days of the week are listed along with a theme, event, location, or time of day. The reader has the option to follow one character's storyline, read the events that happen on any given day, or read for a theme or issue, such as "cultural diversity." While the Contents page promises a clear beginning and end, the HyperContexts promises no such thing. It insists on an excess to the narrative that cannot be contained by the novel and at the same time invites the reader to read the book however they want. For instance, one could look at the HyperContexts map and identify all of Rafaela Cortes's chapters and read the book focused solely on Rafaela (which means reading Chapters 1, 10, 18, 24, 30, 38, and 45), yielding a different focus than reading the book sequentially in its entirety. Similar to Julio Cortázar's 1966 "counternovel" *Hopscotch*, *Tropic* may very well be, as Cortázar states in his "Table of Instruction," a book that "consists of many books."[45] Yamashita herself has cited Latin American literary traditions as formative to her work. While Yamashita might be referential to Cortázar, she does not didactically instruct her reader on how to proceed. For Cortázar, there are "two books above all" in *Hopscotch*. In *Tropic*, any of the seven characters or a combination of them can provide a main storyline. Yamashita proposes an alternative spatial map to the story that invites the reader to consider the endless narratives that can be read out of the text. In other words, the HyperContexts runs counter to the singular, linear logic of the Contents through multiple fragmented narrative threads. The Contents recognizes the possibility of reading this book as a technology of containment; however, juxtaposing the Contents with the HyperContexts, Yamashita innovates the spatiotemporal form of the novel to delineate the limits of "official" or dominant accounts of LA. There is instead an urgency to the simultaneity of plotlines and the various options with which to engage the diverging storylines, similar to the crisscrossing of LA's freeways.

Told from the perspective of seven different narrators over seven days, each character's journey culminates in a multivehicle collision on the Harbor Freeway in 1990s Los Angeles. Rafaela Cortes is a caretaker of a house in Mazatlán, Mexico, who travels back to LA with the migrant caravan. She is married to but estranged from Bobby Ngu, who lives in LA's Koreatown. They share a child named Sol. While Bobby seeks the "American Dream" through hard work, Rafaela is a protestor with "Justice for Janitors" in a demand for workers' rights. Both represent the laboring masses that keep LA functioning. Gabriel Balboa is a Chicano newspaper reporter and noir figure in search of answers. Emi is a Japanese American television producer who both embodies and defies the model minority myth. Arcangel, a character based on the performance artist Guillermo Gómez-Peña, is an immortal superhuman performer who travels north from Mexico to LA, literally pulling up the latitudinal lines of the Tropic of Cancer northward with a group of migrants in his journey across the U.S.-Mexico border to help fight against the U.S. state on the freeways of LA alongside U.S.-based insurgents. Manzanar Murakami is a third-generation Japanese American, exsurgeon, exmodel minority unhoused man who names himself after the Japanese prison camp. He hears music in LA's cityscape and conducts traffic on a freeway overpass. Finally, Buzzworm is an African American Vietnam vet and an informal social worker who roams the streets rescuing abandoned youth in South Central LA.

To navigate the overwhelming quality of the novel, I take up the challenge of Yamashita's Contents and HyperContexts to create my own desired storyline about LA's infrastructural palimpsest by focusing my analysis on Manzanar Murakami's work in conducting the rhythm and soundscape of the city. Attending to the spatiotemporal figuration of Manzanar, I access a palimpsest of LA that is rewritten and remapped to unravel the infrastructure of the aqueduct, freeways, and city life. Standing on the freeway overpass, "conducting" the movement below, Manzanar offers a particular perception of Los Angeles and the layers of struggle unfolding across the landscape. As a conductor, Manzanar serves as a medium and a central axis who provides a means for the unfolding of the narrative and moves the reader through present, past, and future apocalyptic terrains of LA that might otherwise be inaccessible. Yamashita claims that she worked hard to create the rhythmic sound sensibility for her characters to capture various cultural attitudes.[46] Indeed, each chapter is written through the voice of each character and carries with them their own specific beats and intonations. A focus on Manzanar elicits a deep and far-reaching history of LA's infrastructure and the heterogeneous geographies of an Indigenous, multiracial, and settler colonial Los Angeles revealed through their sonic function.

Manzanar Murakami develops an aural mode of perception of LA from his position as a conductor on the freeway overpass. The reader is first introduced to him as a "sooty" unhoused man with a "lion's head of white hair flailing" with a "silver glint of the baton" amid skyscrapers. Manzanar waves his arms from his "concrete podium," hears the sounds of the freeway below as instruments, cadences, and melodies. As a conductor, Manzanar operates as a guide, or "one who brings," "procures," "introduces," "conveys," and "carries" the reader through different strata to other worlds that we cannot see but that nevertheless exist. Ethnomusicologist Stephen Cottrell has argued that the figure of the conductor shares something with the shaman, as a "mysterious, liminal individual who somehow connects us with another world and through whom we are able to communicate with the spirits we believe exist there."[47] The conductor, with the power of his baton, summons the spirit of the dead composer and provides various visions of sonic order. While musicologist and social theorist Theodor Adorno argued that the conductor, as the imago, is an analogue of the capitalist foreman, an authoritarian figure emerging in the nineteenth century who controls the workers' labor, Manzanar is a character who, Yamashita writes, has "side-stepped the system" completely.[48]

Neither foreman nor imago, Manzanar goes against capitalist notions of the conductor as an authoritarian keeper of time, labor, and value. From his position, "he bore and raised each note, joined them, united families, created a community, a great society, an entire civilization of sound. The great flow of humanity ran below and beyond his feet in every direction, pumping and pulsating, that blood connection, the great heartbeat of a great city" (35). Manzanar's work as a conductor is fused with LA, which in turn is enlivened as a being that has a pulse, blood, and heart. LA is transformed through Manzanar for the creation of disparate communities, families, and fields of sociality through the beats and rhythms of music. The city itself is animated through an understanding of its musicality as Manzanar evokes new sonic orders within the existing grid. As a conductor, Manzanar orchestrates stories and his shamanistic power conjures the dead, repressed, and subjugated geographies through multiple, cacophonous, and discordant soundscapes. Manzanar Murakami hears and interprets the residual sounds of the city, unearthing a multiplicity of maps. His special ability to hear, sense, and "see" the maps weaves a "complex grid of pattern, spatial discernment, body politic" that unearths the geology of the land, the artesian rivers, the manmade utility system of natural gas, unnatural waterways of the Los Angeles Department of Water and Power, the sewage, and the poisonous runoff cascading into Santa Monica Bay (56). Conducting the symphony of traffic and geographies below, Manzanar is able to perceive what the "ordinary person" could "never bother to notice." He unearths the ever-present prehistoric grids of plant, fauna, and human behavior and the connection between webs of land use and property. He can locate contemporary infrastructures of transportation (sidewalks, bike paths, roads, freeways), racialized and classed divisions, and past infrastructures that continue to map onto our present.

As conductor, Manzanar serves as a fulcrum that opens onto extratextual forces that take the reader into their own meditative mappings that exist beyond the text. As a place-based character, Manzanar changes his name after his birthplace, the Manzanar War Relocation Center in the Owens Valley, and provides a narrative hinge to the interrelated, yet unequivocal, grids of Japanese dispossession and incarceration, capitalist extraction, Native erasure, and land theft necessary for the rise of LA as an urban center.[49] Rather than asserting the primacy of Manzanar camp, Yamashita positions her character Manzanar the conductor as a shaman and conduit, as the keeper of time and space who ushers the reader in and out of different geographical strata and brings the hinterlands of the Owens Valley into the city. Manzanar's name evokes the Japanese concentration camp located in the Owens Valley, yet Manzanar camp itself is never mentioned. The beginning point of the aqueduct, the Owens Valley was also the location of Manzanar Japanese concentration camp, the first of ten sites of "relocation," between 1942 and 1945, of over one hundred thousand Japanese descendants dislocated from LA after the bombing of Pearl Harbor during World War II. Japanese Americans have long been intimately linked to and overly identified with the area memorialized through an archive of internment documentary photography, most notably by Ansel Adams, Dorothea Lange, and Francis Stewart. The familiar scenes of Adams's happy Japanese gardeners, Lange's dusty landscapes, and Stewart's photos of "evacuees" playing basketball and baseball against the backdrop of a barren landscape currently dominate our knowledge of Japanese American racialized histories. This form of overtly visual memorialization has sealed into a collective U.S. consciousness an overidentification of Japanese Americans with a form of capture and incarceration that renders them passive against an overwhelming landscape.

The switch from Manzanar's visual medium to one of sound in *Tropic* is relevant. Manzanar camp is brought up so subtly in *Tropic of Orange* that the book seems to have very little to do with Japanese incarceration, as Manzanar the concentration camp primarily appears as the utterance of our conductor's name. Yamashita, I argue, intervenes in the hypervisibility and hypervisuality of Japanese American incarceration by offering new temporal rhythms to the place of the Owens Valley, Manzanar, and Los Angeles. The interplay between absence and presence allows for shared forms of survival beyond the confines of the U.S. settler colonial state. If the apocalyptic is about an infrastructural archival mode of erasure and reimagination, Yamashita's play with the absent iconographic histories of the incarceration of Japanese Americans is resignified onto a broader geographic and racialized field. Gayle K. Sato notes that the novel might be the first and only attempt in Asian American writing "to reflect on the memory and meaning of internment through a marked, actually hyperbolic, *absence* of references to Japanese American history, culture, and Redress politics."[50] To overly associate Japanese Americans with Manzanar camp not only limits the spatial geographies of protest for Japanese Americans but also fails to acknowledge the history of land being stolen from Indigenous people, and the erasure of Paiute lifeways under the development of Los Angeles.[51]

At the novel's climax, Manzanar the conductor offers a distinct temporal description of the peaceful encampment on the freeway while overhead "TV and LAPD choppers hover" (169). Manzanar describes this confrontation between the unhoused people's encampment and the police state as a "curious moment of stasis. . . . Not simply a rest or even a coda, but stasis. Manzanar could liken it to a crossover—the pianist's hand flowering to its destination on the opposite end of the keyboard in one breathless extending and endless motion like changing lanes, straddling the dividing line for a sweet, wistful pause before some rude awakening" (169). Manzanar reaches a "moment of stasis," a period of intense slowdown, not pause because there is still movement. During this moment of stasis, fingers are still moving, reaching over to play the next note, combining musical and freeway metaphors, which gives way to an alternate consciousness as he drops his arms and has an out-of-body experience where he sees himself as an old, disheveled "grizzled white-haired beast of a man wielding a silver baton." Memories of his childhood in the camp wash over him. Standing beside himself, Manzanar sees "his childhood in the desert between Lone Pine and Independence, the stubble of manzanita and the snow-covered Sierras against azure skies. He remembered his youth, the woman he loved, the family he once had, a nine-year-old-grandchild he was particularly fond of. He remembered his practice, his patients, his friends" (170–171). This moment of stasis connects Manzanar's intensely personal moment to broader interlocking histories of migration, incarceration, colonization, and imperialism that converge on LA's freeway. Manzanar's musicality taps into the importance of music and musicians, according to Paul Gilroy, generating "especially important resources that have facilitated the difficult procedures of temporal readjustment. It is important to acknowledge their tradition of longing for a temporality that fosters the capacity to see the individual life-course as well as the synchronized movement of contingent lifeworlds."[52] Manzanar does not quite fit in any temporal world and is constantly out of place and out of sync. His work is an expression of the contradictions of his familial history, the U.S. narrative of liberal democracy, and broader histories of California. Yamashita eludes a regulated or sedimented meaning of Manzanar camp and offers a slowed-down moment to recursively grapple with the overlapping places of LA and the Owens Valley, to hold together, and then let go again, different familial and geographic formations.

While stasis can denote a moment of equilibrium, and a state of inactivity, in music stasis is a technique or form that deploys slow musical development. In Black Studies, sound has been importantly theorized as a vocalization of Black fugitive resistance[53]—with hip hop, for example, as naming the ongoing apocalyptic conditions of capitalism.[54] Fredric Jameson argues that modern Western symphony can produce "a new type of perception," emphasizing how instrumental noises and sound patterns have a logic of their own that organize a sign system that activates interpretive nonverbal practices.[55] As conductor, Manzanar has the distinct ability to see the big picture and bring all of the nuanced sounds and pieces together for a palimpsestic perceptual practice in a way that, as Robert Nichols describes *recursion*, combines "self-reference with positive feedback effects."[56] Understanding history as recursive through Manzanar offers a cyclical vision of a time and place that elicits a feedback sound effect, or humming, emanating from the interplay of sound between speaker and microphone, re-amplifying our original understanding of the historical interplay between LA and its hinterlands. In this long, stretched-out moment, Yamashita does not offer a moment of rest, or a coda, or an ending. Instead, the location of Manzanar camp, which Yamashita does not refer to by name, references "manzanita," Spanish for little apple trees, drawing the reader's attention to the cultivation and the land. Manzanar revisits the Owens Valley by bringing the Owens Valley to LA's freeways, during an intense freeway confrontation between LA's unhoused population, workers, migrants from the south, and the LAPD. Providing different markers for Japanese incarceration, Manzanar decenters the camp space for Japanese American politics and offers a moment for something else to erupt and break through. A conductor can be "anything that conducts, leads, or guides," forming a channel, in one sense of the word, "by which water" is conducted, and in this way Manzanar is the readers' guide into understanding two key grids of domination: aqueducts and freeways.

Focusing on the Sierra Nevada, the desert between Lone Pine and Independence, the "stubble" of the trees, and the blue skies, Manzanar's moment of stasis meditates upon the dramatic landscape of the Owens Valley. Although Yamashita never mentions the Paiute in *Tropic of Orange*, I want to take Yamashita's extratextual invitation to recall other historical strata of the Owens Valley that cannot be contained by the text, to ask how the reader can hear and see, as the conductor, what others might not be able to see and hear when contemplating the barren landscape of Manzanar and the Owens Valley. In other words, the palimpsest of waterways, freeways, the Owens Valley, LA, and Manzanar offers a way to call forth elisions within narratives and archives. Rather than cast the Owens Valley as a faraway and disconnected place from Los Angeles, Manzanar brings the Owens Valley to the concrete center of LA, its freeway system, in an unfolding struggle between Asian American, Black, Latinx, and Indigenous communities and the U.S. state.

To take settler colonialism seriously for mutual survival in Asian American studies means thinking simultaneously about Indigenous claims to sovereignty and land, the role of Asian Americans within the settler colonial imagination, and the emergence and persistence of anti-Asian violence. After the Manzanar War Relocation Center finally shut down in 1945, many Paiute Indians contested turning Manzanar into a historical monument. In a 1979 letter to the Inyo County Board of Supervisors, five Owens Valley tribal elders argued that memorializing Japanese Americans would further erase Native presence. They stated, "To develop an elaborate Japanese-American project means the desecration of the spiritual cultural heritage of the aborigines."[57] This moment marks a challenge for comparative racialization. On the one hand, as Thy Phu argues, the War Relocation Authority (WRA) situated Japanese and Japanese American inmates as adventurous settlers, not as incarcerated laborers, who could cultivate the barren land upon which the camps were built *for* Native peoples. Ignoring Native American claims to this land through the forced resettlement of Japanese descendants on stolen land, in a period of rapid urbanization and industrialization, the state erased the history of Indian removal in the late nineteenth century and promoted "the popular narrative that Japanese Americans were solely responsible for agricultural cultivation."[58] The question of memorializing Manzanar as a space of Japanese captivity is debatable, because remembering the Owens Valley as a site of Japanese American struggle calls for the potential erasure of Paiute presence.[59]

On the other hand, a confrontation between Paiute and Japanese American disenfranchisement through Indigenous proprietary and Nativist claims to place that exclude of other forms of violence must be avoided. Women-of-color critique offers a way to think about the production of solidarity against ontological arguments in comparative race study. A differential understanding of racial formation and history, not empty imaginations of solidarity through homogeneity, opens the space for a simultaneity of worldly existence where both Japanese American critique of the U.S. state and Paiute claims to sovereignty can coexist. Indeed, it is noteworthy that Dillon S. Meyer was the director of the War Relocation Authority during World War II and the commissioner of the Bureau of Indian Affairs in the 1950s.[60] Understanding the interrelated colonial infrastructures of incarceration and Native dispossession illuminates the connections between logics of twentieth-century carceral practices within a longer practice of removal. All three texts explored in this chapter continuously revisit the fundamental role of Indigenous dispossession and elimination in the production of Los Angeles. With this apocalyptic clarity in mind, the Owens Valley becomes a palimpsest of U.S. state practices of dispossession and dislocation that intervenes in Asian American politics of incarceration, stolen water, and Paiute annihilation.

Perhaps the most brilliant aspect of *Tropic of Orange* is the way Yamashita provides a mode to call forth the extratextual, the unknowable, and sometimes the unnamable that have been erased time and time again through overrepresentation—like the visual fixation of Japanese descendants at Manzanar camp in photography. While Indigenous presence in 1990s Southern California has been erased or cast to the past, reading Yamashita's work for its extratextual purposes centers Native land, water, and labor in a story of Los Angeles. This particular origin story, which marks the end for so many, can be traced back to the conquest that stole Paiute land, life, and resources, but it can also be traced back to the explosion of capitalist forms of infrastructure. For Manzanar, the Progressive Era was "a time when the V-6 and the double-overhead cam did not reign. In those days, there were the railroads and the harbors and the aqueduct. These were the first infrastructures built by migrant and immigrant labor that created the initial grid on which everything else began to fill in" (238). Within this initial grid of domination, locomotives "cut a cloud of black smoke through the heart of the West," and the "water was eventually carved away from the north, trickled, then flooded, into this desert valley" (238). Recalling a time before the domination of automobiles, Yamashita harkens back to a moment when a new mode of life "cut" and "carved" its way through the valley. The unending transformation of Southern California's landscape violently slashed through by trains and the LA Aqueduct marks an incursion upon the land and the Indigenous population.

Colonial dominance of the region was achieved through military control of the Indigenous nations and through the subsidy of cheap public lands for white settlers. This included the incorporation of Paiute Indians into settler society as wage laborers, and also the destruction of Paiute earthly modes of life.[61] It is estimated that prior to white settlement, two thousand Paiute belonging to the Bishop Paiute Nation, the Big Pine Paiute Nation, the Fourth Independence Indian Community of Paiute Indians, and the Lone Pine Paiute-Shoshone Nation lived in thirty villages throughout northern Nevada and the eastern slope of California's Sierra mountains.[62] The southernmost group of the Shoshonean, the Owens Valley Paiute called themselves *nüümü*, the "People," and had tended their land in the Owens Valley for fifteen thousand years.[63] A philosophy of water is so central to Paiute life that water marks the beginning and the maintenance of life itself. According to the Paiute creation story, once the world was nothing but water. What is now called "Owens Valley" the Paiute called *Payahüünadü*, "The Land of Flowing Water."[64] All the people lived on Black Mountain, the only land above the water, when one day, Hawk and his uncle Fish-Eater, who lived on Black Mountain, sang and shook a rattle, beginning a downpour of dirt until the water began to move down, giving rise to the Sierra Nevada mountain range that held the ocean back. A river soon ran through the valley, and the people found that they had plenty to eat.[65] Gathering pine nuts, grasses and plants, game, fish, and insect larvae in the Inyo and White Mountains, the Paiute developed and maintained sophisticated infrastructural systems of irrigation that tapped creeks running eastward out of the Sierra to flood meadowland plots for several square miles. For the Paiute, water must be scattered. According to Bishop Paiute tribe member Harry Williams, "At one point they had realized that spreading water was life."[66] Williams states, "We looked at everything as a garden. The natives had made this place bloom like a rose," irrigating "wild" seed plants with water, not merely specific farms or plots. For Williams, "The more you spread the water, the more your garden grew: plants, animals, everything."[67] Recognizing that an abundance of water did not come from the sky, but from the Sierra Nevada's snow that trickled into streams and creeks, the Paiute understood how to move the snowmelt and runoff as slowly as possible through ditches, allowing the water to travel and become absorbed into the land, raising the water table for plants and animals.[68] Building dams and digging ditches, the Paiute irrigated the water across the valley for miles and miles, nearly all the arable land in the valley. Managing the water through careful and sustainable water practices, they cultivated wild plants and fruit trees and helped grass, nuts, and tubers grow, which constituted a substantial part of the Paiute diet. Indigenous agricultural technologies and social organization formed a complex farming system based on communal labor and included a head irrigator; dam-building and canal construction; agricultural tools; and harvesting by women, who then re-seeded the ground.[69]

The Paiute belief in water as the basis of creation stands in opposition to the epistemology of the "taking" of water by the invasion of homesteaders and frontier society in the Owens Valley. The transformation of the American West into a settler society during a period of U.S. state expansion and conquest, from 1860 to 1900, set the foundation for later turning the valley into an "appendage of the modern city," from "Native American homeland to metropolitan hinterland."[70] The Paiute clashed with the white settlers and ranchers, whose sheep and cattle consumed the valley's native bunchgrasses, and polluted the waters, all of which were central to Paiute irrigation systems. Furthermore, white settler farmers and ranchers destroyed seedbeds, and Indigenous animals' foraging areas and the piñon nut, the Paiute main food staple, and the water systems that the Paiute followed over their seasonal food-gathering cycles, during which they dwelt near streams and springs in semi-permanent huts built out of willow.[71]

Against the logic of giving back and spreading water, the LA Aqueduct, as Yamashita describes, cuts into the earth, separating water from the land by concrete. Mulholland's logic of "taking" is about the longevity and future of LA inhabitants, centering humans, not the life and landscape of the valley, and it enacts a vision rooted in the growing needs of Anglo settler communities and the disappearance of Native Americans. Oak and piñon trees continue to die in the Owens Valley as willow shoots that traditionally have been used by the Paiute tribes to make baskets have disappeared, and along with them the skill to weave baskets. As the water program coordinator for the Big Pine Paiute tribe, Alan Bacock, states, "Winning more water rights is not a concept that actually helps us to be able to move forward in a positive manner."[72] While the restoration of tribal water rights is promising, as is the return of brine flies, waterfowl, and shorebirds after the *Los Angeles Department of Water and Power* (LADWP) was ordered to remedy the problem, it cannot address Indigenous dispossession and the ecological degradation of capitalism.[73] What does it mean to celebrate the return of birds and flies as an environmental triumph on a lake that remains as stolen land? It's not about taking water away from one population so that one population can thrive over another, nor is it merely about the return of birds. It's not only about giving the water back to the Paiute, who did not understand the water as solely theirs and something to be cordoned off and kept away from others. It is about the fundamental condition of the landscape.

In Yamashita's rendering, the landscape is given primacy. Yamashita tells her reader that after the initial grid of the aqueduct, "nothing could stop the growing congregation of humanity in this corner of the world, and a new grid spread itself with particular domination. As someone said, now the freeways crashed into each other with flower beds" (238). Evoking the visuality of freeways crashing into planted flower beds, the freeway emerges as a continuation and rearticulation of the infrastructural system of the aqueduct, and one that constitutes a new grid. The freeway's particular "modality" of "domination" uprooted neighborhoods and redrew lines of segregation in a period of civil rights and social movement. A destructive force, the freeway in Yamashita's account is reappropriated and taken over by a new mode of life and becomes a site of struggle that gives rise to urban insurgency. Midway through *Tropic of Orange*, unhoused people occupy the abandoned cars left behind by owners after a horrifying freeway crash, "claiming the right to the city" and reclaiming the use value of the freeway, implementing a "Free Zone" and a new social order.[74] Physically and politically pushed to the edges of a gentrified Downtown Los Angeles by the built environment, urban design, and architecture, the unhoused population in the United States living beneath the freeways in cardboard boxes and tents constitutes the largest unhoused population in the United States, doubling in size in the 1990s and rising still.[75] The sounds of the city—the sounds of car doors, hoods, and trunks mix with the "general chatter of festive shopping and looting"—become part of a storytelling project of an emergent place of dwelling in mutual aid. Manzanar reframes "looting" as "one of those happy riots" on the mile-long abandoned freeway (122). Yamashita shifts the perspective of this scene from the car owners—passively watching from TV sets or the freeway canyon, who could only look upon these acts of "looting" and redistribution with sympathy, anger, or impotence, asking "the usual questions of police protection, insurance coverage, and acts of God"—to the "happy" and "festive" perspective of unhoused people (122). Their actions are "happy" and joyful because the freeway and the cars provide them with new shelter, and because their actions create different modes of exchange, production, and artwork through the repurposing of abandoned cars into homes, gardens, and communal spaces. An unhoused performance group called the LAPD, short for Los Angeles Poverty Department, provides arts and culture for the freeway community. Others cultivate urban gardens and grow passion fruit, lettuce, baby carrots, and tomatoes in the trunks of cars as a mode of self-subsistence, transforming abandoned cars from private property into communal property on the freeway.

As palimpsest, the freeway is transformed into sites of subsistent modes of living, and of art and performance, as it gives rise to new conductors, shaman, and geographies of living and knowing the LA landscape anew. After Manzanar's moment of stasis, more grids expand upon his vision. Watching from above, Manzanar sees a "new kind of grid . . . defined by himself and others like him" (239). He finds himself at the heart of an expanding symphony of which he was not the only conductor. He sees on a distant overpass, across the city, on a street corner, on balconies, and on park benches people waving batons, branches, pencils, toothbrushes, and carrot sticks conducting the city's convergence. As traffic stalls, Arcangel and the ensemble of migrants move onto the freeway. Manzanar notes the overlapping "soft angelic quality" from the unhoused people's encampment wafting gently above the "smoking cinders of quenched fires." The choir grows and sound continues to mark LA's transformation as the entire City of Angels opens as a singular voice to "herald a naked old man and little boy with an orange followed by a motley parade approaching from the south. Once again, the grid was changing" (239). At the same time that the Los Angeles Police collide with the unhoused people's encampment, a movement from the South, led by Arcangel, moves onto the freeway. Traveling from the southernmost tip of Chile northward through the Western Hemisphere, Arcangel and his fellow migrant travelers converge on the freeway with the encampment and the police. As the music intensifies, the freeway expands into the city as the parade, described as a singular body, moves and drags its "entire midriff (and maybe even the swaying hips, burning thighs, and sultry genitals) of the hemisphere" challenging the "rational" force of the North, which looked "at the naughty old man who waved his penis around and shook their big collective head," thinking "this was a gesture of war, was it not?" (240). The arrival of the migrant insurgents emerges as the embodiment of the hemisphere, moving its hips, thighs, and genitals into LA, and in their joyous presence, the insurgents are cast as making a declaration of war and as deserving of a full attack from the U.S. military state apparatus.

Turning its military might against its own people, the U.S. state appears as a faceless military behemoth that in this moment can see the strip of freeway and the rise of insurgents only as a colonial space that needs to be conquered. "Despite the celebratory nature of Manzanar's great laboring choir," gunfire breaks out, and the assemblage of military directs its might down at the freeway encampment (240). The people arm themselves with weapons and munitions, as hundreds of helicopters thunder over the freeway, and the overwhelming "coordinated might of the Army, Navy, Air Force, marines, the Coast and National Guards, federal, state, and local police forces of the most militaristic of nations looked down as it had in the past on tiny islands and puny countries the size of San Bernardino and descended in a single storm" (240). By bringing the Owens Valley into the space of the freeway, the lifeline of the city, Yamashita demonstrates how no space can be protected from state violence. The logics that killed Paiutes in LA's hinterlands, or colonized faraway "tiny islands" and "puny countries," is the same force that will dominate foreign and domestic uprisings against U.S. state power. Thus, Yamashita reveals the cyclical temporality of imperialism as she casts LA as one of the many small island countries of U.S. conquest in the long twentieth century. Tapping into the overlayed sounds of the U.S. military, the sounds of antiracist, anticapitalist, and social movement struggles turn the LA freeway into a colonial site of empire on which battles are still waged.

Rather than unending domination, the convergence of unhoused people, southern migrants, expanding freeways, and conductors moves the readers through unending geographies that materialize interminable struggle. Just as LA's insurgent communities retreat against state power, the movement from the South joins the fight: a "rising tide" of Southern hemispheric migration familiar with the "ravages" of war, "never stopped, clamored forward, joined the war with both wooden and real weapons, capital, and plunder. And so, the percussion of war cracked and thundered. Horns trumpeted attack. Strings bled a foul massacre. Oh say can you see by the dawn's early light the rockets red glare, the bombs bursting in air?" (241). The aurality of this scene is palpable and overwhelming. The screams and cries, the percussive "cracks" and "thunder" of war, and the contradictory song of the "Star Spangled Banner" evoked during an attack against its own people are the very things Manzanar hears and "records." The contrast is stark between the might of the state and the wooden weapons of the migrant south fighting a war that is and isn't their own. This struggle on the freeways of LA between the U.S. state and its underclass is connected to the struggles of the migrant caravan, placing the city within a longer colonized history of war—something "not foreign" to the migrants—in the Western Hemisphere. If we can recall Morales's stories of return and reckoning, we can also understand the eruption of migrant insurgents in the urban north as a reckoning with the oppressed people of the hemisphere. This confrontation on LA's freeways is a reminder that the subjugated will not stay away for long. On the freeway, cars have been abandoned and the unhoused people have built an encampment as the force of the U.S. state battles the migrants from the south and unhoused populations, all of whom represent a return of the repressed that connects LA to a longer history of colonization in the Western Hemisphere. In this chaos Emi, who comes to learn that Manzanar is her estranged grandfather, is shot. Buzzworm cradles her and calls to Manzanar to "Go with her!" Manzanar climbs onto the gurney in the helicopter as it takes off and moves along the LA River and over the hills. From this higher perch he witnesses the inflation of thousands of car airbags as they explode against bullets, stopping the war. Nearby, Arcangel wrestles an embodied SUPERNAFTA in a lucha libre match in an auditorium, where they both die. Bobby is reunited with his estranged wife

Rafaela and their son Sol as he struggles to hold together the literal and figurative lines of the hemisphere, of family, and of community. He ultimately questions these lines, lets them go, and embraces the release. And thus, the story ends. Yet, if *Tropic* can be read in a multiplicity of ways, the ending is also unfixed, unfinished, and unbounded, making space for alternative connections that cannot yet be named.

How It Feels to Have No Solid Tierra under You

Following the overlapping pathways of Yamashita's freeway system into Helena María Viramontes's slow and quiet social surrealist 2007 novel *Their Dogs Came with Them*, I confront the material history of the freeways and its burdened symbolism of linear progress, permanence, and stability of a modern U.S. empire. Viramontes was born in East LA in 1954 and raised there, and her oeuvre reflects a place-based writing practice that intersects the questions of race, class, and gender in that specific location of Los Angeles and across Latin America. As Raúl Homero Villa points out, Viramontes's political commitments extend beyond the page. A creative writer, administrator, editor, and critic, Viramontes also coordinated the LA Latino Writers Association, and founded Southern California Latino Writers and Filmmakers. Her work on the barriological literary and artistic anthology *201/Two Hundred and One: Homenaje a la ciudad de Los Angeles* (The Latino Experience in Los Angeles) and her participation in academic Chicana literary and cultural conferences have all cemented her crucial role in the construction of LA's grassroots Latinx cultural world.[76]

Their Dogs provides an account of LA's freeway system as linked to colonial infrastructures of spatial control. Viramontes demonstrates how freeways are a source of violence, segregation, and destruction that can turn minoritized communities into weapons against each other. At the same time, the novel refuses this weaponization and division by refusing colonialist logics of monumental durability. As in *Tropic*, freeways in *Their Dogs* are turned into palimpsestic sites of reimagination. In *Their Dogs*, Viramontes recursively moves the reader back to the 1960s and 1970s to narrate the seemingly quotidian lives of a multiracial community in East Los Angeles in a period of intense freeway construction. Due to an outbreak of rabies transmitted through rabid dogs, the community lives under a public health quarantine and curfew. The Quarantine Authority that is put into place to protect the community in turn polices the boundaries of the Mexican American barrio, surveilling the bodies that leave and enter, while also using snipers to shoot down dogs from helicopters at night to quell the outbreak. Following four Chicanx characters, *Their Dogs* tells the stories of Ermila Zumaya, a high school student who lives with her grandparents and is experiencing a political awakening; Tranquilina, the daughter of missionary Pentecostal Mexican immigrants, who is deeply rooted in her family's spiritual faith and practice; androgynous Turtle, who spends most of the novel on the streets trying to survive as she navigates gang and state violence; and Ana, an office worker taking care of her brother Ben, who is beleaguered by mental illness. The overwhelming presence of the freeways disrupts the realism of the text throughout the novel and is not, as Jackie T. Cuevas argues, "realism, though it is gritty. This is not magical realism, though it flirts with the surreal."[77] Cuevas further notes that *Their Dogs*' themes of historical colonization, forced migration, and familial ties share commonalities with canonized Chicanx literature, but does not "fit squarely within dominant conventions of common Chicanx fictional genres." The novel does not follow an individual developmental journey, nor does is it offer a "collective voice of group identity formation." Neither does the novel present an easily recognizable immigrant or migrant story, a return home, a nostalgia for the homeland, or a story about the "making of an ethnic representative hero/ine."[78]

In naming what the novel *is not,* I am delineating how the novel defies the expectations of the 1960s–1970s Chicano nationalist narratives that seek to valorize Chicano nationalism's past through the evocation of Aztlán as a Chicano homeland and the primacy of Chicano activism as the period's most relevant account. Viramontes evokes symbols and signs of the Chicano movement throughout the novel but also eschews them. Ermila sits in Chavela's house and conjures a connection to an Aztec lineage that is rendered through precariously stacked matchboxes. Later, Ermila participates in student insurrections "for the fun of it" in which she and her friends hold up banners, raise their "fists to demand a better education," and declare "Chicano Power" (50). Midway through the novel, Chicano Power militants on a college campus, echoing the Black Panthers in the 1960s, tell Ben, "If you're not part of the solution, you're part of the problem," as Ben responds that he is not Chicano. Ben is left "confused and terrified by the antiwar salvo of chanting and pro-civil rights demonstrations," the demonstrators, the MEChA (*Movimiento Estudiantil Chicano de Aztlán*, Chicano Student Movement of Aztlán) table, and their brown berets (118). Ben "resisted being lifted up into a gathering mass of swirling political storms. He refused to be clearly defined as a Chicano, and for that, he refused to belong to a fluid movement . . . joining them, joining other Chicanos to become a part, to become a whole and not just stay forever in between" (118). *Their Dogs*'s decolonial imagination moves against a monumental and homogenous historical image of the 1960s and emphasizes the incommensurability of multiple alternative perspectives.

Ben's discomfort decenters a developmental narrative that understands the achievement of a political consciousness as the center for Chicano politics, and Chicano activists as the most important actors. The novel circumvents, as Cuevas argues, a Chicanx coming-to-consciousness narrative, the conventions of "social consciousness literature or social protest literature of the Chicano Movement, instead showing those left behind or unaffected by the movement of the time,"[79] or as Paula Moya notes, "The daily embodied lives of the kind of people who are marginalized within American society is one of its most important decolonial features."[80] By placing the brown berets, Chicano nationalism, and school walkouts in the background, *Their Dogs* foregrounds the politics of "those left behind" by the Chicano movement. Forever caught between the institutions of the state and the radical movements of the left, Ben does not identify as a Chicano, finds Chicano activism frightening, and cannot become "a part" of any whole. And while Ermila experiments with activism, Turtle's world is further politically distanced from the Chicano Movement and the Brown Berets. Turtle experiences Chicano activism, and its desire for activist protagonists, as purely intellectual, inadequate, and far removed from her ambiguously gendered queer Chicanx body.

Renarrativizing the Chicano movement, Viramontes asserts the space of LA as a palimpsestic text for the never-ending project of rewriting the Chicanx archive. Not merely seeing the Chicano movement as asserting rights and civic presence, Viramontes situates the movement within a broader framework of the city's politics and its infrastructural racism. Decentering Chicano activists and social movement as the mainstay of Chicano political life, Viramontes demonstrates how Chicanx literature can function at yet another register—one dictated by the built environment and materials that were literally poured into the development of Los Angeles in ways that were made possible only through the destruction of Mexican American and multiethnic communities. Yamashita's *Tropic of Orange* and Viramontes's *Their Dogs Came with Them* (2007) offer the freeway as a palimpsestic site of progress, "blight," and systematic and methodical terror on Mexican American, Black, Indigenous, and Asian American communities. Both novels refuse to relinquish the apocalyptic site of the freeway and instead reclaim the concrete structures. In *Their Dogs Came with Them*, the freeway system becomes part of a "character-system."[81] In a 2007 interview, Viramontes described how "the list of characters kept increasing and with this increase, the stories multiplied like freeway interchanges. Having this Eureka moment, [she] realized that the structure of the novel began to resemble the freeway intersections."[82] Viramontes follows Ermila, Ana, Tranquilina, and Turtle's movements in the city over the intense decade of freeway construction and dislocation of Mexican American communities toward the end of the 1960s. During this period, new forms of segregation, alienation, immobility, and intercommunity violence erupted through freeway construction. Just as Los Angeles and its freeways are not merely a setting in *Tropic of Orange* and *River of Angels*, neither is Viramontes's East Los Angeles. LA freeways are not merely passive built infrastructure; for better or worse, they are generative and produce disparate systems of relationships and communities. The city's freeways and the novel's character system as palimpsest results in a radical redistribution of, as Moya points out, "narrative space and makes available multiple perspectives on the same event in a way that enables its readers to develop a kaleidoscopic consciousness."[83] Like Yamashita in *Tropic of Orange*, Viramontes holds several interconnected storylines together through the freeways. Never privileging any character over another, the novel is composed of subplots rather than driven by a central plotline.

The novel begins in the 1960s with Ermila Zumaya walking to her neighbor's house, barefoot, "the soles of her feet . . . blackened from the soot of the new pavement" (5). With the new pavement imprinted upon, and soiling, the bottom of 5-year-old Ermila Zumaya's feet, the novel overlays the transformation of East Los Angeles onto the bodies of its characters, such that throughout the novel it is impossible to separate the built environment of East Los Angeles from the material life of the main characters. The reader follows Ermila, with her feet blackened from the pavement soot, from the space of the city into the home of Chavela, an elder who is packing up her belongings before her home is demolished to make way for the freeways. As Ermila sits on a chair and looks around, the narrator lists the many everyday items scattered across the room: match boxes, scraps of paper, taped up reminders, tumblers, cutlery, and souvenir ashtrays. Meditating upon the objects in the room, this opening scene reflects upon and records the life that the freeway will eventually come to demolish and pave over. Chavela's displacement is not easy. The objects gathered over a lifetime could, at first glance, be cast as a junky mess; however, a slower glance poignantly renders Chavela's painstaking organization of belongings imbued with memory and history. Labeling the items with notes, Chavela writes down the contents packed into the pillowcases: "cobijas," "Cosa del Baño," "No good dreses," "Josie's typewriter," "Fotos." Written in Chavela's "toothpick splintery" handwriting, everyday items are heavily laden with memories that appear through their inadequately perfect labels (5). Through their history these everyday objects—blankets, bathroom items, dresses, a typewriter, photos—carry with them a life of their own: the "dreses" have somehow or other led Chavela toward nothing good; a typewriter belonging to someone named Josie is now in Chavela's possession; and fotos that carry with them a host of memories, events, and feelings.

Chavela understands her dislocation in East LA and the presence of bulldozers, or the "earthmovers," in terms of natural disaster and likens her 1960s present moment of dislocation to an earthquake in Mexico that displaced her family seventy-seven years earlier. Seated among her belongings, Chavela tells Ermila what it feels like to be displaced for yet a second time in her life: "I'm trying to tell you how it feels to have no solid tierra under you. Listen to me! Where could you run? The sound of walls cracking, the ceiling pushed up into a mushroom cloud" (7). Chavela poetically renders her feelings: "I cried for so long that if my grief had been a volcano, it would have torn the earth in two." She continues, "My tears could wash away mounds of clay, a flood as dark as blindness pouring from my eyes" (8). Like an earthquake, bulldozers are rendered with the power to seismically shift the ground on which Chavela lives, moving the earth and breaking up the family walls, uprooting her communities. Chavela counters the disruption of her social and physical world by the earthquake and earthmovers with metaphors of grief. Conjuring the intensity of natural disaster—a volcano that could tear the earth in two, a flood that could wash away mounds of clay—Chavela's deep sense of mourning is ready to shatter and flood the earth. Yet, to have "no solid tierra under you" is not merely a metaphorical way of describing Chavela's grief, and the fragmentation of her community, as the actual ground breaks beneath her feet. By the end of the chapter, the houses on Chavela's side of First Street "would disappear forever," (12) making way for the construction of the freeway, which would claim 12 percent of land and dislocate 10 percent of the East Los Angeles population by the 1980s.[84]

While, as Andrew Needham writes, "the arrival of the bulldozer represents the beginning of urban time," Viramontes connects this newly formed "urban time" of demolition and construction to a history of colonization.[85] The reference to dogs is heavily prevalent and continues to haunt the community in the 1960s–1970s, and Chavela likens the bulldozers, or earthmovers, to the conquistadors' dogs, tearing up the earth. In a description of Chavela's home, the earthmovers are described as anchored ships, "their tarps whipping like hanging sails, their bellies petroleum-readied to bite" (12). Like the dogs and the ships of conquest, Viramontes's story of freeway-building represents another moment of conquest.[86] The novel opens with an epigraph that references Miguel León-Portilla's *The Broken Spears: The Aztec Account of the Conquest of Mexico*. In León-Portilla's 1962 translation of Nahuatl accounts describing the Spanish conquest of the Aztecs, the Aztec (*Mexica*) people refer to the Spanish conquistadors as such: "Their dogs came with them . . . running ahead of the column. They raised their muzzles high; they lifted their muzzles to the wind. They raced on before with saliva dripping from their jaws" (*Their Dogs Came with Them*, n.p.). In the novel, dogs are weaponized by the Quarantine Authority to coerce the Mexican American community and are compared to the deployment of dogs by early conquistadores. Just as the conquistadores trained their dogs to savage the Aztecs, especially punishing nonconforming gendered queer Indigenous bodies, the Quarantine Authority shoots rabid dogs and wields the dog's potential threat to terrorize the newly segregated community.

There is perhaps no structure that more forcefully conveys racial segregation in the twentieth century than the freeways cutting through and over Los Angeles. Freeways are, ostensibly, race-neutral structures for transportation, but their construction in the 1950s–1960s displaced and destroyed once-thriving Black and Mexican communities in Downtown and East LA.[87] The monumental concrete freeways are not submerged like the LA River, nor do they exist outside of the city like the LA Aqueduct. Freeways exist so centrally in the lives of Angelenos that it is difficult to imagine contemporary life in LA where freeways did not exist. In the twentieth century, the mass use of automobiles demanded the development of a national highway system within and between metropolitan areas. City officials and the private sector saw this as an opportunity to create jobs, destroy "slums," and generate growth in the cities.[88] The legacy of LA's freeway construction has roots, as Raúl Villa explains, in late-nineteenth-century reformist discourses of the urban "blight" that sought to root out immigrant slums. Connected to the discourse of the LA River and its racialized communities as diseased and ruinous, this representational practice intensified in the 1940s. The notion of "blighted," infected, or detrimental communities by redevelopers took on a pseudoscientific logic by professional planners turned self-proclaimed "surgeon generals" battling for the "physical, economic, and moral health" of Los Angeles.[89] The language of urban blight went hand in hand with the discourse on progress that "emphasized the citizen's willingness to make sacrifices for the city's modernity," which ultimately targeted multiethnic working-class communities as urban blights that needed to be removed in order for a utopian vision of LA to be achieved.[90]

In the novel, the freeway represents not only the characters but the transformation of the city and the passage of time. Their experiences are grounded in a shifting spatiotemporal terrain, which is registered upon Tranquilina's return to Los Angeles, her place of birth, when she and her mother wander through an unrecognizable maze of once-familiar streets. Since they left for Mexico, entire residential blocks were destroyed, as they find themselves abruptly facing dead-end streets. Freeways contributed to LA's modernization, and became a symbol of the city's progress, but did so by "enthron[ing] the machine, not ambulatory human beings, as the arbiter of urban spatial design . . . claim[ing] the authority of reason and science" in its promise to "rescue humanity from its self-destructive attachments to history, community, and identity."[91] Tranquilina remembers how the streets were "once connected to other arteries of the city, rolling up and down hills, and in and out of neighborhoods where neighbors of different nationalities intersected with one another" (32). Recalling the Kosher Deli, the Pandería, the Chinese kitchen, and all of their neighbors, Tranquilina "sees" what is no longer there. Likening streets and roads to arteries that connected disparate ethnic communities across the space of LA, the freeways signify the amputation of connective roads that felt like "phantom limbs in Mama's memory" (33). Cut off, the feeling of what once was there remains. Caught in a rain storm, she looks up and points out concrete freeway walls splattered with gang graffiti. Viramontes does not offer commentary on how Tranquilina might understand the graffiti, and it is uncertain whether or how Tranquilina comprehends the graffiti.

Significantly, the "blight" of gang graffiti is reimagined as an important site of reclamation for the novel's gang members. One evening, the McBride Homeboys claim and welcome Luis Lil Lizard, Turtle's brother, into their gang and set out in search of freeway bridges and sidewalks to tag on with much anticipation of his initiation. In this scene, the freeways as roadways are reimagined as a blank canvas. More than an individualist claim to property, this act is a reclamation of the barrio. Graffiti comes with its own formal aesthetical rules and yet it is also "a new type of imagery irreverent to any rules" that gives way to an exhilarating expression of the McBride Boys' youthful rite of violations against the Caltrans contractor and patrolling sheriffs.[92] There is deep insight into the way tagging is often cast as an urban blight, as threatening acts of vandalism, and as the destruction of public and private property that demands prevention and erasure, and is cast as deserving of carceral punishment. Yet, Viramontes evokes the particular aesthetics of Los Angeles Chicanx politics in this scene through the rendering of West Coast "cholo"-style graffiti that, in LA, is rooted in 1940s Latino zoot suiters. Graffiti art icon Charles "Chaz" Bojórquez asserts that Mexican American gangs developed as a form of protection against a long history shaped by racism, poverty, illegal mass deportation, and beatings of U.S. servicemen during World War II. LA is home to some of the oldest Latino gangs in the United States that grew out of pachucos and zoot suits.[93] Lowrider cars and culture, music, tag names, clothes, and graffiti language grew out of the zooters' pompadours, draped suits, and Caló, a mixture of half-English and half Spanish rhythms.[94]

By calling upon the particularity of LA Chicanx graffiti forms, culture, and codes, Viramontes places the McBride Boys within a long line of Mexican American barrio calligraphers, and as the inheritors of a system of writing that develops and changes through several generations and lives on through its continued practice. The McBride Boys carefully search for a space-turned-canvas on which to "record their names, solidify their bond," and "proclaim eternal allegiance" to each other; the result is what LA gang wall-writers call the *placa*:

MR SPEEDY x POOR x SIDE; BROOKLYN DIABLOS c/s; RUEBEN, ERNIE, RALPH; EL CHINO JOCKEY x Lote M/ LIL LIZARD, SANTOS x McBRIDE QUE RIFA; RUDY LOVES LA CAT BERNIECE POR VIDA. (164)

This *placa*, or plaque, is a symbol that marks territorial street boundaries, pledging an allegiance to their neighborhood and to each other. Referring to SPEEDY as "MR" elevates Speedy to an important status. Usually written in a typeface commonly referred to as "Old English," the *placa* is carefully written with elaborate thin and thick strokes, in uppercase capital letters, square, straight, clean, and "justified" or aligning on both the left and the right: the classic Cholo handstyle. Against a quickly transforming neighborhood, the McBride Boys write in Old English, an elaborate font that only those with time and comfort in the possession of their own territory would dare to complete. In other words, the font symbolizes a slower temporal moment in which they do not have to quickly graffiti because they are in danger of an attack by rivals.[95] The words are stacked and offer its community and the public a formal document that enables the strength of the gang. It produces a quick visual format decipherable to street readers with street gang literacies.[96] The *placa* follows a particular format that includes a roll call list of their gang names: **RUEBEN, ERNIE, RALPH, EL CHINO JOCKEY, LIL LIZARD, SANTOS**; the name and performative proclamation of not only the gang's strength but also their very existence and their commitment to each other; **McBRIDE QUE RIFA** ("McBride rules," or "McBride are the Best"); and older coded mottoes such as c/s, Con/Safos, meaning "with safety," serving as a trademark, a barrio copyright, and a statement that the graffiti is complete and unarguable and that defacement of it should be limited. They tag with the hope of permanence even as they know that it will be written over. A loaded Chicano symbol, Con/Safos presents a code of conduct that demands respect for the *placa*, and in this way it is a claim for respect within a world that deems them illegible or without an ethical code. Written on the freeway, graffiti becomes a public document that concedes the contingency of its own life term precisely because it can be written over, painted over, erased, and rewritten again. It becomes part of a palimpsestic text that calls attention to the surface of the writing, not only its content, and can bear a multitude of competing and diverging meanings that share the same space, and does not obliterate what came before. Thus, their graffiti writing and reclamation of the freeways and neighborhoods call attention to the competing forms of retrieval of the textual surface of the freeway. In this way, Viramontes demonstrates how palimpsestic geographies are not about total erasure, but about remaking the quickly transforming material world of their neighborhood.

Graffiti writing in the novel demonstrates how palimpsest is a spatial surface tied to conflicting notions of temporality. The ephemerality of graffiti disrupts attachments to permanence and presence because the goal is not necessarily to have the graffiti last forever but to create it with the knowledge that it might not even last until the morning because it can be painted over by the city or a rival gang. The goal is to mark their territory for at least a little while.[97] This transient archival act of "recording," "solidification," and "proclamation" signals their graffiti as already a thing of the past. They imagine their names hardening "like sentimental fossils of a former time," "ancient engravings as old as the concrete itself" that are "as cold and clammy as a morgue table." Their writing and the inevitable erasure of it are part of a struggle over territory, not an exception to the rule. Their present actions produce graffiti that will one day vanish, even as it is intended to mark their immortality. Their "eternal bonds" will look "worn and forgotten," disrupting the immortality that the boys seek within a system that constantly reminds them of their imminent premature death, marking the tension between their desire for permanence and their knowledge of their transience. "The boys would never know" that the traffic of cars and pedestrians, earthquakes, and trees would destroy and crack apart the seemingly everlasting freeways. It does not matter that they would never come to know this, because in this moment Luis Lil Lizard's "shadow would rise and appear as a McBride Boy, an infinite part of the freeway" (163–164). Even if their writing is destroyed, its spirit lives on because they were once there and are consequently forever inscribed into the freeway.

Operating on a recursive time that shuttles between the 1960s and 1970s, the McBride Boys are not living or writing for the future, but are meditating on their infinite present moment of preparation. Even as the graffiti represents a proclamation of strength and immortality on slabs of concrete, they too will fade. Bojórquez compellingly explains that Mexican American graffiti in LA is strongly influenced by its location along the Pacific Rim and its proximity to and affinity with Japanese battle philosophy. Japanese war generals were also poets, who would write poetry or draw images in calligraphy to evoke strength or beauty in preparation for battles. Echoing Manzanar's moment of stasis, LA graffiti shares in this idea of long periods of contemplation through writing and drawing before a quick moment of execution.[98] This moment of Luis Lil Lizard's gang initiation and tagging is a period of contemplative meditation that reimagines their familial, gang, and community bonds and boundaries. If the McBride Boys' graffiti writing is an act of meditative recording, one can also understand it as an act of prayer, not only as a wishful act for the future but as one that connects the characters to the past. Viramontes explains that her commitment to "writing is the only way I know how to pray."[99] The prayer in this scene, and if we think of the entire book as a kind of prayer, is about manifesting a desire for the future through meditating upon the ways the characters have arrived at their present moment. Viramontes integrates the boys and their tagging into the language and imagery of urban decline: "trampling," "faded," "old," the morgue; yet, one might also interpret this scene as a moment of contemplation that evokes strength and beauty in preparation for a battle over their neighborhood. Under a system that continually seeks to erase their written words as well as their bodies, the McBride Boys write themselves into existence.

Born into a life of dislocation and the inevitability of premature and brutal death, Turtle and Luis Lil Lizard, even while alive, inhabit a death sentence that haunts the racialized and gendered Chicanx body. At the end of the novel the McBride Homeboys force Turtle to attack a young boy, and Turtle is hunted down and shot by the police. In her final moment, Turtle recalls Luis Lil Lizard's reminder that the two of them "lived in a stay of execution" (324). Tranquilina, having met Turtle only once, runs to protect Turtle, waves at the police, and screams "Don't shoot!" over and over again (324). Chest burning, Turtle drops down to her knees in a puddle, and as Turtle notices someone holding "her as tight and as strong as her brother, held all of her together until sleep came to her fully welcomed," Tranquilina roars toward the shooters, "*We'rrre not doggggs!* . . . Stop shooting, we're not dogs!" (326). Tranquilina's refusal of colonial disciplining, that "we're not dogs," rejects the conditions of a system and a narrative that seek to weaponize the Latinx community against itself. Viramontes's impetus for writing *Their Dogs* against the technology of colonial warfare was to understand why there "was so much brown-on-brown violence." In many ways the book meditates on the questions: "Why are we killing ourselves, and killing ourselves with such brutality? . . . how did we become dogs. . .? If we are treated like dogs, we become dogs."[100] Gang violence is not the only form of violence prevalent in the novel. Within the milieu of the major and minor characters, there is anti-Black racism in the Mexican American community, anti-Chicanx racism in the Asian American community, and histories of anti-Asian racism and incarceration. Viramontes does not remove the effects of colonization by presenting a harmonious gathering of disparate racialized communities. She does not erase the violence of inner-city gangs and cross-racial racism; rather, she refuses a system that would seek to turn them into weapons against each other, to turn them into the U.S. state's attack dogs.

As the sharpshooters steady their guns, Tranquilina summons and embraces her ancestral spirits and the ability to miraculously levitate to escape the authoritarian voices shouting at her to "stay immobile" (325). Refusing the terms of immobility set forward by the state, through her act of levitation, Tranquilina cannot be contained. Her ascension catches the currents of the wind to ride "beyond the borders, past the cesarean scars of the earth, out to limitless space where everything was possible if she believed" (325). *Their Dogs* opens onto a "limitless space" for Tranquilina's levitation and transformation. Similar to *Tropic of Orange* in which the multiplicity of storylines and endings exist in excess to the page, and similarly to the uncontrollable life of Morales's river, Tranquilina levitates past the cut scars of the earth and refuses to be contained by the police state, the concrete structures, and their boundaries. Approaching LA as a site of cultural politics as such opens the city up for new narratives of flight.

Conclusion

What can seem more permanent and unchanging than the mountains, the natural and manmade rivers, the very ground we walk on, and the immovable concrete freeways crisscrossing Los Angeles? Though many think they are permanent and unchanging, the telluric stories of Morales, Yamashita, and Viramontes teach us that mountains, massive infrastructures, the boundaries between manmade and natural resources, and U.S. state claims to permanence and stability that come to organize racial meaning are neither eternal nor stable. Los Angeles itself, over ten million years ago, was under water, and now Angelenos live under constant threat of drought and conflagration. These novels show us what it means to give back, not to only take, and to reach deep down to subterranean levels and across generations of geographies in order to levitate and move beyond the seemingly permanent and stable world in which we live. Morales's, Yamashita's, and Viramontes' texts extend women of color feminist critiques of capitalism to remind us that for many, the end was the beginning of LA as we know it. Los Angeles in all three novels is represented, visualized, and perceived from different locations and scales, from some human and other-than-human points of view. Against any monumental historical picture of Los Angeles, these writers offer heterogeneous and incommensurable perspectives. This multiplicity provides new modes of inhabiting the frenetic spaces of Los Angeles to grasp how disparate visions of the cityscape offer forms and modes of knowledge production to remake the world. The end is already here and has been here for a long, long time, and yet it is a condition in which living occurs, because Indigenous, Hispano, Mexicano, Black, Asian American, and Chicanx ways of life remain. And, one day, the great colonial monuments of the aqueduct and freeways will be written over.

If this current chapter establishes LA's deep colonial history of dispossession as an infrastructural palimpsest, the following chapter extends Yamashita's spatial expansion and contraction of LA as part of an archipelago of U.S. militarism by pivoting southward to San Diego and outward across the Pacific to Southeast Asia to reimagine the condition of refugee arrivancy. As an imperial epicenter, Los Angeles was a port city that promised further expansion across the Pacific.[101] Building upon the position of LA on the Pacific Rim, and following the pathways built between land and water, the next chapter in this book follows U.S. westward expansion across the Pacific to trace LA's position as an imperial metropole.

ARCHIPELAGOS OF REFUGEE WORLDING

SURVIVAL UNDER COLD WAR MILITARY INFRASTRUCTURES

Hollywood, CA
Camp Pendelton
San Diego, CA

• Wake Island   • Hawaii
• Okinawa
• Hong Kong
                       PACIFIC OCEAN
• Thailand   • Guam
• Vietnam   • Philippines
• Malaysia   • Samoa
  • Singapore
SOUTH CHINA SEA
  • Indonesia

2

> Movies were America's way of softening up the rest of the world, Hollywood relentlessly assaulting the mental defenses of audiences with the hit, the smash, the spectacle, the blockbuster, and, yes, even the box office bomb. It mattered not what story these audiences watched. The point was that it was the American story they watched and loved, up until the day that they themselves might be bombed by the planes they had seen in American movies.
>
> —Viet Thanh Nguyen, *The Sympathizer*

Lê thi diem thúy's hauntingly beautiful 2003 novel *The Gangster We Are All Looking For* opens with a seemingly linear refugee journey in the aftermath of the U.S. war in Vietnam. It offers a story about a family of Vietnamese refugees who flee their homeland and move across harrowing landscapes toward resettlement in San Diego, California. Upon closer look, though, the reader will notice that lê's imaginary eludes any teleological story of arrivancy that also avoids any Hollywood "smash," "spectacle," or "blockbuster" "American story." Instead, the novel initiates an oceanic chain of constant displacement that connects San Diego, Los Angeles, the oceanic, and Southeast Asia. *Gangster*'s unnamed narrator begins the novel by locating herself and her family, always on the verge of eviction, in Linda Vista, a community in San Diego; or where they first lived, in the "Green Apartment on Thirtieth and Adams, in Normal Heights." Before that, the young narrator tells us, they "lived in the Red Apartment on Forty-ninth and Orange, in East San Diego," and before that their familial connections were different. On the other side of the Pacific Ocean, they "weren't a family like [they] are now." The narrator, Ba, and Ma were separated, waiting for each other, with Ma on the other side of the ocean and the narrator and Ba in Southern California with four strangers. She was connected to these four uncles "not by blood but water" and the experience of "stepp[ing] into the South China Sea together," escaping on the same boat. While water takes the place of blood in the new formation of familial ties, it is also a marker of separation, wrought by warfare, that breaks apart and displaces the family unit. Shuttling between the past and the present, the narrator moves the reader through various entry points, vehicles, and spaces. Mirroring the ebb and flow of the ocean, the narrator moves the reader even further back in time through the bonding force of water as they enter the sea onto a fishing boat, and then entering the hold of a U.S. Navy ship, before arriving at a refugee camp in Singapore. There, they are given papers and processed before they "entered the revolving doors of airports and boarded plane after plane" that "lifted [them] high over the Pacific Ocean," and through "clouds, ghost vapors, time zones." In San Diego, the narrator, her Ba, and uncles "were carried" through unfamiliar streets, "delivered to the sidewalk" in front of their sponsor's house "whose door [they] entered" (3–4). Within this constantly transforming world, the narrator places herself within a never-ending journey of movement and familial realignment across water and land, within continuous and intermittent spaces of U.S. militarism. Emphasizing the significance of linked places—and not naming the narrator, her parents, or uncles—the narrator defers the knowledge of who constitutes the collective "we," delaying, or refusing to provide, a clear figuration of the refugees who live in a constant state of dislocation even after resettlement. She narrates a perpetual state of waiting, the deferral of time, and the breakdown and regeneration of familial kinship across oceanic and landed spaces against any notion of linear certainty. While the use of passive voice at first might appear to submit to the objectification of refugees as passive objects to which "things were done," waiting for something to happen for or to them, lê's use of passive voice throughout this beginning rehearses an oceanic story of escape and arrival through an archipelagic imagination. Although the family resettles in San Diego, I approach *Gangster* as a Los Angeles archipelagic text that demonstrates how LA operates as an imperial metropole through its military-oceanic infrastructural connection to San Diego and Vietnam.

This chapter continues the previous chapter's study of deep imperial dispossession by pivoting outward across a militarized Pacific to examine Los Angeles's infrastructures of war and the condition of refugee arrivancy to open up new configurations of relationality across the imperial metropole and seemingly distant geographies. Inspired by Third World radicalism and anticolonial internationalist ideals of transnational solidarities, I argue that *Gangster*'s oceanic language uncovers the imperial circuit of warmaking infrastructure between LA, San Diego, the Pacific, and Southeast Asia, revealing in the process an archipelagic militarized cartography to Los Angeles. Reimagining LA as part of a San Diego-Pacific-Southeast Asian archipelago constitutes LA differently as part of what Tongan writer Epeli Hau'ofa calls a "sea of islands."[1] Archipelagic thinking, as Édouard Glissant illuminates, considers the mainland as part of a capacious territory in relationship to other islands, providing physical, geologic, cultural, intellectual, and spiritual encounters to reconfigure new forms of relationality across disparate geographies.[2] And, in critical refugee and transnational Asian American studies, Patricia Nguyen, Erin Suzuki, and Evyn Lê Espiritu Gandhi have further theorized the oceanic and archipelago as critical and dynamic sites to analyze relationality. In this way, archipelagic thinking has been crucial to retheorizing Asian American and Indigenous Pacific subjectivities in the wake of militarized colonial conflicts across the modern Transpacific to understand their differential histories and the possibilities of alliance within the shared geopolitical space of the Pacific.[3]

Lê works with an archipelagic spatial logic to disrupt U.S. state, Hollywood, and popular visions of Vietnam as an apocalyptic backdrop that was crucial to Cold War narratives of freedom. The Cold War was a pivotal moment in the reimagination of the planet through a masculinist apocalyptic visual aesthetic that was formulated around the justification of U.S. violence of militarization, soldiers, and warfare. In popular culture, LA's Hollywood mythmaking machine intensified the apocalyptic vision of the "Vietnam War" by making Vietnam synonymous with war through films that centered U.S. soldiers and the failure of U.S. imperialism.[4] Vietnam has been represented, as the title of Francis Ford Coppola's 1979 film suggests, as an "apocalypse now," transforming the apocalyptic not as a disaster to come but as an end that has already happened, "over there" on the other side of the world. Apocalypse over there, in this logic, must take place in order to preserve "our" freedoms and progress over here, creating a cartographic narrative of discrete spaces. Cold War apocalypticism is a regime of destruction that is tied to the specter of warfare as well as residual regimes of anticolonial counterinsurgencies that connect seemingly separate and disparate spaces. *Gangster*, as I argue in this chapter, unsettles the dominant representational practices of the Cold War and instead unearths a submerged military infrastructure that Cold War apocalypticism suppresses. Lê's novel interrupts dominant and popular visual logics of Vietnam as an apocalyptic space, and unsettles the linear path of refugee arrival, instead revealing the infrastructural intersections of Cold War militarism.

While the Hollywood machine of Los Angeles constructs a Vietnam spectacle and the liberal narrative of heroism and freedom, *Gangster* offers an occasion to ruminate upon the LA-San Diego corridor as also being the repressed site of massive defense-industrial production, highlighting the infrastructures of U.S. militarism to which Vietnamese refugee worldmaking is bound. In this chapter, infrastructure references the actual materiality of war armament and bombs, and the militarized spaces of battle, imprisonment, and refugee resettlement across an archipelagic imagination. A stronghold for the U.S. Navy and Marine Corps, San Diego is home to Camp Pendleton, one of the largest and significant Marine Corps bases in the United States and the site at which fifty thousand Vietnamese refugees arrived over a period of six months after the "fall" of Saigon, resettling throughout Los Angeles, San Diego, and Orange County. In the aftermath of the U.S. war in Vietnam, Vietnamese refugees were rerouted through the very places that were crucial to the devastation of Vietnam. Each year Camp Pendleton trained over forty thousand active-duty and twenty-six thousand reserve military personnel. Marines prepared at the camp with replicas of Vietnamese jungles and villages before heading off to Vietnam. Out of Camp Pendleton, the 1st Marine Regiment waged war across Vietnam and in 1971 it was the last Marine infantry unit to leave Vietnam.[5] Camp Pendleton and the Pacific military bases of Clark and Andersen Air Force Bases were positioned as places for Vietnamese refugee resettlement even as they were part of a broader destructive infrastructure of warmaking that instigated the refugees' displacement. If LA is the representational site of the fantasy of the U.S. war in Vietnam that projects outward Hollywood spectacles or military armaments, then San Diego is the militarized real with entanglements in longer histories of total colonial warfare.

In this chapter, I focus on *Gangster*'s figurative language to ask, "How does lê build for refugee survival in the face of the apocalyptic logics and effects of Cold War militarization?" To think through this question, the three sections of this chapter consider the apocalyptic logic built into a proliferation of Cold War military infrastructures. The first section engages with the visual regime of the Cold War and the contradictory discourses of the U.S. racial liberal state, the white supremacist movement, and anticolonial struggle surrounding the U.S. war in Vietnam. Refusing any singular hegemonic narrative of the war, I counter the Cold War apocalyptic visual representations and its ocularcentric productions—images produced both by photojournalists and by LA's cinematic Hollywood machine—through lê's use of ekphrasis, metaphor, simile, and imagery. Such a focus offers an archipelagic imagination to symbolically deterritorialize LA, revealing LA as an apocalyptic cultural screen connected to material sites of war. The second section continues with lê's archipelagic imagination by transforming Vietnam's jungle, the infrastructures of weapons, bombing, and camp spaces by remaking the space of Vietnam into a field of intimacy, sociality, and kinship. The third and final section considers infrastructures of resettlement found in the debris and spillage of oceanic waterways, war and refugee camps, and life in Vietnam and San Diego. *Gangster* begins and ends with metaphors of water for the imagination of a refugee worldmaking where trauma, memory, and grief are associated with the atemporal boundlessness of the oceanic, spilling across the ocean and throughout the mainland as a horizon of possibility, connection, and placemaking. In this sense refugee worldmaking, like the ocean, has no beginning and no end, challenging the teleology of singular apocalypse, evoking an archipelagic landscape of living, working, and dying within the paradoxical and unresolvable spaces surrounding war, resettlement, and belonging.[6] Realigning nation and homeland with the fluidity of water makes the concept of dwelling shapeless, flowing, and unstable, and recasts the imperial metropole of LA's cultural force as part of an archipelagic chain of U.S. militarism to defy a neat linear narrative of rescue and resettlement.

Vietnam Is a Photograph: The Visual Politics of the Cold War, the White Supremacist Movement, and Third World Archipelagic Imaginaries

Narrated through a first-person point of view, *The Gangster We Are All Looking For* is composed of nonlinear events, broken time, and memories that transport the reader back and forth between life and death in Vietnam and in the United States. Brushing up against the autobiographical and bildungsroman, the novel mirrors certain aspects of lê's life. Like *Gangster*'s narrator, lê was born in Phan Thiet, Southern Vietnam, in 1972 during a hot summer in the countryside amid attacks from Northern Vietnam. In 1978, at the age of six, lê escaped with her father on a boat, just as the narrator does, and is placed in a refugee camp in Singapore before they eventually move to the naval base city of San Diego, California, through sponsorship. While *Gangster* represents one of the first novels from the generation of "boat people" of the late 1970s–early 1980s and vaguely mirrors lê's life, the novel's work on figurative language yields a refugee worlding practice beyond the promise of knowledge about a concrete universal refugee subject.[7] I argue that *Gangster*'s use of figurative language intervenes in the visual regimes of U.S. Cold War infrastructure to create a relational politics between Vietnamese refugees, LA's fantasies of war, San Diego's militarized infrastructures, and a world brimming with ghosts, the reanimation of dead things, and of the jungle. Language in this chapter reimagines war not in order to make war artful, but to engage with the ways U.S. militarized infrastructure, and its justifications, went hand in hand with U.S. cultural practice and representations of warfare.

In the aftermath of the fall of Saigon, Vietnam has become, in the words of Rick Berg, a "resource for the American culture industry," where the "fragments" and "ruins" of Vietnam are "unrepressible and endlessly recuperable."[8] One of the most devastating wars, the U.S. war in Vietnam was also the most photographed, "the most chronicled, documented, reported, filmed, [and] taped" wars in U.S. history.[9] Hollywood in particular tethered the war and the nation of Vietnam to an imagination of total warfare that firmly fixed Vietnam as an apocalyptic backdrop in the second half of the twentieth century. Through this narrative of devastation Hollywood films have, as Viet Thanh Nguyen described, "dehumanized" and "de-realized" Vietnamese people in order to humanize the U.S. soldier and defend U.S. ideology and culture.[10] Vietnamese men are depicted in film, television, the news, and photographs as cold-blooded and brutal Viet Cong, or as useless and dishonest South Vietnamese. Vietnamese women are hypersexualized fetish objects for Western consumption who entice U.S. soldiers in Stanley Kubrick's *Full Metal Jacket* with the memorialized phrases "Me so horny! Me love you long time. Me sucky sucky." For a long time, and still today, when the United States thinks of Vietnam, it is alluded to only as "the war," and "our," the United States's, loss.[11] These representations of Vietnam, as John Carlos Rowe argues, betray an "unconscious" epistemology through the guise of realism that casts Vietnam to the past while affirming an American individualism.[12]

While the photographic documentation of war and combat has existed since the mid-nineteenth century with the Crimean War, photography during the war in Vietnam for the first time functioned as a significant means to shape U.S. national opinion and culture. Dubbed "the living room war," visual imagery served to evoke feelings of shock and terror over the violence enacted by U.S. military presence in Vietnam but also over the harm inflicted upon U.S. soldiers, sowing divisions within the country. Indeed, visual representations of the war were essential to the production of a Cold War racial liberal state that promised the spread of capitalist democracy against communist threats abroad and at home in a period marked by the waning of an official white supremacist U.S. state and the emergence of a prescribed U.S. antiracist liberal-capitalist modern state formation, a U.S. state-recognized form of antiracism.[13] The suturing of U.S. state capitalist democracy to the containment of communism justified war and U.S. militarization at home and abroad. In this formulation, destruction was necessary as a means for the maintenance and futurity of democracy. The specters of war and U.S. militarization formulated critical spatial logics that in this critical period of the twentieth century restructured epistemologies of the end of the world. Seen through this worldview, Vietnamese people and Vietnam are transfixed into an empty homogeneous space, overvisualized through the U.S. military-industrial complex and erased through a U.S. nationalist narrative of catastrophic warfare as a tragedy for the United States and its soldiers. The photographic capture of Vietnam as apocalyptic sign, icon, and referent was significantly linked to U.S. racial liberal Cold War cultural practices of hegemonic governance and dominance that sought to contend with institutionalized racism domestically while justifying U.S. occupation abroad. Photographs of Vietnam was also part of, according to Thuy Linh Nguyen Tu, an "authorized account of war" that testified to U.S. suffering and heroism.[14] The war consolidated a narrative of the United States as savior of democracy while also offering an "opportunity" to systematically and scientifically cohere a Cold War system of knowledge through the collection and study of soil, plants, and other elements of the landscape.[15]

At the same time, the war and its aftermath led to the intensification of a new white supremacist movement that viewed the war through a cosmology where white Americans saw themselves within a race war that marked the end times. Movement leaders such as Louis Beam returned from Vietnam and turned to the popularization of "common" elements of the "Vietnam War experience" and warfare violence through films such as *Apocalypse Now*, *The Platoon*, *Deer Hunter*, and *Full Metal Jacket*.[16] Vietnam was seared into Beam's memory so much that "even after all this time there seems to be no way we can forget or let Vietnam descend into the past.... There is no relief, and can be none. We are forever trapped in the rice paddies and skies of Vietnam. We can neither go back or go forward, suspended for eternity in the place that they put us.... Forget? Not even if I could."[17] For white supremacist activists, the war served as a catalyst—and a persistent image of horror and danger—and white soldiers served as an army that unified different U.S. white supremacist constituents in a continuation of the war stateside. Betrayed and abandoned by the U.S. government, soldiers returning home fueled a critique of the U.S. politicians and military leaders for not recognizing their sacrifices. By the end of the 1970s and in the war's aftermath, according to Kathleen Belew, white nationalism cohered white power groups striving for a revolution that would bring about separation and a white utopian nation. The loss in Vietnam, social movements of the 1960s for racial and gender equality, the passing of civil rights legislation, the expansion of immigration laws, shifting liberal state institutions, income inequality and unemployment, and prevalent distrust in the government consolidated white nationalism across heterogenous groups of Klansmen, neo-Nazis, and suburban Californian skinheads, white supremacist congregations, and southern separatists, fueling a public and underground white power movement that increasingly viewed the U.S. state, nonwhites, and immigrants as their collective enemy. United by a common desire for a white homeland against the "threat" of Viet Cong and Vietnamese refugees across national boundaries that would unite white people globally, the white power movement fought against the perceived governmental eradication of whites in the United States through interracial marriage, rape, birth control, abortion, immigration, and the resettlement of nonwhite people.[18]

While the U.S. war in Vietnam was used to formulate a new notion of white supremacist worlding, it also mobilized a new anticolonial Third World archipelagic imaginary. Anticolonial struggle was crucial to toppling white supremacist versions of the war. Perhaps one of the lasting critiques of internationalist antiwar movements was the ways these movements laid bare the contested signifier of Vietnam and denied the hegemonic racial liberal and white supremacist visions of the war. U.S. governmental acts of repression, and the remarkable demonstration of state power, fanned the flames of revolution across feminist, Black, Asian, Latinx, and Indigenous movements that linked the United States's racist interventionist practices, the maintenance of U.S. white supremacy, and global uprisings abroad. Third World radicalism innovated critiques of empire and war through a new archipelagic imagination of global struggle. Black liberation movements understood the war in Vietnam to connect the Black power movement at home to a broader international struggle against imperialism. At the same time that the racial liberal state was passing the Civil Rights Act of 1964, local police and state law enforcement agencies collaborated with U.S. military and FBI intelligence to enact an anti-Black militant agenda, targeting the Student Nonviolent Coordinating Committee (SNCC), the Congress of Racial Equality (CORE), the Southern Christian Leadership Conference (SCLC), the Black Panthers, the Nation of Islam, the Mississippi Democratic Freedom Party, and the National Association for the Advancement of Colored People (NAACP).[19] U.S. communists were identified as "subversives" and were purged from service, underwent loyalty tests, and were heavily surveilled at the local, state, and federal level.[20] Between 1956 and 1971 the furtive and extralegal work of the Counter Intelligence Program (COINTELPRO) infiltrated, disrupted, undermined, and surveilled "subversive" domestic feminist organizations, anti-Vietnam War organizers, civil rights activists, the Black Power movement, the Communist Party USA, environmentalist and animal rights groups, the American Indian Movement (AIM), and independence movements such as the Young Lords and the Puerto Rican Socialist Party. COINTELPRO assassinated roughly twenty-nine Black Panthers and imprisoned hundreds of other members. By 1968, the growing unpopularity of the war conjoined U.S. domestic questions of racial justice with international critiques of U.S. militarism.

    I return to this earlier contestatory era to think through the durability of Third World radical critique imagined across an archipelagic cartography of revolutionary thought. Officially beginning in 1955 and ending in 1975, the war seemed to signify the end of the world for U.S. power, but for anticolonial movement and new forms of white supremacy it also marks the beginning from which new worlds emerged. Internationalist anticolonial struggle against U.S. Cold War empire generated a defensive panic and paranoia about an aligned Third World/Black insurgency that instigated an apocalyptic mentality. Vietnamese endurance against U.S. intervention sparked anticolonial revolutions against forms of Western capitalism. The proliferation of rebellions across the globe, as Jeremi Suri highlights, provided ethical, intellectual, and revolutionary sustenance throughout Africa, Asia, and Latin America.[21] The Vietnamese revolution symbolized a triumphant victory against the military strength of the United States and inspired other Third World revolutions. Along with Cuba, Vietnam inspired, as Odd Westad points out, a new Left that saw Soviet development and foreign policy as "too dogmatic, too self-satisfied, and too timid."[22] Vietnam became a model for a more efficient win over imperialism, especially after Hanoi's successful military and political victory over the United States after the 1968 Tet Offensive. Revolutionary movements in Southeast Asia (Malaysia, Thailand, and the Philippines) learned from the North Vietnamese and the National Liberation Front (NLF) how to wage warfare like the peasant guerilla. In the United States, the Panthers were inspired by the guerrilla Vietnamese fighting tactics that demonstrated how smaller forces can achieve small victories and disrupt the image of an invincible U.S. military campaign. Inspired by anticolonial struggle across Africa and Asia, Black civil rights and radical activists have long integrated a global outlook to U.S. struggle. SNCC and the Black Panther Party yoked the 1960s racial urban uprisings to Vietnam's NLF. From the 1950s to the early 1960s, military service represented a significant employment option for African Americans, and the Black community saw military service as an opportunity out of impoverishment and to demonstrate their "valor" and "honor" as a GI and "good soldier." By the end of 1966, sixty thousand Black soldiers were based in Vietnam.[23] The NAACP, the Urban League, and civil rights moderates supported the U.S. military abroad, but by the end of 1966, as Black Americans were disproportionately dying in Southeast Asia, these groups raised concerns in Black communities in the United States. By the late 1960s and early 1970s, Black activists from Martin Luther King Jr. to SNCC recognized the Vietnam War as racist and imperialist, with excessive Black deaths, abroad and domestically, fueling opposition to the war.[24] King proclaimed the irony of "Negro and white boys on TV screens as they kill and die together for a nation that has been unable to seat them together in the same schools. We watch them in solidarity burning the huts of a poor village, but we realize that they would never live on the same block in Detroit."[25] Black radical insurgency challenged the U.S. state's claims to an emergent liberal capitalist position as "leader of the free world."[26] Student activists of the 1960s made links between the U.S. "military-industrial complex" and the contradictory predicament of African American soldiers fighting in a U.S. imperial war.[27] SNCC activists in this moment began to question Black politics, and they put out a statement against the war as part of an understanding that Black struggle was linked to a "much larger struggle than we had all anticipated in the beginning."[28] Electrified by the Vietnamese insurrection, U.S. social movements drew on Third World internationalism, its analytics of power and domination, and archipelagic collective imagination for revolutionary practice.²⁹ For the U.S. state, anti-imperial struggle was something to be contained to pull the world back from utter annihilation. For anticolonial struggle, the end is not the end but a place and time for the breaking and making of the world through a new relational geography for racial solidarity.

The release of *Gangster* in 2003 demonstrates the ways antiwar critiques of Vietnam continuously re-situate U.S. imperialism and Cold War visuality across an archipelagic literary imagination for anticolonial thought. Lê's literary work can be seen as innovating Third World radical cartographies in a confrontation with a racial liberal visual regime to reimagine, as lê does elsewhere in other forms of writing, how "Vietnam is not a war."³⁰ In lê's 1993 poem "Shrapnel Shards on Blue Water," the speaker addresses her "sister," Lê Thi Diem Trinh, and outlines what "vietnam is not." Vietnam is not a word, world, love, family, or fear that should ever be buried by a definition of Vietnam demarcated by the United States, a "foreign land" that has overdetermined "Vietnam" through war.³¹ Lê uses capital letters, and emphasizes through a series of repetitions, to "let people know/VIETNAM IS NOT A WAR." In doing so, lê seeks to supplant the oft-repeated images of Vietnam as war through language, making Vietnam artful and therefore multivalent. To "let" people believe this, to allow people to see Vietnam as only a war, is to bury the various valences of Vietnam. To correlate Vietnam only with war presents a mode of perception, or a reading, that makes Vietnam overwhelmingly visible only through destruction and acts of forgetting. In order to survive, one must "never forget" the meaning of Vietnam within a broader system of Cold War worldmaking. She ends by opaquely explaining that Vietnam is "a piece of us, sister" and even then,

we are
so much

more

The space between "much" and "more" entails a period of waiting through which something "more" might emerge. This space does not ultimately define Vietnam, nor does it need to be filled, but evokes a series of paused relationships between words, worlds, love, family, and fears. The pregnant pauses testify to the obscuring work of language and the never-complete definition of Vietnam, drawing Vietnam into a discursive formation of simultaneous erasure and emergence. Lê's insistence undoes the metonymy of Vietnam as war and reinvents Vietnam as a different kind of signifier for reimagining war and displacement.

Lê revisits this earlier Cold War moment through *Gangster*'s diegetic setting, the 1970s–1990s, and continues to explore the artfulness of "Vietnam" as a countervisual narrative to the ocular capture of Vietnam. A beautifully quiet text, *Gangster* stands in stark contrast to U.S. representations of the Vietnam War, a cultural-political visual phenomenon that has overwhelmingly locked our apocalyptic senses of perception into one of total warfare and annihilation in the twentieth century. The genius of *Gangster* lies in lê's use of figurative language to unsettle "Vietnam" from the iconography of Cold War racial liberal apocalyptic imagination that fixes it as a distant landscape of military intervention.[32] *Gangster* approaches the social and cultural fields embedded within descriptions of and acts of perceiving photographs as a disruption of apocalyptic visual practices surrounding the U.S. war in Vietnam. One day, while living with her family in San Diego, a black-and-white photograph of the narrator's grandparents arrives in the mail. This photograph in particular is referred to in different sections throughout the novel, disrupting and collapsing the narrator's spatiotemporality of her present moment in San Diego with her family's past life in Vietnam. Through its fragmented representations the reader, along with the narrator, pieces together the story behind the photograph, which begins to take on a life of its own. The narrator shares, "Vietnam is a black-and-white photograph of my grandparents sitting in bamboo chairs in their front courtyard" (78). Claiming that Vietnam "is" this photograph recognizes how Vietnam has been made static by ocular images. This "image," however, is rendered through the language of metaphor. In this way, metaphor becomes the language of relationality. The metaphorical use of "is," according to Paul Riceour, is the copula of the verb *to be* and signifies simultaneously what it "is not" and what it "is like," establishing a condition of similarity and dissimilarity, enabling us to see two things in one. Saying "Vietnam is a . . . photograph" marks an encounter between two words ("Vietnam" and "photograph"), and initiates a deviation from the ordinary usage of both words.[33] The resignification of the word, and the semantic innovation of Vietnam as photograph, exists ephemerally, for a mere moment, as it is resignified.[34] Likening Vietnam to a photograph seems to make Vietnam static, but through language, "Vietnam" is animated and abstracted from a referent through tropological substitution. As such, Vietnam, to borrow from Riceour, "dissipates itself in ornamentation"; it is never fixed as it is "allowed to run free" and "[lose] itself in language games."[35] Lê's use of metaphor gives rise to a worlding practice that constitutes a "displacement and an extension of the meaning"[36] of the words "war" and "Vietnam." Through the level of the discursive, lê disrupts any singular notion of Vietnam as romanticized homeland or apocalyptic war zone.

Lê's figurative language arises as an infrastructural foundation, or as linguistic building blocks, for refugee survival that counters the linear apocalyptic visions of Vietnam as a place of ruination. Playing with the metaphor of photography opens onto ekphrasis as a literary practice that offers, in W.J.T. Mitchell's words, a "verbal representation of a visual representation."[37] Lê's artful description of the photograph of her grandparents performs the function of ekphrasis as she offers a different way of "seeing" the image through figurative language to offer a simultaneity of nonsynchronous time. Joseph Darda has recently argued that racial liberal temporality "registers in the figurative language most Americans, including conservatives and radicals, use to address race" through metaphors of "antiracism as war, as reform, education, and integration."[38] The moment of "seeing" of a "still moment" that lê offers is not only a visual experience but structures language into formal arrangements that "still" the "movement of linguistic temporality into a spatial, formal array."[39] This shaping entails not only vision, but "stasis, shape, closure, and silent presence," in other words "stillness," as the aims of a general understanding of ekphrasis.[40] The interplay between verbal and visual representation becomes, according to W.J.T. Mitchell, "practically endless" as the imagetext or verbal icon overtakes the image/text divide.[41] In this scene, Vietnam as photograph cannot be stilled as other imagetexts are. Verbal icons are substituted for the still image of the narrator's grandparents, and for the narrator the photograph captures not only a moment of her grandparents sitting in their courtyard but the moment of her mother's loss.

Lê rethinks the visuality of the Vietnam War through figurative language to render a story about trauma, loss, and regeneration across the geopolitical terrains of the United States and Vietnam. The narrator describes the photograph in great detail, describing what she can and cannot see. Her grandparents' stature is tall and proud, and they wear thin sandals on their feet. Her grandfather's forehead is broad and shiny, and her grandmother's eyes are "famous[ly] sad." Chickens and roosters surround the two figures, "oblivious" to what has transpired and what is transpiring in the country at large and the family in particular. These are the images that are obvious to the eye; however, the photograph also loudly pronounces an absence: her mother. The supposed transparency of the photograph is undermined by what the field of visuality cannot capture. Her grandparents disowned her mother, "a Catholic school girl from the South," when she married her father, "a Buddhist gangster from the North." This is "not visible to the eye," nor are the impressions in the soft dirt of the courtyard from the day her grandfather chased her mother out of the house, beating her with the very broom with which she would use to sweep the courtyard (79). Turning to the literary to "see" her grandparents and Vietnam presents and, as Kandice Chuh writes, "thus makes present—that which is normally construed as bygone."[42] The static image of her grandparents, the animals, and the house around them is brought into the space of the family's present-day life in California, rupturing the veil between the past and present. The distance between the United States and Vietnam signals how the losses of the past remain unresolved for the family.

Lê reveals the literary effects of figurative language to be a space of refugee worlding that makes legible fields of sociality that are typically elided within U.S. narratives of freedom. Grappling with past trauma in *Gangster* is not about escaping to the U.S. and into the future away from Vietnam. The photograph exceeds an understanding of the photograph as marking a past moment, the rejection of her mother by her family, or the referents in the photograph: her grandparents. Instead, this moves beyond a neat temporality of the past and present and marks a spatial movement. At first glance, the photo looks like her grandparents' wedding portrait, but in actuality it is a photograph taken for their children in their final years. This is an image that should be "moved in" to their children's house, to be placed on an altar with incense, fruit, and water, for ancestral worship, so that they can live beyond their humanly death, and be taken care of by the daughter they disowned. And, in return, the ancestor will continue to care for their family and descendants. For the narrator, this photo signals a "beginning. To or toward what, [she doesn't] know, but always a beginning" (78). Engrained within the narrator's description of the photo is a sense of time, in which the end of her grandparents' life is embedded into a vision of a beginning, even if she does not yet know what it is. If Vietnam "is" this photograph, then Vietnam marks the beginning of the end of her mother's relationship with her parents and a reconciliatory and irresolvable marker that continues with her grandparents, who travel through this photograph, across the ocean to be with their family in San Diego.

As the narrator grapples with the photograph, Vietnam emerges as a place of survival, love, and family, offering glimpses of life that exceeds destruction and forgetting. Her parents' love story, for instance, emerges within the narrator's description of the photograph, and the photograph comes to tell the story of Ma's family breakdown as a result of her relationship with Ba. The photograph arrives in the chapter entitled "The Gangster We Are All Looking For," from which lê names the entire novel. For the narrator, Vietnam "is" this photograph because it represents what Vietnam means to her—a familial history of breakdown that exceeds official and mainstream accounts of "seeing" Vietnam. Following her description of the image, the narrator shares how Ma "followed [Ba] in circles through the forest, supposedly in search of the clearing that would take them to his aunt's house. They wandered in darkness, never finding the clearing much less the aunt she knew he never had" (81). In the darkness of the jungle, they hold hands, and stand on the brink of war and love. Ma studies Ba's face, memorizing the scars on his face. Intertwined within her parents' courtship are her mother's dreams about the end of the war: foods she would eat, songs she would sing, movements she would dance. While Ma hoped for the end of war, war also operates in an archipelagic circuit across Vietnam, the U.S., and Southern California where war and their struggle to survive continue.

Bombing, Camps, and Kinship

Lê's archipelagic imagination captures and transforms U.S. infrastructures of weapons and warfare as they take shape through chemicals, bombs, and militarized camps. Lê's artful linguistic confrontation with the photographic image confronts technologies of weapons and prison camps as she readjusts her relationship to the nonhuman world of the jungle and war camps in a cycle of warfare. While Nora Alter suggests, "It is as if Vietnam had no history before the American occupation and nonethereafter,"[43] in *Gangster*, the jungle exists long before the war, exceeding the temporality of U.S. modern warfare, and is rendered through disparate refugee intimacies and familial ties. When Ma daydreams about Ba at the beginning of their courtship, she begins to ponder what the forests were like before the American planes began to rain "something onto the trees that left them bare and dying" (81). The presence of the U.S. military is felt through the landscape of the dying trees, making the effects of war concrete. Vietnamese people were, as Thuy Linh Nguyen Tu points out, "left with the lingering effects of wartime ruination, with an ecology gravely altered, and with bodies still containing alarmingly high dioxin levels."[44] More explosives, according to Yến Lê Espiritu, were dropped onto Vietnam, a country smaller than all of California, than in the totality of World War II.[45] To this day, the poison released from carpet-bombing and chemical defoliation contaminates Vietnam's ecosystem. Three million lives were lost to U.S. military policies of search-and-destroy missions, systematic deforestation, chemical defoliation, the razing of Vietnam's countryside, and the contamination of the air, land, and water. At the same time, lê's linguistic renderings reclaim the dead and Vietnam by realigning the relationship between Vietnamese bodies and the jungle.

Lê transforms the material infrastructures of war—planes, weapons, and bombs—through the depiction of the jungle. Lê's literary landscape of the jungle offers a contradictory place of ruination, richness, and abundance in contrast to Hollywood representations of the jungle as a solely nightmarish space of trauma and death for the white U.S. soldier. Personifying the jungle, Ma recalls her father's stories of a time when the leaves smiled broadly and the jungles were thick from the richness of the soil. The jungle is imagined as a productive landscape of intimacy and regeneration in which her parents wander and fall in love, and not only as a place of illness and disease that threatened U.S. soldiers. Warfare in *Gangster* is not a singular moment of catastrophe but an ongoing condition where toxins and chemicals rained down by U.S. planes were absorbed into the bodies of Vietnamese people. Whereas Hollywood and popular representations of warfare offer singular visions of war infrastructure as necessary to liberal democracy, lê offers a pluriversal world through the lush Vietnamese jungle to counter and set in relief what is repressed and can survive through the violence of war.

The breaking and making of Vietnamese families, and her parents' recollected love story, is about survival and what can grow out of the devastation of war. The narrator shares that on the night of her birth, Ma watches a news story on the TV about a girl from a nearby town who is killed in a napalm bombing, which immediately shapes Ma's fears of giving birth. On the night of the narrator's delivery, Ma fills in the news story with her own narrative of the girl's death. She imagines the girl walking to the beach "to cool her feet in the water." In the very next sentence, her lifeless body is found "floating on the sea." Ma is not physically present for this young girl's death but she grapples with it through a series of images. She imagines how the girl's body glows "like a lantern" from the napalm's phosphorous, and serves as a source of light in the water that casts napalm differently, as illumination, within a cycle of death and life. Ma builds "in her mind" a canopy for this young girl, who could be any Vietnamese girl, including her own infant daughter. This scene evokes one of the most famous images of the war in Vietnam, "Napalm Girl." Taken by photojournalist Nick Ut while he was working for the *Associated Press* of Los Angeles, the 1972 Pulitzer Prize–winning photograph was captured in the southwest village of Trang Báng. Originally called "The Terror of War," the photograph shows a nine-year-old girl Phan Thị Kim-Phúc running without clothes on, with her arms splayed, away from a South Vietnamese napalm strike. Apocalyptic images such as this flooded millions of homes in the United States through the increasing popularity of television and the nightly news, and were reprinted in newspapers and in magazines such as *Time, Life,* and *Newsweek*. Through these media, American viewership witnessed the first "television war" from a distance and from the comfort of their living rooms.[46] While the images of wounded and dead U.S. soldiers, destroyed villages, and Vietnamese bodies burned by napalm explosions garnered antiwar protest, the onslaught of media coverage turned violence and tragedy into commodified representations for U.S. consumption. The world-destroying use of 388,000 tons of napalm, or "liquid fire"—a sticky combustible material that was weaponized to burn, asphyxiate, and kill during the Vietnam War—is silently rendered in lê's passage through the girl's body. Lê gives texture to this single casualty of combat by avoiding the masculine aesthetics of war that focuses on the soldier, GI, and weapons to confront the killability of noncombatants by the U.S. state. During the war, the number of Vietnamese killed in combat, or in the U.S. Army's terms "body counts," measured the advancement of war. The goal was to maximize the kills of enemy combatants—a category used by the Geneva Conventions to justify war—and their civilian allies so that Vietnamese soldiers would surrender.

Lê demonstrates how the violence of the war revises the category of "enemy combatants" as it spills over onto entire worlds of people and landscapes. Ma makes sense of war's violence by imagining the beach as a "badly burned arm of a dying giant buried in the sand" who had either been buried and was trying to escape or had buried himself for protection from the bombing but could not shield his arm in time for the attack. The absent presence of the dropping of the bomb and the moment of killing happens in the space between the first two sentences: the girl walks to the beach, and then her body is floating. The napalm appears in this moment only through her glowing body and the burnt giant's arm—both "bodies stopped in mid-stride, on their way somewhere" (86). What becomes important and centered is the girl—her intentions to cool off on a hot night and then her floating body. Although she is unnamed, her story affects Ma so deeply that the story marks how this young girl—who could also very well be her own child—cannot be ignored or cast off as an unnamed, faceless casualty of war. At the same time, the beach—something commonly seen as background or "mere" landscape—is personified and made alive within a new social relationship with the young girl. This memory is enduring because of the way language makes the destruction of the beach just as important as the death of the girl.

Lê transforms the terms of war through incoherent metaphors, giving it many shapes throughout the novel, to capture the entirely incomprehensible violent acts of empire and remake its very infrastructures. In the novel, war is light, it is a bird, it is air, it is a boat. Though the war in Vietnam is commonly depicted through aerial shots of fire-bombing, the novel offers a different bird's eye view through Ma's metaphorical perspective. According to Ma, "war is a bird with a broken wing flying over the countryside, trailing blood and burying crops in sorrow. If something grows in spite of this, it is both a curse and a miracle" (87).[47] Ma's insight—that what can spring from the devastation of war can also be a miracle—is profound. Whereas a curse is typically an utterance that invokes the power of an otherworldly being to punish, a miracle signals a welcomed unexpected divinely constituted occurrence. This dialectic of curse and miracle stages the continual destruction of war as constitutive to the growth of something new. This is to say that something both cursed and miraculous can grow "in spite of war," and not that war is needed for growth. Transforming war into a bird gestures toward military planes or the aerial warfare that the United States fought, but here the bird is wounded and broken and is placed into a relation with the natural world through a series of off-balanced and broken images. Stating that war "is" a bird, lê challenges the visuality of aerial shots, the aerial bombing of Vietnam, and the images of the jungle being fire-bombed below, and draws attention to the effects on the landscape, covering it and living beings in this delicate ecosystem with a contradictory sorrow. Employing the word "is," rather than using the more suggestive simile "like," emphatically overrides any singular ontological meaning of the war and Vietnam.

And yet "in spite of" war, both miracles of regeneration and the curses of war are possible and inseparable. Through Ma's account of the narrator's birth, the war becomes a contradictory condition that exists all around and in the very air they breathe. Throughout the novel, the narrator integrates destructive acts of war and the presence of U.S. weaponry into the family's daily life. Lê changes the terms of war by transforming war into vapor that ethereally pervades their very bodies, thus capturing the totalizing effects of war's technologies of destruction and the ways it infiltrates entire life systems. Bombs are not singular explosive events, but carry chemical agents that destroy entire ecosystems that continues generationally. The narrator is born amid the curse of war, without which there would be no storyteller to reimagine her family's life in Vietnam. She recalls: "When I was born, [Ma] cried to know that it was war I was breathing in, and she could never shake it out of me. Ma says war makes it dangerous to breathe, though she knows you die if you don't" (87). In this passage, war is overwhelming and unavoidable and exists in the very air one breathes. The narrator's birth marks a moment of mourning for Ma, where the fact of being alive—being able to breathe—already marks a danger and threat to life. The war lives on and becomes engrained in the baby's body, which, Ma realizes, can never be separated from the destruction of war. The narrator has only known what it means to live and breathe in a state of war. Ma considers throwing her newborn against the wall, stomping on her tiny body and dancing on the baby to get rid of the war inside of her that "is killing us all." The language of love and care, and the "miracle of life," between a mother and a newborn is refashioned through a discourse of death and danger wherein life also signals the curse of war. The violence of war changes the terms of motherly love, invoking a desire for Ma to commit violent acts toward her newborn out of love and a fear of what she sees as an inevitable death. The narrator then muses that Ma did not carry through with those thoughts because "Didn't I know? War has no beginning and no end" (87). This is a spatial recognition that the boundaries between the baby's body and the ongoing war cannot be separated. So too is it a realization that even if she kills the war inside of the baby, war could not be ended as such. There is no end to war, because the war's effects will continue through her child and in other ways that cannot yet be grasped.

Gangster offers a scalar language that breaks war down into the very dust that Vietnamese people breath into their body, casts war as a continuous looping temporality, and as spreading across oceans and national boundaries through metaphors of a broken boat. Ma builds on her insight that "war has no beginning and no end" as it "crosses oceans like a splintered boat filled with people singing a sad song" (87). War itself becomes an effect in the shape of a disintegrating boat of people who carry with them sad stories. Song is story for lê and war is transformed into story that crosses vast bodies of water. The young narrator attempts to make sense of her family and their dislocation in ways that do not fix any meaning, moving and flowing like water, with "no beginning and no end." War becomes a boat that, no matter how splintered, physically carries fleeing refugees. Lê is able to transform the infrastructures of war into vessels of escape through the force of figurative language. The boat, the ocean, and water offer a simultaneous space of dwelling and movement, of an intense coming together and violent separation. Lê does not offer any easy or finite answers for a group of people who arrive on the other side of the ocean, within the national boundaries of the U.S. empire, in the wake of the brutality of war. She does offer language to reimagine war's contradictory terms. By conjoining war with a bird with a broken wing, burnt beach, a wounded giant, a murdered young girl, her doomed newborn, and a splintered boat, Ma marks the continuous nature of war, as well as modes of modes of survival and escape.

What emerges powerfully from Ma's language around war is the different senses evoked against the ocularcentricism of Cold War apocalypticism that debilitates other senses. Lê's language reconstructs a relationship to aurality and the haptic in order to reimagine kinship structures destroyed by war. In the same chapter in which the grandparents' photograph arrives, the narrator describes her "first memory" of Ba's face as one "framed by the coiling barbed wire of a military camp in South Vietnam" (82). This "framing" of Ba's face is quickly interrupted by Ma's voice as a scene of synesthesia where the sound of Ma's voice at the camp mixes with the narrator's vision of Ba's face. The narrative effect of synesthesia in this scene produces language and storytelling as acts that are, as Trinh T. Minh-Ha argues, "transmitted from mouth to ear, body to body, hand to hand. In the process of storytelling, speaking and listening refer to realities that do not involve just the imagination. The speech is seen, heard, smelled, tasted, and touched."[48] Ma's voice "crosses through the wire. She is whispering his name and with this utterance caresses him. Over and over, she calls him to her, 'Anh Minh, Anh Minh,'" in such a way that Ba's name "becomes a tree she presses her body against," intersecting the sense of sound with touch to reimagine their encounter (82). Ma tenderly mixes in her own name with Ba's, "Anh Minh, em My. Anh Minh, em My," "like a pebble in a well," playing with the sound of their names, the sound of a small rock dropping in water to express a desire to be consumed and enveloped by Ba (82). Ma's voice touches Ba like a "caress" through the barbed wire "like a warm breeze," engulfing them both (82). Her repetition of words and act of naming serve as a reminder of the connection between Ma and Ba's names, where the play with the sound of their names is an act of meditation that pulls the family together across the partition of the camp's barbed wire and gates. When the gates open they fall into each other's arms, "always meeting for the first time, savoring the sound of a name, marveling at the bones of the face cupped by the bones of the hand" (82). Combining the image of Ba with the sound and "touch" of Ma's voice, the narrator provides entry into her parents' intimate world amid the chaos of war, leaving the narrator "trail[ing] behind them." Likened to "the tip of their dragon's tail," she is "drawn along, like a silken banner on the body of a kite" (82). These mixed metaphors of tree, dragon, silken banner, the body, and kite and their synesthetic effects realign their familial kinship and mode of survival with the mythic and natural worlds that exceed the war camp.

The figuration of the gangster—a criminal and fugitive entity—contradictorily emerges as a central axis for familial destruction as well as refugee survival. The image of Ba as gangster breaks Ma apart from her family, and yet it becomes the stuff of stories and legend, of persistence, and of familial realignment. The narrator comes to know her "gangster" father through another black-and-white photograph and through rumors. In the photograph he is sixteen years old, his head is cocked, and his "expression . . . wary"; his arms are crossed as "one hand balled into a fist. In this picture, what reveals him most is the will to give nothing away" (63). Mixed with this "image" of Ba are a set of "mysterious and mundane" rumors. The narrator describes Ba as almost a stranger from a time before she knew him: "Before he was my father, he was a skinny kid in the South Vietnamese army. He was a heroin addict. He was a gangster. . . . He ran away from home. He was part of a select unit trained by the Americans. He jumped out of airplanes and disappeared for weeks into the jungles and hill towns. His friends fell around him, first during the war and then after the war, but somehow he alone managed to crawl here, on his hands and knees, to this life" (103). Anaphorically repeating the pronoun "he" throughout the description of Ba, lê offers contradictory images of Ba, allowing the reader to anticipate and participate in the discursive production of Ba as gangster. Keeping the focus on her father, the narrator stares at the photograph in an attempt to understand and pin down a clear image of Ba. The rhythmic use of "he" with the past tense reinforces the description of Ba's past life that does not stay in the past but incurs in the narrator's present, establishing a distance between Ba and the narrator. Ba as gangster contests the narrative of the "good refugee" bounded within the national confines of the United States. He is transformed into a linguistic figure for familial reconnection across vast spatial distances. Ba is transformed into a necessary figure—the gangster that we all must be in search of—and signals a method of survival that necessitates fragmentation and breaking away from established demands of being the right kind of Asian refugee. While the model minority stereotype first racialized Chinese Americans and Japanese Americans in the 1950s–1960s, in the aftermath of the Vietnam War, Vietnamese refugees were represented through the trope of the "good refugee" in a way that recuperated the morally bankrupt and unsuccessful Vietnam War in the late 1980s. The "good refugee," according to Yến Lê Espiritu, buttressed the "good war" narrative of post–World War II, in which the United States was cast as the savior, protecting others from tyrannical governments by enfolding "good refugees" into a "nation of refuge" in a postwar democratic world. In this narrative, the United States emerges as a place of salvation for war refugees, and as "triumphant *and* moral," legitimizing and valorizing "U.S. militaristic intervention around the world then and now."[49] This is a recuperative story that serves to justify the failed U.S. military offensive in Vietnam. Granting Vietnamese people the "gift of freedom," the United States has recuperated its power through erasing Vietnamese people, who continue to be "unmentioned" and "unmourned" and merely seen as victims who have been "rescued."[50] A rejection of the "good" model minority refugee, and the embrace of the "bad" refugee and the acceptance of their broken family, moves against liberal narratives of the model minority as the "good refugee" to be saved, and is foundational to survival. Ba as gangster is storied and mythical, and what the narrator really knows, ultimately, is that this gangster managed to survive death. The narrator promises that when she grows up she is "going to be the gangster we are all looking for" (93). With all of its connotations of violence and criminality, the gangster is transformed through linguistic repetition and imagery into an aspirational figure of fugitivity and survival across the ocean.

Infrastructures of Resettlement and the Spill of Oceanic Debris

Throughout the novel, the destructive agent of napalm, the glowing bodies of people, and bombs are deemphasized in lieu of water, where the ocean is the site of dramatizing Vietnamese refugee flight and escape. Turning to the ecological, cartographic, and elemental space of water disrupts a linear narrative of escape as the reader is pulled through the atemporality of an oceanic imagination that spills over and connects the archipelago of Vietnam, the Pacific Ocean, San Diego, and Los Angeles. My study of *Gangster* frames LA as part of a broader "archipelago of Vietnamese resettlement," building upon

Evyn Lê Espiritu Gandhi's conceptualization of *nu'ô'c* where water is not "in opposition to land" but "connotes fluidity, fugitivity, movement, and connectivity—the erosion of borders by the constant waves of the sea."[51] Lê tells us in *Gangster*'s epigraph that "in Vietnamese, the word for *water* and the word for *a nation, a country,* and *a homeland* are one and the same: *nu'ô'c*." This opening frames the importance of *nu'ô'c* as a term and concept that undoes the separation of land and water and brings disparate geographies and meanings of home and transitory spaces into relation. Holding onto the ambivalent term *nu'ô'c*, not letting it go or forgetting it in their displacement, lê translates Cold War oceanic passages into the Vietnamese word for *water*. Burdened with the act of translation, lê's narrative strategies draw on the ambiguity of language to reconsider an archipelagic politics in the making and unmaking of kinship, nonnational politics, and refugee arrivancy through oceanic crossings.

Refusing any fixed notion of the war, Vietnam, settlement, or Vietnamese arrivance, the limitless conditions of the ocean are crucial to an imagination of refugee worldmaking that has no beginning and no end. The narrator recounts the night she fled Vietnam and tells the reader, "It was my father who carried me down to the beach and placed me on the fishing boat. During hours that must have been ones of fear, anxiety, and desperation, my only memory is of how calmly I sat waiting for him" (105). Leaving her in search of Ma, Ba returns to the boat in a panic. On this occasion—unlike the camp scene—Ba cannot hear Ma's voice over the multitude of voices calling for help. The narrator recalls waiting on the boat in the dark with others, but she only remembers her father: "He walked slowly toward me, gently pushing everyone else aside. He picked me up and kissed my hair. He stroked my face and rocked me" (108). In contrast to the fast and wildly extreme portrayal of Ba as a gangster, here Ba is rendered in a different temporal mode to emphasize his care for his family. He is "slow," "gentle"; he affectionately reassures her with kisses and hugs as they escape. At the refugee camp in Singapore, she is woken up by the sound of her father's crying: "Time stopped. Then—inexplicably, incredibly—it continued" (109). The narrator conjures the stillness of the moment, captured as a moment of stasis and pause like a photograph of her father's sadness, expressed after the moment of separation from Ma. The sea is a contested space of competing claims of sovereignty and unclaimed spaces for refugees; it emerges in *Gangster* as the place of destruction, a dangerous place where it is estimated that 10 percent of boat people were lost, attacked by pirates, drowned, and died of dehydration.[52] In this escape scene, time stops and carries on, tracing the colonial and militarized infrastructures of refugee resettlement, where Vietnamese refugees were commonly relocated to a refugee camp in Hong Kong, Thailand, Malaysia, Indonesia, or Singapore, then transferred to a U.S. Air Force base on Guam, the Philippines, or Wake Island before arriving at Camp Pendleton in Southern California, Fort Indiantown Gap in Pennsylvania, Eglin Air Force Base in Florida, or Fort Chaffee in Arkansas.[53] Moving from one military base or encampment to another, the narrator, her father, and their fellow travelers renegotiate an infrastructure of resettlement as fragmented, nonlinear, and never fully settled even upon their arrival in San Diego.

A focus on San Diego expands the archipelagic reach of LA's militarized cultural imagination and at the same time connects San Diego to a history of total war and occupation. The site of human armaments and a port for the arrival of refugees as people who represent the collateral damage of U.S. imperialism, the Marine Corps Base Camp Pendleton is a 125,000-acre military base on the coast of San Diego, California. Connected to a long history of U.S. imperialism and conquest, Camp Pendleton was developed over the homelands of the Juaneño, Luiseño, and Kumeyaay tribes. These tribes were first "encountered" by the Spanish in the late eighteenth century; then Anglo American settlers occupied the area for roughly a century, all the while blocking federal ratification of treaties with Native communities, leaving the tribes without use and legal claims to the land. With the rise of Progressives, anti-Japanese hysteria in California ignited San Diego's militarized economy after 1915. With increased geopolitical tensions across the Pacific and "war scares" with Japan, the Pacific Fleet was created to "safeguard" California against the "yellow peril" that followed the anti-Chinese and anti-Japanese movement. Imported into San Diego as a source of cheap labor, the number of Chinese workers increased with the construction of the railroad, where hundreds were working in 1884. Progressives in Southern California promoted the exclusion and incarceration of Japanese residents who had first come to San Diego in the 1880s, making charcoal or working as waiters, fishermen, cannery workers, shopkeepers, and farmers. San Diego was indeed built as an Anglo-Saxon haven free of a disruptive working class. San Diego politicians courted admirals and generals for naval investment in the city, seeking a landscape for training camps, defense plants, bombing ranges, airports, and parade grounds. This modernization of San Diego provided the U.S. military with land, but was not structured to shelter workers and military families. The post-1945 ascendancy of the United States as a global power was fortified through the strengthening of a military-industrial complex as well as the assertion of U.S. inclusion and liberation politics. Housing and highway policy in the United States encouraged the growth of white suburbs to build property equity for working-class and lower-middle-class whites; however, urban renewal served commercial, commuter, and business interests and built freeways and tramlines that destroyed black, Asian, and Latinx neighborhoods.[54] While admirals and generals were included in the elite classes of San Diego, the militarized city by design favored the Anglo elite, and in the mid-1960s

San Diego was deemed by the Fair Employment Practices Commission as one of the most segregated cities in the United States.[55] In 1942, the U.S. Marine Corps acquired the prized land that became Camp Pendleton, with its seventeen-mile shoreline and diverse topography for combat training.[56] It was here, at this first U.S. mainland military facility to house Vietnamese refugees, that the largest Vietnamese population outside of Vietnam began.

Gangster upends this U.S. militarized space of reunification by turning to the oceanic as a contested site through which territorial national sovereignty is questioned, where kinship is reimagined, and where the memory of escape continues even after the family is reunited in San Diego. Years later in San Diego Ba would recall his and the narrator's moment of escape through the voices of escaping Vietnamese people as a "seawall between Vietnam and America or as a kind of floating net, each voice linked to the next by a knot of grief" (105). Their moment of escape by boat leaves behind Ma amid a mass of voices wailing for help that is likened to the oceanic infrastructure of a seawall—a large structure of concrete erected along the shore of a beach to protect the mainland from storm surges, muffling their calls for aid, rendering their individual voices indiscernible. These voices emerge as an erect structure that is folded into a logic of portioning between Vietnam and the United States. Simultaneously representing displaced people in need and a structure that comes between their journey to the United States, refugees in the boat are cast as an oceanic surge that must be stopped from hitting the U.S. mainland. In addition to the imagery of the concrete structure of the seawall, the voices are also likened to a "floating net," a porous object that is meant to catch and sift through debris while allowing water to pass through. The net here is composed of refugee grief. Displacement and the effects of war in this linguistic logic become the very things that represent Vietnamese refugees as oceanic debris that form the very infrastructures of partition between land and water. As such, refugee conditions are enfolded into the very infrastructures of separation. The voices simultaneously are a barrier and a linked entity of survival. This image of the floating net and the seawall emphasizes the place of water and the oceanic for a Vietnamese refugee worlding project for continuance.

Lê effectively conjures the imagery of refugees as fragments of ocean debris, left over from the wreckage of war after crossing the ocean, that are swept up onto the coastline. They are torn apart, in pieces, not wholly present, just like the broken images of war, the bird, the newborn, and the jungle, but will inevitably become something else. In this way, lê's figurative language emphasizes constant transformation, incessantly in process of becoming and never settling into a permanent condition. Her images of fragmentation, of broken human and nonhuman subjects, are reflected in the broken temporality of the novel, which moves back and forth between the past and the present and between Vietnam, refugee camps in Southeast Asia, the ocean, and San Diego, California in ways that break with the linear time of U.S. narratives of resettlement. In Black diasporic studies, the geographical space of the Atlantic Ocean has deeply informed Black cultural production, transatlantic intellectual life, and the theorization of modernity where the oceanic constitutes "the sublime force" of the ocean, its passages, and its itinerant dwellers as, in Paul Gilroy's formulation, a fluid "counter-power that confined, regulated, inhibited, and sometimes even defied, the exercise of territorial sovereignty."[57] In critical refugee studies, scholars argue that the refugee condition poses a challenge to the very possibility of the nation-state because the paradigm of the refugee indicates an aberration in the "nationalist order of things," and makes apparent the arbitrariness of borders and signals "a transgression of the social contract between a state and its citizen."[58] Survival in *Gangster* is established through a reimagination of familial ties created through the language and imagery of water over blood, eschewing the paper trail of citizenship and reimagining infrastructures of resettlement. In this way, water challenges the juridical understanding of citizenship and belonging. Both time and spaces of statelessness and unbelonging—not the narratives of nationalism and recuperation by the U.S. Cold War state—bleed into each other and become the worldly formation of a Vietnamese refugee condition.

The inseparable relations of land, water, and homeland open onto a consideration of the nonnational framework of refugee worldmaking as a relational politics that does not fold all refugees into a homogeneous group. Critical refugee scholars have offered important relational politics through the insight that we must not, as Yến Lê Espiritu argues, "integrate" Vietnamese refugees for the purpose of racial equality for Asians living within the U.S. nation-state, but must understand their particular racial formation within the context of U.S. occupation and warfare throughout Southeast Asia.[59] For Espiritu, Asian American studies' pan-Asian framework have folded and suppressed particular histories and epistemologies, creating a hierarchy within Asian American studies by absorbing Vietnamese and other Southeast Asians into a predominantly East Asian framework. Describing the place of her relocation, lê's narrator says, "We live in the country of California, the province of San Diego, the village of Linda Vista," reterritorializing the United States, breaking it up into different regions. She continues, "We live in old Navy Housing bungalows built in the 1940s. Since the 1980s, these bungalows house Vietnamese, Cambodian, and Laotian refugees from the Vietnam War," connecting the ways military infrastructure becomes repurposed within the logic of U.S. resettlement and linking refugee housing to a history of warfare. The narrator continues to describe the way they live alongside "Navy people." At school, Navy people's children are considered the "Most

Popular, Most Beautiful, Most Likely to Succeed" (89). And, even though there were more Vietnamese, Cambodian, and Laotian kids at the same school, "they call us Yang because one year a bunch of Laotian kids with the last name Yang came to our school. The Navy Housing kids started calling all the refugee kids 'Yang.' Yang. Yang. Yang" (89). This is an acknowledgment of how U.S. "Navy people" are defined as successful, beautiful, and popular against Southeast Asian children. Furthermore, relationality in critical refugee studies excavates the category of Asian American beyond a unified signifier where within the category of "Southeast Asian refugee" Vietnamese, Cambodian, and Laotian people should never be collapsed together. This relational politics demands an attention to the heterogeneous populations of Southeast Asians in Southern California and challenges the solidity and homogeneity of "Asian American" politics and the possibility of comparing entire Southeast Asian groupings as predetermined positions arriving from across the Pacific Ocean.

The ocean is a place and an entity that reorients Vietnamese refugee journey and escape beyond the stereotypical narrative of "boat people." Water in the novel guides their escape, while also moving them further from their family and the nation-place of Vietnam. Water in *Gangster*, according to Brian G. Chen, is an "unfathomable material with which the narrator's family develops an ambivalent relation" that serves as a "metaphor for their wandering state of mind that oscillates between their old memories back in Vietnam and their new identities in the United States."[60] San Diego is not an endpoint, or a place of safety for the narrator's family, but is repositioned within a refugee world of sociality. The narrator's opening description of her family's movements stands in contrast to a vision of Vietnamese refugees as helpless and deviant populations cultivated by U.S. racial liberalism. The Russells, a white family living in San Diego, decide to sponsor the narrator, her Ba, and four uncles in the wake of the war. Living in San Diego in 1978, retired Navy man Mr. Russell, who was stationed in the Pacific and had fond memories of the "small and kind" people there, learned of the "Vietnamese boat people." He lay down at night haunted by the homogeneous "nameless, faceless bodies lying in small boats, floating on the open water" (5). In contrast to the intimate and particular details of the narrator's familial memories and recollections, the "Vietnamese boat people merged with [Mr. Russell's] memories of the Okinawans and the Samoans and even the Hawaiians" (4). One night, Mr. Russell dreams that "the boats were seabirds sitting on the waves. He saw a hand (4) scoop the birds up from the water. It was not his hand and it was not the hand of God. The birds went flying in all direction across the blinding blue sky of Mr. Russell's dream, but finally he saw them fly in only one direction and that was toward the point where in the dream he understood himself to be waiting, somewhere beyond the frame" (5). Mr. Russell's vision is one that imagines a clear singular direction out anywhere from Vietnam, to Okinawa, to Samoa, or Hawaii, and to an endpoint, himself in the United States. In his vision, he and the United States are not part of the chaos—they exist "beyond the frame"—and instead mark a destination of refuge and safety. Mr. Russell enfolds Vietnamese refugees into a longer history of militarization across the Pacific. From 1898 with the Spanish-American War, President McKinley's U.S. empire spread through the Caribbean and the Pacific as the United States colonized Puerto Rico, Cuba, Hawaii, Eastern Samoa, Guam, Wake Island, and the Philippines, altering them into tactical sites for expanding U.S. military and economic benefit. Throughout these islands militarized infrastructures of communication, harbors, and coal stations were established for U.S. imperial domination, with detrimental effects on the local community, economy, and ecology.[61] Lê returns refugee worlding to a different temporality and spatial politics by placing the U.S. war in Vietnam within a longer history of U.S. military warfare. Mr. Russell's romantic vision of war finds comfort in war for the way it defines a "good" U.S. national subject. In the calm comfort of his home, Mr. Russell is positioned against the unruliness of Vietnam. The image of hands scooping up and rescuing the seabirds of small boats activates a universalizing myth of the United States as the savior of refugees from war-torn countries. Mr. Russell's vision is one devoid of the differential scales of war and its impact upon Vietnam, its people, their bodies, and escape, but takes up a racial liberal narrative of U.S. freedom. Just as the novel constantly moves and transforms the representational circuits of war and San Diego, so too does it reanimate Vietnam. Lê's insight that war has no beginning and no end opens onto the ways the Cold War is part of a longer model of total warfare that extends from Spanish colonization but also takes on a new dimension through the expansion of U.S. empire and territorial conquest across the Pacific.

Gangster is in many ways a novel drowning in its sorrow, memories, and the traumas of warfare that spill out through each character. Through the ghostly waterlogged spectral presence of the narrator's brother, Ma's vision of the napalm girl, and Ba's scenes of unrestrained grief, the ocean spills out of them, marking their trauma. At the same time, the oceanic serves as a horizon of placemaking for refugee worlding. Attempting to remember Ma, the narrator tells us that "if [she] never see[s] her again, [she] will know [her] mother by the smell of the sea salt and the prints of [her] own bare feet crossing sand, running to and away from, to and away from, family" (95–96). For the narrator, Ma becomes synonymous with the sea, marking a refugee condition that moves in and out with the tides of the ocean. The smell of the ocean, the images of sand and the narrator's own feet, more impactfully capture her memory of Ma than the sight of Ma's face, placing Ma within a series of relationships with the narrator's body and the interstitial space of the beach, of the ocean, and land. Lê's family photograph of her grandparents invokes a familial negation, in which Ma is excised from her biological household because of a breach in parental approval and of national lines. As a novel about "running to and away from, to and away from family," *Gangster* follows an oceanic movement of ebb and flow as a constant condition of refugee worldmaking where home is never stable (96).

Within *Gangster*'s world, San Diego is not a haven or refuge, nor is Vietnam solely a place of utter annihilation and death; instead they spill into each other through the oceanic, offering a revisualization of war's spectral presence and linking war's dislocation to their constant condition of displacement. Fences emerge as infrastructures of separation in San Diego, serving as a counterimage to the boundless sea. After their eviction, the family stares at the "tall, silver, and see-through" chain-link fence circling their block, "like a bad dream" (96). At night, they return with the three uncles and cut a hole through the fence, breaking into their house to "steal back" their belongings. At the sound of police cars, they flee, they "tumble out the window like people tumbling across continents. We are time traveling, weighed down by heavy furniture and bags of precious junk" (97). Ma cries, "What about the sea?" In despair she cries out, "I want to know, I want to know . . . who is doing this to us?" She demands to know why there is "always a fence" and why they must constantly leave "like this?" (97) They learn in the morning that they were evicted for the building of condominiums, town houses, and family homes. The fenced-off block assumes the image of an entire flat world through which they search for their "blue sea" as they watch a wrecking ball destroy their house. Ma calls out and whispers, "'Ma/Ba, Ma/Ba,'" evoking and transporting the reader back to the moment of the camp in Vietnam in which she attempts to find connection with Ba across a fence. As objects from their home float out "across the surface of the sea," this scene emphasizes the ocean and the spilling over of Ma's despair and the limits of placemaking (99). The fence and sea here are metaphors for displacement and yet the sea is ceaseless and limitless, reclaiming this displaced place for an archipelagic entanglement between land and water where what is destroyed is buried but still present.[62]

The oceanic becomes a timeless figuration through which the narrator is haunted by familial ghosts. The novel closes with the chapter entitled "nu'ô'c," where the adult narrator is living on the East Coast, estranged from her parents. Interspersed with memories of her brother's deadly drowning in the South China Sea, the narrator overhears women discussing her brother's death. Jumping from boat to boat, he must have slipped, some women claim. According to those whispers, the water "dragged" him, causing him to "plunge straight down . . . into a hole in the water" (146). Curiously, against these violent recollections of her brother's death the narrator transforms the hole into "a room and the room was in a house" like her home in San Diego. Her brother's house was darker and colder, filled with fish instead of chickens.

She imagined him rolling and turning until, "like the shells my grandfather had given me . . . his body became as smooth and brilliant as polished bone" (146). The narrator transforms the place of her brother's death—the sea—into a place of dwelling, and one that connects, and brings, him closer to their life in San Diego. The sea is not only a place of trauma and death but a home for the dead to reach the living. *Gangster* constantly confronts us with the dead, and what we must do with them after they have passed. Grandparents join and move into their new home across the world through a photograph. A drowned brother lives on in the place of his death. He does not stay intact but changes forms. Lê beautifully describes his body as becoming "smooth" and "brilliant" like a "polished piece of bone," and not through decay. In the absence of flesh, he becomes a new entity altogether, "like a seashell," that belongs to the ocean. His glow is reminiscent of the glowing dead girl killed by napalm and lit as a lantern. Her brother, too, "glows" in the darkness of his home in the ocean and shines in such a way that "knowing that in time he would not fade at all; he would only shine brighter" (146). The narrator tells this story as an adult, estranged from her family. Transforming her brother's death into a light that will continue to shine, she does not blame the sea, but embraces it as a place of transformation and habitation.

The family does not end in a fully formed, cohesive unit, but is rendered through a continuous flow of unification and fragmentation, marked through the fragmenting and unifying symbol of the ocean. The novel turns toward the elemental as a way of countering midcentury visions of an apocalyptic Vietnam, and U.S. statist and white supremacist masculinist notions of the end of the world, that would see the end of capitalism, or Vietnam and its threat to western masculinity, as an end to "mankind." Enfolding embodiment and the elemental rethinks the apocalyptic in this novel as an account of perception that stretches beyond the racialized and gendered enclosures on the human. In this way, lê's figurative language gives a window into the elemental force of *nu'ô'c* in the constitution of human and nonhuman kinship. This is a revelatory brink that exists on the edges of land and water. *Gangster* and the final chapter, "nu'ô'c," end with a memory from the narrator's childhood during that first spring in California when her father wakes her and Ma up to go to the beach. She recalls how they walked toward the water, mirroring the napalm girl's walk to the beach. She remembers the silence after the sound of waves crashing. This time, the phosphorescent light emits from tiny silver fish, not from the body of the young girl from Ma's neighboring town. In this final scene, the young girl's story is allowed to continue beyond a napalm attack. The fish in this scene gestures back toward the fish in Ma and Ba's fight scene, but this time the fish turn toward the full moon, brightening and writhing. Mother, father, and daughter smile at the fish familiarly "as if [they] knew them" (158). The narrator tells us,

> My father remembers stroking my mother's face.
> My mother remembers wearing my father's coat.
> I remember taking off my sandals and digging my heels into the wet sand.
>
> As my parents stood on the beach leaning into each other, I ran, like a dog
> unleashed, toward the lights. (158)

And so, the novel concludes with this joyous memory, on the Californian side of the ocean, along the water, with different sources of light: the full moon and the fish. Nothing short of a miracle sprung from the curse of war, Ma, Ba, and our young narrator, whose story is not "stopped short midstride" as she leaps forward, "unleashed," and unbounded. The constant references to fish, water, light, phosphorescence, and the young girl killed in the napalm bombing, across different characters and scenes, point to the cyclical, interconnected, and knotted traumas of the characters in the novel. The reader is asked to return over and over again to earlier passages, recalling other memories, searching for mnemonic devices, patterns, tropes, and symbols that in each iteration change. The repetition of the word *remember* reminds the reader at the end that the entire book is composed of the narrator's memories, and her granular transmission of a world-historical moment, that reimagine "boat people," refugees, and their escape from war to the United States. *Gangster*'s figurative language remaps Cold War infrastructures of war to name the simultaneity of worldbreaking and worldmaking; thus we can see how the visual sphere of U.S. capitalist state power tried to subdue and dismantle anticolonial revolution to open onto pluriversal epistemologies that come out of refugee worlding practices. The ending ambiguously offers an opening that reinvigorates the politics of apocalypse so that one may retheorize acts of perception and the historicity of our senses, to imagine a "home" within a scorched landscape and the curse of war, and to seize on fear, pain, anxiety, and loss to imagine miracles and more just ways of living in worlds that are falling apart. Constantly unmoored and always-ever attempting to locate herself (in Vietnam, across Southeast Asia, on the ocean, and in Southern California), the young narrator of the novel challenges any fixed notions of national borders and poses a new political model that inhabits and names a wider set of broken and displaced worlds. This political worldview insists upon not leaving Vietnam in the past and elsewhere but holds onto seemingly impossible radical visions of building beyond basic survival.

By meditating upon lê's mobilization of figurative language and imagery, this chapter has considered what it means to survive and create in the face of war. In the vein of feminist critical refugee studies, I advance refugee worldmaking as a project of building sociality and relationality through the wreckage of war. *Gangster* transforms a politics of Cold War racial liberal apocalyptic visuality through ekphrastic memory to formulate a dialectical relationship of destruction and regeneration that causes one to feel the need to run away from and run to. The novel's representation of infrastructural circuits across Vietnam, the war, the jungle, Vietnamese bodies, the gangster, water, and the ocean simultaneously destroy and provide a means for survival. *Gangster*'s figurative language enters the visuality of the Cold War through a different register, and it ultimately remaps Cold War infrastructures of war to move beyond the grievances of U.S. combatants, the casting of Vietnamese refugees as objects to be saved, the United States as savior, and the justification of militarized warfare. In their place, *Gangster* offers stories that cannot be accounted for by official narratives of the U.S. state and advances a story of refugee worldmaking as a site of critique, where the figure of the refugee is not an object of study or recuperated within any nationalist framework. Instead, the novel's aesthetical literary paradigm critiques the racialized and gendered logic of U.S. militarized state violence. By the end of the novel, the infrastructures of war and resettlement are resignified and the imperial metropole of Los Angeles can be traced southward to San Diego and across the Pacific Ocean to Vietnam. Lê's landed, oceanic, and aerial pathways reveal how the long *durée* of modernity inscribes U.S. militarism and the colonial archive into one of the largest U.S. metropolitan cities. The following chapter follows the archipelagic imperial system of Los Angeles to the Sherman Institute in Riverside, California, an Indian boarding school located just northeast of San Diego and southeast of Downtown LA. The U.S. war in Vietnam during the Cold War marks an intensification of counterinsurgent strategies that drew upon earlier forms of Indian warfare. Combining the techniques of U.S. militarized warfare against Native Americans (the breaking down of kinship networks, and the destruction of ecological systems) with anticommunist ideology, the U.S. war in Vietnam reformulated Cold War state-making practices. In the next chapter, I study Diné poet Esther Belin's works to consider survival under genocidal policies and to consider her reimagination of the disciplinary infrastructures of termination, coloniality, and U.S. empire.

INFRASTRUCTURES OF TERMINATION AND ESTHER BELIN'S IMAGINATION OF DECOLONIAL MOBILITY

- University of California Berkeley

Dibé Ntsaa •
(Hesperus Mountain)

• Sisnaajiní
(Blanca Peak)

• Four Corners Power Plant

Navajo Nation

Dinétah

Dook'o'oosłííd •
(San Francisco Peaks)

• Institute of American
Indian Arts (IAIA) - Santa Fe, NM

Los Angeles, CA
• Sherman Institute - Riverside, CA
• Perris, CA

• Tsoodził
(Mount Taylor)

New Mexico

Southwest Oklahoma

3

> Raised urban among Los Angeles skyscrapers, Mexican gangs, Vietnamese refugees, eating frybread and beans. Middle child. Father from Birdsprings. Mother from Torreon. Daughter of Eddie and Susan. U.S. Federal Indian Relocation Policy placed them into boarding schools away from the rez. Five-Year Program at Sherman Institute, Riverside, California. Goal: annihilation of savage tendencies characteristic of indigenous peoples. New language. New clothes. New food. New identity. Learn to use a washing machine. Learn to silence your native tongue, voice, being. Learn to use condiments without getting sick. Learn a trade and domestic servitude. Learn new ways to survive.
>
> —Esther Belin, "In the Cycle of the Whirl" (1999)

Born in an old Indian hospital in Gallup, New Mexico, on July 2, 1968, and growing up in Los Angeles, California, Diné (Navajo) poet and multimedia artist Esther Belin identifies her distinct experience within a multiracial landscape as writ within the epigraph above from her 1999 collection of poetry and essays, *From the Belly of My Beauty*. Locating herself within the milieu of LA in a string of words—"Raised urban among Los Angeles skyscrapers, Mexican gangs, Vietnamese refugees, eating frybread and beans"—Belin connects her LA existence as a self-proclaimed "urban Indian" to the cityscape and other displaced racialized communities.[1] Information about her family quickly follows. She is the middle child, the daughter of Eddie from Birdsprings and Susan from Torreon who, under the federal government's Indian Relocation Act of 1956, were placed within the Five-Year Program at Sherman Institute, an Indian boarding school in Riverside, California. A crucial component of termination's infrastructures for over a century, hundreds of thousands of American Indian children were forcefully sent to Christian boarding schools beginning in the 1870s. At the Sherman Institute, Diné, Hopi, Paiute, and other Indigenous children who were taken from the areas now called Arizona, Utah, Nevada, and California were prohibited from performing their rituals and religions, speaking their languages, and singing their songs, in an effort to assimilate American Indian children during a period of intensifying U.S. imperial expansion. An image of the skyscraper is juxtaposed to her distance from the Indian reservation system, which she re-terms "the rez," reflecting the way Belin was raised far away from

Dinétah ("among the people"), the homeland and point of entry for the Holy people when they left the prior world for the existing world. "Dinétah" also refers to the reduced area of the Navajo Nation, the largest U.S. Indian reservation located within the Four Corners region.[2] In contrast to these bordered definitions of the reservation, Belin understands it as such: "Navajo Reservation. Definition: place where the sun toasts your skin with color from its painted desert after spring showers and the oozing silence thunders with your heartbeat" (69). Her final sentence after the cycles of U.S. violence reads as follows: "learn[ing] new ways to survive," rerouting termination's infrastructures in the aftermath of the Indian boarding school system toward new pedagogical modes of endurance. Positioning herself within a familial genealogy of movement through and around Dinétah and Los Angeles, Belin expresses a vision of Southern California and its distance from "the rez" that is reconceived as a place of mobility through which to claim Diné sovereignty against fixed ideas of Native immobility, termination, and extinction.

Under the Bureau of Indian Affairs' (BIA) Termination era policies of relocation, education, and resource extraction, the U.S. Congress attempted to terminate federal commitments and promises to tribes. Dillon Myer, director for the incarceration of Japanese Americans during World War II, deemed relocation as a corollary to the Indian Termination period of the 1950s, which enabled policies by the federal government to end its relationship with Indian tribes by removing Indian land from trust status in order to stop providing tribes with services. Cold War ideologies of national and cultural homogeneity fueled assimilation policies that underpinned federal Indian policy that began to unofficially relocate Native people after World War II and officially, in 1952, absorbed 1,279,000 acres of land and reduced health, education, and other social services that were an element of treaty rights. As U.S. global expansion looked outward to reconfigure its power, the U.S. nation-state reconfigured Native nations to redraw its own internal borders and boundaries. In 1953 Congress passed legislation to "terminate" tribal recognition and facilitated Indian relocation to cities in an effort to disband over one hundred Indian "bands" and "tribes," declare them "extinct," and sell their land in an effort to eliminate Native governance, depopulate reservations, and "integrate" Native Americans by making them "self-sufficient" and no longer dependent upon the federal government.[3] The Indian Relocation Act of 1956 initiated Native American movement off reservations and into urban areas such as Seattle, San Francisco, Chicago, New York, and Los Angeles. Hailed as "the urban Indian capital of the United States," Los Angeles experienced the greatest increase in American Indian urbanization. The Indian Relocation Act of 1956 was, therefore, the culmination of broken promises and treaties, and the decimation of Native American life that required termination infrastructures—boarding schools, resource extraction, bureaucratic and built systems of relocation—as a continuation of Indian warfare and U.S. imperial expansion.

This chapter engages with Belin's two Native American feminist books of poetry, *From the Belly of My Beauty* (1999) and *Of Cartography* (2017), to consider its invocation of the nascent role that Los Angeles plays in U.S. infrastructures of Indian termination. While Belin's poetry explores the violence of the assimilationist Indian boarding school system and relocation, distance from Dinétah and her elders, and the destruction of Diné territory by energy extraction and the detonation of the atomic bomb, her work also utilizes the spatiotemporal precept of "the whirl" in such a way that redefines what it means to adapt and exist within interstitial spaces in the construction of "urban Indian." Urban Indian, in this way, is less an identity category than it is a confrontation between LA's modernity and Native life in the city. Ned Blackhawk has usefully cited the ways Donald Fixico and Kenneth R. Philp produced monolithic representations of American Indians as victims of federal policy whose experience in urban America is one of only suffering, broken traditions, and inferiority. Casting American Indians living in the city as a tragedy, Blackhawk continues, can be noted in N. Scott Momaday's *House Made of Dawn* (1968) and Leslie Marmon Silko's *Ceremony* (1977). In both Silko's and Momaday's novels, Los Angeles is marked as wholly unfamiliar, foreign, and alienating. Only upon leaving LA and returning to their homelands can the novels' protagonists have resolution.[4] Appearing most explicitly in the final piece of *From the Belly of My Beauty*, "In the Cycle of the Whirl," the notion of the whirl appears throughout Belin's poetry. Not linear or simply repeating, Belin's "cycle of the whirl" casts U.S. infrastructures of termination as fortifying and magnifying colonial technologies. Sweeping the reader into the unpredictable, tumultuous, discombobulating, dizzying, and disorientating "whirl" of termination's infrastructures, Belin's poetry ruptures and overturns the interlocking spaces of U.S. white heteropatriarchal norms of the military, religion, education, and domesticity.

Against the colonial spatial capture of Native people on and off the reservation, and against fixed romanticized notions of the homeland, I argue that *From the Belly* and *Of Cartography* draw upon Belin's family's experiences to reimagine LA and the Southland as a zone of decolonial mobility that challenges fixed ideas of Native termination, that Native Americans must be solely nonurban, are of the past, disappeared, or immobile. Belin's poems about the road and travel recast Native mobility within and beyond LA's association with the linear progress of urbanism, automobility, and infrastructural "modernity."[5] Through motility, Belin's politics of urban Indigeneity bridges the spaces of the roads between the "rez" and Los Angeles and connects termination to the intimate spaces of family and domesticity, and to far-reaching grids of energy extraction of the Southwest by Los Angeles. Thinking through and against settler colonial infrastructural constraints—of Indian boarding school, interstate automobility, and energy extraction—Belin enacts new modes of adaptability and survival beyond settler colonial terms of Indigenous annihilation through the routes between the Sherman Institute, the Ethnic Studies department at UC Berkeley, and the Institute of American Indian Arts (IAIA) in New Mexico. Her familial movements within the whirl of Los Angeles, the Four Corners region, and the heterogenous spaces and places in between reroutes the project of colonization as unfinished and incomplete. In this sense, her poetics of the whirl enacts a decolonial mobility to offer a unique insight into the politics of being "on the road" as a Native person, naming immobility as termination, and shifting its colonial infrastructures of segregation, dispossession, removal, and extraction for the worldmaking capacities of Native people.

The Immobility of Termination

Throughout her poetry collections, Belin's aesthetics of the whirl traces two infrastructures that tumultuously exist within one another: first, the world-ending termination pedagogy of the Indian boarding school system; and second, a regenerative and reworlding Indigenous feminist decolonial pedagogy of mobility. Her poem "Atmospheric Correction" from *Of Cartography* weaves together an account of Native incarceration, Indian boarding schools, and Los Angeles that understands the attempt to capture and render inert Native life as a correlative to the progressive temporality of the U.S. nation-state. Preceding the poem is a statement describing a black-and-white photograph from 1895 of nineteen Hopi men who were imprisoned on Alcatraz Prison Island off the coast of Northern California because they would not place their children in federal boarding schools. The Hopi men were initially believed to be Apache but were labeled as "Moqui Indians" in the photo (66). Typed in italics, this opening statement is separated from the rest of "Atmospheric Correction," which claims poetic license over the incorrectly labeled photograph that would arrest the nineteen Hopi men in a certain place and time as "Moqui Indians, 1895" and as criminals in need of discipline. The poem follows the statement by moving the reader into the main body of the piece, overlapping and shifting temporalities of capture through poetry.

Belin integrates nineteenth-century quotes from *The San Francisco Chronicle*—espousing the civilizing mission of education that justifies the incarceration of the Hopi—across a series of locations (LA, San Jacinto, Alcatraz, and the Sherman Institute in Riverside) and temporalities (1895, 2016) that refuses a capitalist temporal-spatio demand to "stay" "until" they "appreciate" the "advantages" of federally run boarding schools and their farming techniques. "Urban Indians, 2016" is overlaid onto "Moqui Indians, 1895," connecting Belin's own history to that of the Hopi men through a play on their labeling, or mislabeling. In doing so, Belin unfixes the Hopi men from Alcatraz, 1895 and a colonial narrative of carceral correction and reeducation. The "transparent and syrupy" atmosphere places the Hopi men in LA's setting, exceeds the boundaries of their imprisonment, and embeds them into the very "atmosphere" of Los Angeles. Their imprisonment in Northern California is connected to Southern California and remaps twentieth century incarceration in relationship to federal boarding schools. Belin's remapping of incarceration and the reproduction of this historical event is an invitation to rethink Native incarceration as a multi-temporal and multi-spatial experience that reorganizes the past and present in a reclamation of kinship.

In contrast to the generalized and false statements about the Hopi prisoners, the speaker summons some of them by name—Masatiwa, Sikyakeptiwa, Lomayestiwa—and claims their disobedience as part of her own genealogy, fusing their fingerprints and "their heritage" to the walls of Alcatraz and her own "blueprints." In doing so, she places herself in a longer history of federal boarding school education and Native capture that perpetually sought to immobilize Native Americans. The parallel imagery of the atmosphere as fading "LA smog" at the beginning of the poem is reiterated through the image of the "Fading Indian" at the end of the poem, evoking a disappearance that is not wholly gone but is transformed. Invoking the Sherman Institute in Riverside, California—one of the biggest off-reservation Indian boarding schools in North America—as part of the BIA, the Department of War, and the incarceration of the Hopi men in Alcatraz, Belin's historical position as an "urban Indian" is located within the intersection of termination and LA and a Native history of refusal and of movement.

Repositioning the photo and the Hopi men's presence through LA's thick atmosphere of smog, into San Jacinto and the Sherman Institute in Riverside, Belin offers a cartographical vision of a wide-reaching capitalist infrastructure of termination, linking Native incarceration to the boarding school system across California. Originally established in 1892 as the Perris Indian School, just south of Riverside in the rural area of Perris, California, the Sherman Institute represented the U.S. government's flagship Indian school from 1903 until 1971. Now named the Sherman Indian High School, the Sherman Institute operated the Special Navajo Five-Year Program—the very same program in which Belin's parents were enrolled—between 1946 and 1961. In 1903, Harwood Hall, the Sherman Institute's first superintendent and an Indian Office career agent, aspired to move the school to a growing city; he cited access to a sufficient supply of water as an excuse for its relocation. Frank Miller, a local Riverside entrepreneur in need of cheap labor and a tourist attraction of Indian students for his growing business, "The Mission Inn," worked with Hall to establish the Sherman Institute in Riverside. In the 1890s, Riverside was a citrus empire and the richest town in the United States, cultivating and cultivated by the image of Southern California as a paradisiacal Garden of Eden and utopian retreat filled with clean water and clean air. In the post-1950s era, however, Riverside would come to exemplify Southern California's imperial failures. At the crossroads of empire, contemporary Riverside is now marked by a reputation for meth labs, prisons, and brutally hot summers, and is seen as an epicenter for the nation's mortgage crisis, epitomizing, as Karen Tongson describes it, "a world after the fall."[6]

At the opening of the Sherman Institute on July 18, 1901, Senator George C. Perkins declared to those in attendance that the buildings erected "will stand for the redemption of a race" and will help the "Indian, who can no longer exist in a wild state . . . meet the requirements of modern progress . . . [and] secure for himself the best there is in our civilization." The presumably benevolent educational act of assimilation and redemption, or assimilation as redemption, was undertaken, Perkins declared, "for the glory of the great God whom we all revere," for "our Father and the Father of all races of mankind."[7] Tacitly driven by a biblical notion of progress that situated Native Americans as a catastrophic presence whose "wild state" threatens not only themselves but "modern progress" and "civilization itself," the only recourse to the supposed destructive state of Native Americans is, for early twentieth-century reformers like Perkins, a system of formal reeducation grounded in a Euro-American messianic vision of redemption that universalizes the Christian God as savior. Modeled after Spanish and French missionary schools beginning in the colonial era, Indian boarding schools followed Catholic priests in the practice of separating Native American children from their families, tribes, and culture in an effort to instill more "civilized" Christian values. In contrast to the early Bible-focused education of Indian students at schools such as the Catholic Indian boarding school Saint Boniface in Banning, California, the U.S. government–run Indian boarding schools fused Christianity to assimilate Indians into U.S. citizens, which could not happen apart from "Christian morality."[8] Impediments to capitalist futurity and progress had to be eliminated in order for capitalism to overwhelmingly assume the U.S. nation's providential history. In the second half of the nineteenth century, Indigenous peoples were reduced by disease and warfare to a "manageable" number. As a rejoinder to church reformers and liberal politicians, policies under President Ulysses S. Grant shifted from outright annihilation to assimilation, and education constituted "*the* . . . key ingredient." Indians had to be "weaned" of their traditional ways of life in order to participate in the "vortex of euroamerica's emerging capital-driven wage labor economy."[9] Capitalism was configured as the path to victory, liberty, and justice and became sutured to a "divine order" against the "forces of evil."[10] Throughout the Allotment and Assimilation period in American Indian history (roughly between 1879 and 1934), former policies targeting Indian populations for extinction were replaced by the "systematic conversion of communal Indian land and cultural practices" into individuated "civilized forms" that were more amenable to market capitalism and liberal democracy.[11] While U.S. federal reform in 1934 shifted from the individualizing politics of the Allotment and Assimilation era, the "Indian New Deal" sought to recognize the political, socioeconomic, and cultural communities of tribes across the United States, providing funds to support tribal reservation economies through the Indian Reorganization Act of 1934. Despite this seemingly altruistic framing, Indian child removal was an extension of colonial military campaigns that found in Indian family separation a powerful technology for domination and stifling rebellion that in many ways was more effective than direct warfare.

This system of Euro-American education was affirmed and reinforced by the authority of an emerging U.S. capitalist state's role as benevolent father and redeemer, and Native American children, like their adult parents, were cast as wards of the state in need of rescue. Beth Piatote advances that "Indian wars are wars on Indian families" in which Indian families and networks were central sites of settler contestation to eliminate the tribal-national polity.[12] The Indian boarding school's weaponization of kinship was, according to George E. Tinker, "a product of nineteenth century liberal inclinations born of roughly four centuries of evolution in eurowestern theology and philosophy."[13] And in Margaret Jacobs's study of Captain Richard Henry Pratt, the superintendent of the first U.S. Indian boarding school—the Carlisle Indian Industrial School—Jacobs writes that it was not just education that would deter resistance, but that the officials learned from Pratt the practice of breaking up Indian families to quash Indian resistance to American conquest. A former army captain and prison warden, Pratt developed his assimilation philosophy directly from militarized tactics of warfare and the innovation of Native incarceration.[14] As superintendent, Pratt believed in strict disciplinary reform that would "kill the Indian and save the man," a pedagogical refrain that continued to guide Indian boarding schools throughout the earlier part of the twentieth century.[15]

Through cultural conversion, isolation, a system of corporeal punishment and policies, Pratt believed that Indian children would not only advance and "uplift" themselves but would advance civilization as a whole. Armed commanders and cavalry men were supplemented with protestant missionaries and federal agents who propagated notions of federal paternalism and the sanctity of domesticity that turned the domestic into the very definition of American femininity, marking the renewal and reformulation, not the end, of conquest. The struggle to assimilate "Indian economies, lands, kinship, systems, languages, cultural practices, and family relations" turned the space of the Indian home into a major site of struggle, marking the continuation of conquest through an assault on the domestic front.[16] Indian family forms of kinship, nonnuclear family gender roles, and marriage practices were cast as aberrant forms to define the institution of white male citizenship through a relationship to private property, labor, and the nuclear family structure.[17] Students at Sherman would, school and religious leaders hoped, leave as Protestant missionaries to the reservation to convert larger populations of Indian people for Christ. In this way, the boarding school system served as a crucial infrastructure in a paternalistic teleological apocalyptic temporality of "progress" grounded in a messianic notion of time that was "called" to annihilate Native American cultural life.

In the poem "Euro-American Womanhood Ceremony" in *From the Belly of My Beauty*, Belin confronts the capitalist infrastructure of Indian termination by shifting the terms of domesticity, a central tenet of racialized gendered capitalist forms of labor that revolves around the achievement of Euro-American womanhood by Native women. Remapping domesticity onto a cartography across Southern California, Belin moves Indian warfare into the space of the kitchen, the family, Diné women's bodies, and the homes of white families in Sierra Madre. Beginning the poem with the phrase "some say," the speaker introduces the multiple perspectives surrounding the Indian boarding school system. From the opening line, Belin eschews any set poetic form, and refuses to provide the poem's readers with any singular experience of Indian boarding schools, releasing female "students" from the achievement of a formalized Euro-American Womanhood project. At the same time, a tone of doubt arises around the intentions and the success of the boarding school experience as the reader waits in anticipation for what the speaker will surely tell the reader about what others might have to say about their experience. Beginning in mid-thought, or mid-conversation, the poem identifies an unknown source that believes that the boarding school "wasn't that bad" because they learned a trade. After a slight pause the speaker continues, "at least the men did." Native women are introduced after a long pause between the first two stanzas, mirroring the gendered division of labor under federal Indian and assimilation policies that placed Native women firmly in a devalued space of domesticity. In contrast to Native men, Native women were "trained" to "mimic" the rituals of Euro-American domesticity, transforming themselves into copies of white women, and "to be happy servants" for white families before their own.

"Euro-American Womanhood" is a historically laden term and racial formation that intersects the colonial trajectories of capitalism, labor, conquest, education, femininity, and domesticity. Scholars of sentimentalism have illuminated how nineteenth-century U.S. sentimental literature, as a genre that made legible the experiences of love, connection, and sympathy, elevated maternal love that racially differentiated forms of motherhood. The "Republican motherhood" of white woman was regarded as the most precious and, according to Amanda Zink, "valorized mother love . . . to protect and uplift the home and nation."[18] Republican womanhood presents an ideology and rituals that white heroines can impart onto nonwhite women so that they could "master a particular brand of American femininity."[19] Sentimental patriarchal Christian discourses of Republican motherhood promoted feelings of sympathy to naturalize, according to Beth Piatote, a "tiered maternalism" that upheld white heterosexual women and their family units as the apex, establishing a system of disciplinary paternalism and racial hierarchy of motherhood that subordinated tribal familial forms to settler nuclear families.[20] The white Christian loving and competent mother of sentimental fiction in the nineteenth and twentieth centuries served as the "bearer of sentiment," and conversely the Indian mother was cast as "savage and incompetent . . . without access to public feeling," securing social positions for white women under the terms of benevolence. By giving birth and nurturing men and the nuclear family structure, women were integral to propagating the U.S. nation's morals and values of citizenship, labor, private property, and belonging.[21] In this way, colonization worked precisely through the reorganization of gendered logics within everyday and seemingly mundane practices of labor and familial life. In his study of nineteenth-century antislavery reform, Kevin Pelletier proposes that we rethink the genealogy of sentimentalism as a negotiation of seemingly oppositional emotional economies of love and fear, not as competing, but as imbricated in what he calls "apocalyptic sentimentalism." Pelletier advances "providential history, not antiracist liberalism" as the "master narrative" for early nineteenth-century abolitionists who promoted social transformation by means of feelings of love and interpersonal connections, but also the threat of God's vengeance and terror.[22] This vision of U.S. colonial settler apocalypse in Southern California draws upon sentimentalism as a redemptive mediating genre to rationalize termination through Indian removal, boarding schools, and Native erasure.

In the twentieth century, I argue, an early form of antiracist liberalism *as* providential history is the master narrative for reformers of the boarding school system. While genres such as science fiction, dystopia, disaster, noir, and detective fiction have been more typically poised as archetypal genres of Los Angeles as a place of destruction, posing apocalyptic sentimentalism as a key LA genre, or as a precursor to these latter genres, opens onto a history the apocalyptic genre as a master narrative to infrastructures of termination. Building upon apocalyptic sentimentalism's visions of destruction, fear, redemption, and love and notions of futurity, later twentieth-century LA genres are tied to a longer histories of settler colonial discipline in the formation of the U.S. capitalist state.[23]

Motivated by discourses of God's love and wrath, apocalyptic sentimentalism was undergirded by Christian morality that sought redemption for Anglo American genocidal violence and the redemption of Native people from their so-called savagery. Christian apocalyptic stories understand redemption as a narrative in which, after a great destruction or "the end," a "revelation" arises, and God's love and salvation will manifest the emergence of a new world, heaven, and earth. The persistence of Native American lifeways is cast as the impediment to God's love and the providence (or historical necessity) of the second coming of the messiah, or in this instance, the manifest destiny of the U.S. capitalist nation-state. Sympathy alone could not sufficiently enact transformation and the imminent terror of God's wrath was a prerequisite, catalyzing calls for feelings of redemption, sympathy, and love, following a key Puritanical understanding: that "forming a just community sometimes takes some coercion."[24] While Western masculine capitalist progress was grounded in the "rational" domination of imperial conquest, a particular notion of feminine progress, defined through Christian mores, was conjoined to white bourgeois feminine domesticity and the production of the nuclear family as a central purpose and grounding for U.S. modern life.

The opening stanzas of "Euro-American Womanhood Ceremony" establish the differential education of Native men and women as they have been inculcated into a patriarchal structure of labor and servitude that was necessary for white families in the Sierra Madre to thrive, as well as a language of domesticity that became central to assimilative practices. Re-formulating notions of education, redemption, and progress of feminine Christian morals as a critique of U.S. settler colonial apocalyptic domesticity, "Euro-American Womanhood Ceremony" summons a history of the Sherman Institute's gendered curriculum that trained boys to be saddle-harness makers, cobblers, masons, farmers, electricians, printers, and blacksmiths and trained girls in domestic sciences. The assimilation of Native Americans through paternalistic relocation policies fostered patriarchal nuclear families that positioned women within secondary positions in a moment when U.S. reformers and officials increasingly sought to define the country as a Protestant nation.[25] Denied opportunities for vocational training, women were positioned firmly within the domestic spaces that imagined Indian men as the heads of the households. The language of "learn[ing] a trade" masks the labor exploitation of the boys, and it exempted Native children from child labor laws under the guise of their training as laborers, not professionals, for a sustainable future.[26] The repetition of the infinitive "to"—"to specialize in domestic household work," "to mimic the rituals of Euro-American women," "to cook roast beef and not mutton," "to eat white bread and not frybread," "to start a family and not an education"—initiates stops and starts between the unconjugated verbs to pause between the new set of capitalist rituals that are articulated through a series of negations. The excision of traditional foods (mutton and frybread) and the introduction of new foods (roast beef and white bread) ritualizes Native women's domestic training and mimics Euro-American womanhood.[27]

The transformation of Indian occupations and economies into capitalist domestic and manual wage labor involved "outing programs" that placed Indian girls and young women with local non-Indian families to immerse them into a new "civilized" Christian way of life.[28] In exchange for their childcare and domestic labors, young Indian women were placed in middle-class farm homes in Riverside to earn a small wage and to learn firsthand Anglo American cultural practices. Outing programs, as David Wallace Adams notes, soon "degenerated" into a system that provided white families with "cheap Indian labor."[29] Girls cooked, washed, cared for white children, and cleaned white homes as domestic servants to fulfill Riverside's growing labor needs. At the Sherman Institute, which reportedly provided the best diet out of all of the Indian boarding schools, malnourished students worked and were not able to benefit from their labors; instead, their earnings paid for staff salaries and produced luxury items in the form of baked goods, produce, dairy, linens, and clothing for the school's surrounding white community, making the school "financially self-sufficient" and profitable.[30]

The word *ceremony* appears several times in the poem, and is given ample space, to intervene in the capitalist rituals of the Indian boarding school system. Occupying its own lines, Belin emphasizes how ceremony cannot continue if it is not constantly practiced (20). By calling Euro-American Womanhood a "ceremony," Belin names the rituals, processes, and practices that have changed Native femininity and destabilizes any idealization of womanhood. The speaker of the poem recognizes that Native women who were being forced to mimic Euro-American womanhood were taken from the rez too soon, and did not complete the physical and spiritual ceremony of "fasting and sweating and praying and running" (20) that they would have completed had they not been removed from their homeland. Organized around obedience, servitude, and domesticity, Euro-American Womanhood ceremony is set in relief against Diné notions of a womanhood ceremony that centers seemingly mundane acts of running, sweating, and praying that are tied to a sacred matrilineal genealogy. Living off "the rez," Belin references the ways urban Indian women were cut off from ceremonial practices such as the Kinaaldá, a ceremony that "recognizes and celebrates the reproductive and regenerative powers of women" during her first two menses, which according to Diné belief is when the young woman's unique power is the most potent and is in a special state.[31] Based on the traditional stories of Changing Woman, one of the most critical Diné deities, the Kinaaldá is a ceremonial practice in which Navajo women are molded into Changing Woman's image to represent the transformation and the change in seasons and life. She grows old in winter and young again in the spring and she never dies. Changing Woman is not "woman" in a biological sense, but is the embodiment of a different social world of good will and nurture, the rebalancing of male and female energies. Changing Woman embodies the creation of the Navajo's ancestors—women and men out of her own skin—and was the first to have Kinaaldá in the world of the Holy People, on top of Dzilná'oodilii. After twelve days she was found matured after preparing herself, her clothes, her hair, running for four days in the four directions, molding and stretching herself throughout the run. During her self-preparation and run Changing Woman created songs that she sang for energy to help prepare her for her very existence.[32]

For the young Diné girl, family surrounds her to help support her preparation—especially her female kin, who cook, gather wood and water, sing, wash her hair, parting it into womanhood, and tie it in the style of Changing Woman, signifying her focus and determination. Recognizing the temporary condition of life and the body, they stretch, massage, and mold the kinaaldá's body so that as she grows old, her body will be strong and healthy, balancing her spiritual, emotional, intellectual, and physical life, and have a strong voice. She then, over the course of four days, runs in all four directions so that she can be quick and can run without tiring during war time, without hesitation, and so that the Holy people will notice her running and will provide help in her time of need.[33] The woman's matrilineal kin grind corn, and make a corn cake batter to bake overnight. The next day, the Kinaaldá ends with the Blessingway, where guests are offered pieces of the corn cake, which represents Mother Earth because the corn came from the earth as Changing Woman was able to make food out of the earth.[34] Jennifer Nez Denetdale has pointed out how certain Western Marxist paradigms interpret the Kinaaldá as a "ritual designed to bind Navajo women to the inferior domestic sphere," but that Navajo social organization, "with its focus on matrilineality, continues to confuse non-Navajos who privilege males and can only interpret women's experiences in relation to the patriarch."[35] To be attentive to termination's infrastructures of Indigenous people, both at the level of national policy and in the most intimate spaces, is to understand how the world-ending sentimental logics of paternal benevolence, maternal sympathy, and Republican motherhood, seep into, and violate, the sacred spaces of Native life. At the same time, in this poem, Euro-American Womanhood ceremony is but a momentary system within a longer and ancient practice that extends back to the creation of Diné people and is not a sustainable and everlasting.

Instead of the "molding" practices of the Kinaaldá that emphasize the movement of running and strength, under shifting forms of capitalism Native women were taught to change their relationship to their bodily forms for assimilation within the confines of the boarding school and household. Embodying an incomplete form of womanhood within Belin's poetic imagination, those women "never really became women" in the Diné sense because of their forced distance from the reservation and because of the wounds and imposed rituals of Euro-American womanhood (20). The listing of domestic duties—set the table, vacuum, iron, nurse, and feed—and the repetition of giving birth "and birth and birth" (20) express an exhausted state of repetitive labor born of the rituals and expectations of a patriarchal U.S. capitalist system. Simultaneously, it alludes to the constant regenerative force of Native femininity. Belin refutes the common lasting lie of U.S. domesticity that scholar Amanda Zink relays: "that indigenous women have no values or rituals of domesticity and thus need the intervention of white women."[36] Clifford E. Trafzer, Matthew Sakiestewa Gilbert, and Lorene Sisquoc remind us that

> Indian education did not originate with Europeans and Americans at colonial mission schools or federal boarding schools. Native education was indigenous to the Western Hemisphere. All of the Indigenous peoples of the Americas had their own systems of education long before non-natives arrived. For thousands of years, Native fathers and mothers, grandparents, aunts and uncles had taught their children medicine, mathematics, literature, science, music, dance, history, and a host of other disciplines.[37]

But, once the rituals of Euro-American womanhood and its heteropatriarchal aims can be named, one can see what remains, what cannot be extinguished, and how U.S. settler colonialism contradicts and subverts its own vocations and creates its own world-ending conditions.

Rather than understanding Native women as poor reproductions of white femininity, Belin's poetry of the whirl as constant movement recasts their "adaptability" as a decolonial transformation that can reinvent the ritualistic terms of Euro-American womanhood ceremonies. One way to understand ritualization is as an indirectly coercive process that hides coercion. The domestic reorganization of Native families linked Christianity to the paternalism of the nation, which was key to consolidating a U.S. state power undergirded by ritualization, repetition, formalization, and tradition.[38] Yet, this is not the only way to understand ritualization. Talal Asad argues that ritualization can also speak to the "self's potentiality—its ability to obey and to command, to adapt and to stand firm, to please and to offend. In other words, the achievement of ritualized practice is itself essential to what the self becomes, helping to form or to deform it."[39] Indigenous feminist whirls of repetition are never quite the same as they renegotiate and deform social, historical, and political worlds as rituals and as a set of practices.

Decolonial Pedagogies of the Road: Power Lines, Ethnic Studies, and the IAIA

While "Euro-American Womanhood Ceremony" exposes how the racialized and gendered violence of the boarding school system has been deeply embedded in the U.S. narrative of dispossession, it also importantly explores an Indigenous infrastructure of study rooted in a retrieval of urban Indigenous modes of education and study through movement. While the first half of the poem demonstrates the speaker's deep knowledge of the rituals of Euro-American domesticity, the second half of the poem reclaims the spaces in which they live and their bodies, shifting colonial visions of domesticity. Within the cycle of imposed Euro-American domesticity, Belin imagines an emergence of "a new nation of mixed bloods and urban Indians" (20). "Sobering" up from the intoxicating disease of Euro-American womanhood, Indian "mothers/providers/wives" planned road trips, and provided new connecting lines, between the city and the reservation to heal from the Euro-American ceremony. The imagery of Euro-American ceremony as a wound opens onto the possibility of something else to grow from and scab over, and it casts aside the sacred purity of Euro-American womanhood, the myth of a pure Native womanhood or homeland, and the healing Christian narrative of feminine redemption. Belin rewrites the terms of womanhood by reclaiming women's multiple positions as "mothers/providers/wives." And thus, "Euro-American Womanhood Ceremony" ends by linking Native mothers to the space of the road, moving the work of motherhood onto the connecting pathways within her family's travels back and forth between California and the reservation in New Mexico.

The movement between the city and the rez creates a different ceremonial space—a different form of education that I name a "pedagogy of the road"—that takes the work of women outside of the home, beyond setting the table, vacuuming, ironing, nursing, and giving birth. A pedagogy of the road transforms termination routes and forced relocation and reeducation. Rather than wholly casting aside Euro-American effects and resurfacing a nostalgic return to an original past form of Native life, Belin honors the importance of syncretic forms of urban Native motherhood that regenerate from the devastating infrastructures of termination. Native motherhood here becomes less about asserting feminine domestic spaces of birthing and raising men and good citizens for the U.S. nation, and more about rewriting domesticity for the reclamation of Native sovereignty that undermines settler coloniality and its intimate forms of conquest. "Healing" is also a demand for the end of capitalist rituals, which for Belin is an opening of new ceremonies and rituals of decoloniality. In his discussion of ceremony, Opaskwayak Cree Shawn Wilson cites Minnecunju Elder Lionel Kinunway's belief that a ceremony is not merely a "period at the end of the sentence. It is the required process and preparation that happens long before the event. It is . . . *dadirri*, the many ways and forms and levels of listening. It is . . . Ways of Knowing, Ways of Being and Ways of Doing. It is the knowing and respectful reinforcement that all things are related and connected. It is the voice from our ancestors that tell us when it is right and when it is not."[40] Ceremony in this sense, as opposed to Euro-American ritualization, does not have an endpoint, but is instead found within the preparation and process of stepping out of the everyday and toward a higher condition of awareness for the extraordinary and the miraculous.[41] Building on the spatial and journeyed dimensions of ceremony, Wilson further explores the concept of ceremony through the Maori, who "do ceremonies . . . to eliminate the space between people. So the space between people is Kapu, is sacred, and you go through a ceremony and respect each other's space, but the ceremony brings us together so that we occupy the same space."[42] For Wilson, the Indigenous concept of place positions humans and the environment in a shared sacred relationship where ceremonies actively "do" bridging work. In this way, Native belonging is imbricated within and between the settler colonial grid of Los Angeles and "the rez." The multiple work of Native women as mothers/providers/wives is reimagined in Belin's poetry as bridges tied to acts of healing from dislocation, assimilation, termination, their removal from their homeland, and its ceremonies. New ceremonial practices emerge within the interstitial space between the rez and the city, and women here are valued in a reformulation of reproduction and motherhood as adaptable, and regenerative in the afterlife of Indian boarding school systems. Belin continues the ceremonial work of bridging Los Angeles and the reservation in New Mexico, where urban Indigenous knowledge exists on, and in the very transitional and divergent spaces between, the reservation and the city.

While colonial modes of Native education have been tethered to acts of annihilation, Belin does not abandon the question of learning. At the same time, Belin refuses to stay within the confines of termination's immobilizing infrastructures. As such, I follow the educational trails between and through Los Angeles, UC Berkeley, the reservation and the Institute of American Indian Arts (IAIA) in Santa Fe, New Mexico, to seize upon alternative Native-centered pedagogical spaces as ceremony. Belin's pedagogy of the road continuously uses syncretic matrilineal storytelling practices for regeneration and decolonial education through varied landscapes as a way of rerouting the violent infrastructures of colonial apocalyptic domesticity. Throughout *From the Belly* and *Of Cartography*, Diné mobility in and around LA offers new revelations about the U.S. Southwest's cartography. In the poem "Directional Memory" the speaker locates herself in Western, Northern, Southern, and Eastern coordinates by rollerblading, walking, and driving through Southern California. Her "awe" of downtown LA intermingles with ghosts of her "native brothers and sisters" whom she never learns about in school because she grew up far away from "Indian land," which was "far away in another world, across state lines where/grandparents plant corn and herd sheep on a brown-eyed/blue-eyed horse." Her recollection of "Indian land" allows her to see LA anew, and with astonishment—"I always forget L.A. has sacred mountains"—as she is constantly reminded of what is there but too easily forgotten (9). The poem "Night Travel" also offers a sustained deliberation on traveling to LA where the notion of "home" is not marked by Dinétah. At the same time, LA as home is also impure. "I like to travel to L.A. by myself," the speaker shares, where it is polluted, smoggy, hazy, and ultimately "healing" because "being urban I return to where I came from/My mother/survives in L.A./Now for over forty years" (56). She continues to recollect her memories of her dad's truck and of sleeping in their camper with her brother, sister, and parents. The roads in and out of LA are what she "knows" as they "[swim] through her veins," are "dark like [her] skin," "floods [her] liver," "Pollutes [her] breath," she "still witness[es] the white dawning" (57). Driving is turned into a bodily experience where the roads become embedded in her veins, skin, organs, and breath. Polluting and flooding her body, the roads offer another way of thinking about the persistence of Diné sovereignty and kinship beyond the space of Dinétah as she finds home in bodily practices of mobility.

"Study on the Road to Los Angeles" offers a different perspective of the city, from the vantage point of driving back into Los Angeles from Diné country, but it also explicitly names decolonial mobility as a mode of study and learning. Belin begins the poem by portraying an extractive relationship between Southern California and Diné land in New Mexico. The speaker casually mentions driving past the power plant, but notes its extractive positioning: it is "tucked in" New Mexico but "lights up Southern California." "Tucked" away, far away from Southern California, it is the region's light source. Without naming the power plant, the speaker locates herself in a geographical landscape that more than likely places her driving past the Four Corners Generating Station, a power plant built on land leased from the Diné Nation, near Fruitland, New Mexico. Just a few years after the Indian

Relocation Act of 1956, the Four Corners power plant was established in 1963. There, burned unearthed coal releases nitrogen, sulfur dioxide, heavy metals, and carbon dioxide into the sky, where mercury and ash then falls back onto the ground, into the soil, and into the bodies of humans and animals, in its generation of electricity for far off places. According to the Mercury astronauts, the plume pouring out of the Four Corners Generation Station is one of two human-made entities that can be seen from space.[43] Unleashing coal's energy, spinning magnets conduct the flow of electrons from atom to atom, between copper wires, sending electricity surging through circuits into homes far away from Diné territory.[44] The emergence of urban centers materially taps into nature by harnessing the combustion of prehistoric fossil fuels and transforming coal and water's kinetic energy for electricity. For Belin, the phenomenon and usage of electricity and its environmental effects appear in everyday conversations about the "hot and dry desert," which are "as common as morning greetings:/ *Yá'át'ééh abíní*, good morning/ *Aoo', yá'át'ééh*, yes it is good." The poem's speaker moves on to the common "talk of the hot and dry desert" that becomes as familiar as daily greetings. In a reorientation of her drive back to Los Angeles, the road becomes a mundane place of study, one in which the speaker tracks the relational spaces of, and extractive relationship between, Southern California and its hinterlands.

The space of Los Angeles is a compelling space of politics that reorients one's relationship to the landscape and to Diné territories, as the placemaking project of modern LA exists on water stolen from Paiute land in the Owens Valley, but also on electricity generated on Diné land. As Andrew Needham illuminates, in the Termination era, by replacing federal authority with state authority over reservation lands, officials asserted their power over the resources of remote territories in order to meet metropolitan demands. This is, as Barry Goldwater stated in 1950, a process of "unlock[ing] the natural resources known to exist on the reservations."[45] Energy supplies on Navajo land were crucial to the expansion of the urban Southwest, which resulted in social and environmental inequalities between metropolitan development and Navajo underdevelopment, transforming and drawing Navajo land into a reconfigured relationship with the city center.[46] The proliferation of power plants is a continuation of colonial conquest in the west that reorganized the relationship between the Navajo Nation and surrounding cities. "The Southwest" is a regional description but also the political reorganization of space that turned it into a place in order to claim and redistribute resources.[47] An Angeleno's ability to flip on a light switch is directly linked to LA's extractive relationship to the Diné reservation. By integrating and calling upon U.S. place-names—Southern California, New Mexico, "American" Southwest, the rez—within an energy grid that destroys Diné land and people, Belin reframes this colonial mode of extraction as unsustainable.

Moving the space of education outside the realm of domesticity, outside of schools, and off the rez, Belin realigns "study" with conduits of travel as a perpetual movement between the natural and human-built surroundings. The speaker decenters herself and focuses on her surroundings as the source for study: the Chaco River and its mountain snow from the north, heading west, but first traveling south. Once the speaker hits Newcomb, New Mexico, she sees *dootl'izh* "all around." In the English language, the noun *turquoise* might come closest to the meaning of *dootl'izh*, but there is still a differentiation between blue and green. In Navajo, *dootl'izh* is a word for a family of blue/green colors, where color is a state of being or action; functioning as a verb, it creates and forms objects. For example, *dootl'izhii*, meaning "that which is turquoise colored," is a reference to mined turquoise. Belin recognizes the ubiquity of *dootl'izh* as the optics through which the speaker sees and experiences her surroundings in the summer sagebrush, mile markers, sky, mountains, truck, and even in a spare tire. Including Diné words and concepts such as *dootl'izh*, Belin offers a perceptual shift in seeing and understanding the surrounding environment. Driving into Sheep Springs, the speaker notices the pavement, and the way "the HUD housing marks the turn-off to the paved road that divides the Shuskas," as the sun provides "perfect light and shadow" through the cracked windshield. She notices a lone hitchhiker, an elderly woman, holding out her thumb, and a tribal police car. One UPS truck sits at the Crownpoint turnoff as Torreon lies further east (36–37). The simple act of looking out a car window is reframed through *dootl'izh*, remaking the terrain and its objects into active beings. Belin's perception of color offers a much more capacious way of perceiving the world and its inhabitants than settler colonial lexicons of relocation and transplantation.

The visual spacing of the poem slows the poem's tempo down so that the speaker and the reader may deliberate upon and reconnect with memories of her family, intertwining the landscape with her father, mother, and grandmother. The placement of the poem's lines mirror a windy road as it describes the family driving through the roads that lead in and out of Los Angeles. Driving west on Interstate 40, Flagstaff is 185 miles ahead, as "memories of *shizhé'é*," her father, erupt alongside the "rugged" Arizona desert. The line breaks and spaces in the description of the desert force the reader to consider the landscape through the words "untamed," "rough," "unbearable," and "free," and as something that cannot be domesticated. Desert time, as considered through this Native driver's perspective, is an alternative temporality marked by nature, the temperature of "hot days" and the "coolness" of the night. Time is recast by the "glow" of the sunset and the "forgotten" heat of the day in such a way that renders the linearity of capitalist time inadequate. At the end of the trip, and in the final stanza of the poem, the speaker finds *hózhó* (beauty and peace), centering this landscape of time on the Navajo philosophy of living in harmony and balance. A poem about the multidirectional paths between Los Angeles and Navajo territory in New Mexico, there is no linear trip from Torreon to LA, but instead there are stops, musings on environmentally disastrous infrastructures, disruptive memories, and meditations on the mundane life on the road, and there is also the beauty and life of *hózhó*. The passage of time of the road trip, the speaker's destination, and LA are all rerouted through the life of her surroundings and the pedagogies of the road (38).

Central to Belin's decolonial unlearning and ritual remaking on the road is the rediscovery of the "landscape" of her writing and within her storytelling practices the language of *shimá* (mother) in a refusal of U.S. infrastructures of termination that sought to dislocate and breakdown Native families. Engaging in a longer genealogy of domesticity to reimagine its terms, Belin populates her writing with feminine ancestors and names a broader network of Indigenous feminine kinship through her mother, her aunt, her daughter, her grandmother, and their mothers as travelers. "In the Cycle of the Whirl," the final piece in *From the Belly of My Beauty*, with which I began this chapter, takes the reader on a familial journey. "In the Cycle of the Whirl" is a composite of essays, autobiographical writings, and poetry that allows, according to Belin, to pop "in and out of the poetic form" and not worry "about its mechanics." She found in essay writing a way to combine "objective and subjective voice" in order to create and write Native American history as storytelling, not ethnography. For Belin, "We are storytellers, so our work can go in any direction."[48] Similar to the "rugged" Arizona landscape I discuss in "Study on the Road to Los Angeles," "In the Cycle" is "untamed," "rough," "unbearable," "yet free" to offer a pedagogical space of the road to rethink storytelling practices.

Against the logic of Euro-American womanhood that centers womanhood for patriarchal aims, Belin centers motherhood within a matrilineal logic of storytelling and language. Rather than seeing the imposition of "the enemy's tongue" as a total loss, the speaker is able to "use" and "manipulate" English, which mixes with the "tribal language" "scrambled within" her. The speaker acknowledges her mother's "sacrifice," that there was much for her mother to lose, in "allowing" her to "use the enemy's tongue." English moves beyond punishment, and is something Belin uses on her own terms, for indeterminate ends as noted in the repeating words "perhaps" "to reverse," "to change" the process; "perhaps" so she could "survive the process easier" (67). Belin's poetics reroutes coloniality through a relationship to the English language that is different from her mother's. At the same time Belin's mother is transformed into the speaker's story itself and gives way to new forms of language. Story here does not exist in linear time of cause and effect, but a whirling cyclical tumultuous spinning unpredictable time of coexisting worlds and histories within which Belin and her mother are caught. Understanding language in this way is "her-story," and also her way of "re-telling" her mother, or *shimá* (67–68). Belin draws upon knowledge of Diné in the textual form of the English language to reimagine how one lives on through the repurposing of language.

Belin moves away from a singular way of understanding of "mother" and embeds it into a Diné epistemology of relationality. Belin understands her story, her writing, her use of language as indebted to a longer genealogy connected to different worlds. After the opening **"RE-ENTRY"** she writes, "In the beginning, there was darkness. But by the time we emerged to the Fourth world, many things existed. Especially grandmothers" (67). Gesturing toward the First, Second, Third, and our current Fourth World in Diné cosmology, Belin links her mother to her mother's mother, and their mothers before. Her grandmother, *shinálí*, "said prayer is part of our survival, giving thanks, manifesting our destiny. Many of the things given to us contribute to our survival—not because we deserve it, but because our creator planned it" (67). Reconfiguring and playing off of linear colonial notions of Manifest Destiny, Belin decenters herself as the main object of the entire story, and focuses on a longer creation story of survival and adaptation. The force of Belin's writing, her recollections, her emphasis on words and language serve a pedagogical function of decolonial mobility that reroutes survival as storied practices instructed out of scrambled understandings of the Navajo language. Belin writes: "I only remember listening to the nasal low and high tones sounding like a chanter speaking powerful words. I would see the words flow over my body, tingling my skin. My recollections come from the instructions I received as a child. Instructions in the husky syllables of the Navajo language. Instructions familiar and natural" (67). The link between her grandmother and prayer appears as an instructional memory that intertwines survival and forms of embodiment. Even as her "tribal language is scrambled within" her, she understands the powerful words of the chanter as the prayer evokes a sensorial reaction. The familiarity of "husky" syllabic Navajo words moves over her body, making her skin "tingle," moving her back to the original moment of instruction as a child. The sensorial nature of this memory makes this moment of instruction for survival, for "manifesting" their destiny, by linking the sensation of the speaker's body to the sounds of her grandmother. With this recollection, Belin demonstrates how decolonial mobility, and its refusal to "stay," is mired in an instructional function. Her body's haptic memories and sensorial inhabitation are written against colonial erasures of the Native body and language.

In the poem, distance between the reservation and Los Angeles is marked through instructional knowledge. Grandmother reminds her not to fear toads and spiders, but to talk to them and recognize that they have something to teach. Grandmother shares a set of instructions on what not to kill, because not only is everything a living being but these living beings are familial and familiar ancestors. Her instructions on human and animal relationships opens onto a network of kinship in a stream of sentences, packing in as much information as she can before the speaker leaves the reservation for LA. Throughout her works there is tension between learning and forgetting, and the necessity of learning "the ways of the bilagáana [white man]" and knowing her language as a way to keep her connected to her clan. Belin's knowledge of her clan's language is erased through her distance from the rez and proximity to the urban center. Simon J. Ortiz has argued that it is crucial to understand that

> the indigenous peoples of the Americas have taken the languages of the colonialists and used them for their own purposes. Some would argue that this means that Indian people have succumbed or become educated into a different linguistic system and have forgotten or have been forced to forsake their native selves. This is simply not true. Along with their native languages, Indian women and men have carried on their lives and their expression through the use of the newer languages . . . and they have used these languages on their own terms.[49]

Her cyclical returns to the reservation are neither simply repetitive nor reproductive of Diné culture. Instead, she dwells in the in-between spaces between the rez and the city and within the languages of English and Diné.

Belin reengages and relearns Dinétah through imaginative ways that access hybrid urban Indigenous knowledges and unexpectedly arrives at Chinese to find new answers. In an interview, Belin states, "I wanted to understand why the English language is so dominant so I studied linguistics, and I studied the Chinese language. Chinese is an old language, a pictorial language. You appreciate the drawings and how you put words together. Studying Chinese has helped me with Navajo, and I really like seeing the relationship among languages. In the English language I often find two answers. In Dinétah, there is one answer, one tradition."[50] Against the binaristic "two-answer" logic of the English language, the visuality of Chinese helps Belin to access and imprint Diné language and epistemology. In *Of Cartography*, Belin includes a poem by Tang Dynasty poet Wang Wei, entitled "Apricot-Grain Cottage," as an epigraph in the section "bundles are bundling." A poet, painter, musician, politician, and Zen Buddhist, Wang Wei was a master of short imagistic landscape poetry and painting during the Tang dynasty.[51] Resonating with Wei's landscape poetry that moves beyond words on the page, the Diné also consider language to be creative and effective in creating life beyond the page. Belin builds upon the imagery of water found in Wang Wei's "Apricot-Grain Cottage" and follows the images of Wang's cottage, its eaves and roofbeam, clouds, and rain.

Belin begins with an image of herself as wooden, which then becomes soaked with rain as she grapples with her own habits and children as the "product" of a René Descartes Cartesian coordinate system based on a horizontal X axis and vertical Y axis. Images of more water—she "feels like the flood waters"—lead to feelings of repulsion for their "accommodation" to an antediluvian temporality, conjuring the biblical fall of humankind and the great flood. More images flood this poem—a blank journal, twisted cords, mythic tangles, damp soil, and rabbit holes—that intertwines her need to write with imagery in order to make sense of—and remake—her family as "products" of a Western biblical and scientific tradition of time (10). For Belin, writing poetry in English, mixing in American Indian English and Navajo, while drawing on Chinese landscape poetry allows her to change the forms and functions of English, rather than "succumb" to the linguistic erasure of the boarding school system.

For Belin, language is a syncretic practice to imagine alternative landscapes and modes of writing. Its value lies in its impurity and its ability to adapt and to provide an entry point for conjuring historical copresence. The potential for the triangulation of Chinese-Diné-English languages and cross-racial activity builds beyond the spaces of Euro-American education and institutionality. This moment of cross-racial practice does not collapse or assimilate Chinese or Diné identities or beliefs into the other, but is a commitment to an expanded epistemological relationship to language that harkens back to women of color feminist calls to create bridges across racial division.[52] This is a bridging that acknowledges the limits of one's own practices while paying deference to and recognizing the value of simultaneous systems of knowledge. Hers is a constant life practice of reeducation to reverse and violate the violent educational structures imposed over Native families for generations.

Although Belin recognizes the potential for cross-racial linguistics, "In the Cycle of the Whirl" continues the speaker's journey of reeducation and unlearning into the spaces of University of California, Berkeley, a contradictory place that had not fully reckoned with Native sovereignty and Native gendered racialization within its classrooms and hallways. UC Berkeley, in the piece, is interconnected to the educational institutions she and her mother and father inhabited. She recalls the moment she was asked to speak at her commencement ceremony:

> Every time I tried to write, all I saw were faces, not words. Shináli at dusk, sitting, pushing up her wire-rimmed spectacles, my mother shuf-

fling around in the gray hours of the day, me in the halls of UC Berkeley saying "sorry" with my body as I move out of the way to allow others to pass; my father sitting in his armchair where I massaged his shoulders. After dinner while watching the news, he'd massage his own feet. His body wearing thin from work. (75)

Belin's pedagogies of the road reroute the reader through the landscapes of elite public institutions of higher learning, and emphasize her embodiment within them. She tries to make herself small in order to make way for others at Berkeley, apologizing for her existence, even as her body ruptures the popular lie that Native Americans are all dead and gone. The friction between Belin's bodily experience and memory at UC Berkeley connects the site of the university to a longer history of colonization. As she tried to write her commencement speech, the English language cannot inspire her to write. Faces and images of her family appear instead of words. The face of her shinálí and her mother, and finally her father sitting in their home, interrupt the space of UC Berkeley, as Belin considers her experiences at UC Berkeley alongside her parents' experience in boarding school. Even as Berkeley is not equivalent to the explicit violence of Indian boarding schools, Belin helps the reader understand how UC Berkeley stands as an educational institution rooted in settler colonial logics of racialized erasure. If the goal of Indian boarding schools was to wipe out the ability to speak one's tribal language and to erase Native bodies from U.S. social life, termination's goals continued at UC Berkeley as Belin confronts the continuance of Native erasure in its halls. Acknowledging the lack of Native students, especially students indigenous to California, the speaker recalls how there were no Native dorms or clubs, or Native student orientations as there were for Chicano, Black, and Asian students, highlighting Native erasure within particular practices of multiculturalism and diversity.

Even as UC Berkeley is a limited space of confinement and erasure, Ethnic Studies provides the speaker of "In the Cycle of the Whirl" with the opportunity to theorize how liberation is never settled and is always up for contestation. For the speaker, Ethnic Studies is not a remedy, as she expresses a deep tension within her studies at UC Berkeley, the storied site, along with San Francisco State, of emergence for Ethnic Studies in 1969. Born out of a coalitional student movement of Black, Asian American, Chicano, and Native American students, the emergence of Ethnic Studies was part of a demand for changes to the curriculum, hiring practices, and admissions that would address the needs of Black, Native, Asian American, and Chicano communities. In her recognition of the differential experiences of students of color, Belin expresses an ambivalent relationship to the Third World student movements in the 1990s. She describes how, in the spring of 1990 at Berkeley,

Third World students organized to demand diversity among the faculty and the student population. She further recollects that while the Native population was small, other students of color encouraged Native students to express their demands (76). Still, Belin did not "fit in" within the student movement. Rarely, she states, did the students, whom Belin identifies as middle-class, speak of class differentials and the lengths that certain working students had to go in order to pay tuition. Colliding with student movement leaders who were often able to cite Third World leaders, Belin realized that her Diné philosophy and worldview lived in friction with other student activists whose radicalism had a different approach.

In this recounting, Belin opens onto a different nonlinear demand grounded in Indigenous time. Her classmates "had no concept of natives, especially those indigenous to California. With such huge cities as Los Angeles and San Francisco, many non-natives considered themselves native because of the few generations their families had resided in the state" (76). With this, Belin conceptualizes a politics of urban Indigeneity as part of "a voice silenced for hundreds of years. My voice and the voices of other natives on campus were not simply our own. We speak the voices of our nations, our clan relations, our families." Their story is long and predates the civil rights movement, she claims, and cannot be reduced to the word *genocide*. Hers is a collective voice: "mixedblood, crossblood, fullblood, urban, rez, relocated, terminated, non-status, tribally enrolled, federally recognized, non-federally recognized, alcoholic, battered, uranium-infested" (76–77). By noting the erasure of Indigeneity within Third World politics, the speaker is able to name a heterogeneous collective account of Indigeneity that cannot be accounted for within the radical temporality of the student movement. Indigenous philosophy and worldviews predate the civil rights movements of the 1950s and Third World liberation movements of the 1960s. At the same time, Belin does not dismiss these latter formations nor their effects. Her courses in the Ethnic Studies department, she acknowledges, taught her how to reroute and "re-create images, to re-tell stories" of colonial domesticities, and she found the department to be a crucial site for decolonial studies of empire, colonization, race, gender, and sexuality (75).[53]

The contradictions of cross-racial solidarities in the late 1960s continue through her writing to open up spaces to dwell in the mobilizing and generative properties of tension that she feels within the heterogenous categories of being Diné. The "travel" home emerges as a space that teaches Belin the differential experiences between herself, her mother, and her family still living on the rez. Recognizing the differential experiences of a collective Native story, Belin does not position her commencement speech, or her ability to graduate from Berkeley, as marking her exceptionalism; instead, her accomplishments are part of a longer story that will engender more stories, supported by the generations that came before. Belin ends her meditation on her experience at UC Berkeley, crediting the different and united collective "journeys" of "native nations" with her ability to graduate (79). Drawing on the stories of her mother, grandmother, and aunt, and on her own stories, Belin does not collapse them into a homogeneous experience of Native womanhood. She realizes that her mother labors under two jobs, while Belin receives grants to study literature and "theories of Manifest Destiny," at an elite institute. She is "silenced" by the irony found in the contrast between, on one hand, her perceived "success" and, on the other, the menial labor of her mother fostered through her reeducation at the Sherman Institute (78).

Belin's journey ends with "In the Cycle of the Whirl," in a section entitled "Homeward," narrating her enrollment at the Institute of American Indian Arts (IAIA) in 1992, ending the text with an alternative space of institutionalized education. Founded in 1962, and set on a 140-acre campus in Santa Fe, New Mexico, IAIA explicitly prioritizes Native American and Alaskan Native people with the following guiding goals: "empowerment through education, economic self-sufficiency, and expression and enhancement of artistic and cultural traditions."[54] Surrounded by Native students, something Belin had never experienced before, she discovers a unique community that provided her "with a safe house to re-cover, un-cover, and dis-cover. Self, Voice, and existence have all been nourished and battered" (84). And so *From the Belly of My Beauty* finds in the whirl a space of re-covery, un-covery, and dis-covery. At IAIA, Belin is inspired by a working model that "from the center of its skull," deep in the school's bones, "houses a furnace of voices, scrambled with signs of recovery, gagging on oppressors' tongues, a hope chest treasured with stories" (85). The IAIA is not an endpoint for Belin, but it is a decolonial homecoming through which recovery can take place and subjugation can be transformed through language and story.

Journey as Home

In 2004, a gathering of Southern Paiute people from the areas currently called Arizona, Utah, Nevada, and California converged at the site of the Sherman Institute Cemetery in Riverside, California. The group of Paiute elders, children, and singers sang salt songs to bless the site so that the souls of buried Indian children who were taken away from their families and reservations could make their sacred journeys home. Instantiating a ritual of mourning for a group of people who died from tuberculosis, pneumonia, whooping cough, influenza, typhoid, and other forms of abuse far away from their homeland and people, the salt song singers sought to guide Native students' transitions to the next world and to help their communities heal. Published around the same time at the turn of the twenty-first century, *From the Belly of My*

Beauty (1999) and *Of Cartography* (2017) can be read, in many ways, as salt songs of worlds that have ended and that also continue onward. Through a network of roadways Belin refuses to allow Native students to die within the confining spaces of Indian boarding schools. Re-navigating the domestic space of the home, of the roads between and through the reservation and Southern California, the Four Corners, Los Angeles, and the spaces of education, Belin reimagines Native American womanhood and motherhood, hers and that of others, as decolonial spaces for movement grounded in a particular urban Indian epistemology that does not see apocalypse as a time to come, or Native people as objects in need of redemption. Reeducation through the deployment of Euro-American sentimental motherhood crucially redefined Native life, womanhood, and motherhood in ways that served extractive practices for urban development, U.S. capitalism, and military expansion within the domestic United States as well as across the Pacific. As such, the imperial enforcement of the "domestication" of Native women is part of a broader infrastructural project of empire-building overseas. As Mishuana Goeman asserts, Native people were far from isolated from U.S. global expansion. Foreign policy, according to Amy Kaplan, was directly tied to the expansion of the U.S. nation-state as a civilizing project routed through ideals of Euro-American domesticity to "conquer and domesticate the foreign," in which anything external to the home of the nation was cast as "alien and threatening" or "savage."[55] Feminist scholars such as Kaplan, Denise Cruz, Haunani-Kay Trask, J. Kēhaulani Kauanui, Maile Arvin, and Noelani Goodyear-Kaʻōpua have all also demonstrated the ways U.S. state imperial power doubled its territories throughout the 1830s to the 1850s, across the Spanish borderlands of Mexico, Texas, Oregon, California, and international spaces through "the empire of the mother" of white middle-class woman and the discourse of Manifest Destiny across the Pacific.[56]

More than relaying individual experiences of relocation and the boarding school experience, Belin's poetics is part of a wide-ranging and heterogeneous "new tribal consciousness," to borrow from Gerald Vizenor.[57] This is a critique, following Mishuana Goeman, gendered settler colonial orderings and mappings of early- to mid-twentieth-century federal programs that sought to restructure U.S. territoriality and eliminate Native presence that was pivotal to the U.S. nation-state's rise to global power in the twentieth century.[58] Writing for Navajo people who were relocated and returned, who struggle with the Navajo language and are disconnected from the reservation and its rituals and ceremonies as a consequence of boarding school education, Belin understands herself "as an interpreter of what happened in [her] parents' generation."[59] Esther Belin is not alone in this journey homeward and is part of a broader cohort of Indigenous writers and poets, such as Leslie Marmon Silko, Paula Gunn Allan, Joy Harjo, Luci Tapahonso, and Nia

Francisco, who continuously reinvent the terms of colonial systems of culture practice, education, motherhood, movement, and labor. As such, Belin is a part of a cohort of Native women writers writing after, for, and about the generational legacies of Native people surviving under the violent infrastructures of Native termination. Haunted by assimilation practices, Christianity, and education systems that have been used to destroy the competing national sovereignty of the tribal-national polity, her work continuously refuses to cede her Indigenous feminine ties, as she constantly recalls her mother, her grandmother, her mother's sister, and her daughter.[60]

Belin refuses and reorganizes the redemptive logic and time of Euro-American Christian domesticity that finds its way forward as an uncontested logic of apocalyptic temporality. Dwelling within the in-between spaces of the Southwest, and within the contradictory accounts of the apocalyptic, Belin continues the story of disobedience of the Hopi men who were incarcerated on Alcatraz for refusing to submit their children to the U.S. government with which I began this chapter. Through this disobedience, Belin comes to terms with her loss under U.S. capitalist settler colonial infrastructures, and finds regeneration in the hybrid urban Indigenous spaces she occupies. The following and final chapter of *Worlds at the End* studies Octavia Butler's seminal text *Parable of the Sower* to take up the question of survival on the road through Black feminist interventions into the apocalyptic infrastructures of Los Angeles within and after capitalist breakdown.

- Acorn

Interstate 5

State Route 156

INFRASTRUCTURES
OF FLIGHT
LIFE ON THE ROADS OF
A DISINTEGRATING WORLD

California 101

Robledo •   Los Angeles, CA

California 118

California 23

4

> When civilization fails to serve, it must disintegrate...
>
> —Octavia Butler, *Parable of the Sower*

To say that Octavia E. Butler was ahead of her moment is an understatement. Though neither was she a wishful prophet. She was, rather, a reader of the signs of her place and time who meditated profoundly on "failure" and "disintegration." Born in Pasadena, California, on June 22, 1947, Butler was the first living child of Octavia Margaret Guy and Laurice James Butler's five pregnancies. Laurice, who died when Butler was seven years old, worked as a shoeshine. Her mother Octavia labored as a housemaid and, with Butler's grandma, raised her in a Baptist household in an integrated neighborhood in Pasadena. Growing up in Southern California, Butler acutely felt the intensifying political economic shifts between the civil rights period and the mid to late twentieth century. Often hailed as a visionary, Butler's force lies in her ability to study the rise of neoliberalism as a conjunction of racial capitalism, environmental catastrophe, the privatization of the public arena, and the deregulation of the Reagan-Bush era in order to create, in Butler's words, "worlds... born out of the chaos of [her] reading and living."[1] As her archive at the Huntington Library elucidates, Butler was a rapacious reader and a writer-scholar who studied and wrote about the warnings of environmental devastation and the backlash of neoliberal conservative politics of the 1980s and onward. According to Butler, she "kept hearing or reading" in the news cycle a contempt for public education and enthusiasm for the expansion of and filling up of prisons. She recalled that incarcerated people could not take classes because they should not "benefit" from committing crimes. She read that schools did not have enough resources and books and were dangerous spaces that were falling apart; public colleges and universities discontinued remedial classes that could support struggling students, who were forced to go elsewhere "or nowhere." In Butler's California, voters attempted to pass an initiative that would bar "illegal aliens" from schools and hospitals.[2] She understood the deepening divide between the rich and the poor, and understood racial conflict not as a singular "explosion," "big crash," or "sudden chaos," but as "things [that] are unraveling, disintegrating bit by bit" (*Parable of the Sower* 110), slowing down the temporality of catastrophe for her readers through the production of and breakdown of Southern California's infrastructural systems. Presciently unfolding ongoing and imminent catastrophe through her writing, her insight is a refusal of neoliberal capitalism as a historical end goal. It is fitting, then, to end a book on Los Angeles, infrastructure, and apocalypse with Octavia Butler, one of the greatest apocalyptic thinkers and writers of the twentieth and twenty-first centuries.

In Butler's futuristic vision of Los Angeles 2024 in *Parable of the Sower* (1993), liberal state governance has collapsed even as a veneer of liberal democracy continues; new forms of enslavement and company towns proliferate; loved ones disappear daily; conflagration is ongoing while "safe" enclaves are in constant threat of being torn down by those living on the streets beyond their gates within a deepening division of the "haves" and "have-nots." Spanning the years 2024 to 2027, *Parable of the Sower* is told through a series of journal entries by fifteen-year-old empath Lauren Olamina as she escapes up the coast of California on foot with a group of travelers through the highway system after her community of Robledo is burned to the ground. Part road narrative and part pseudo-scientific-religious text, *Parable of the Sower* is a modern revision of the apocalyptic narrative that draws upon the mythic forms of the Bible and the scientific death theory of entropy to question the linear logic of transformation of either Christian salvation of humanity (through the grace of God) or scientificity (entropy's imminent disintegration of the universe). Composed of Lauren's writings, *Parable* is a collection of diary entries and verses, detailing her revelation of "Earthseed," a belief system of her own invention that follows a singular but expansive tenet: "The only lasting truth is change; God is change." "God is change" reconfigures the object of worship and actors of transformation through a zealous embrace of malleability. This move away from modern linear stories of the end times offers overlapping apocalyptic genealogies of Christianity, Black radicalism, and scientific discourses of entropy in ways that demonstrate how no singular apocalypse is totalizing and completely world-ending. In this way, malleability and the inevitability of nonlinear change in infrastructure is Butler's way of thinking about worlding after the end and in the aftermath of collapse.

This last chapter ruminates upon the postapocalyptic infrastructures of LA's freeways and roadways as pathways of forced migration and colonization as well as escape, providing an optic for what has, and will, come to pass.

In *Parable*, freeways are no longer coherent and dominant through their automobility, but instead are disintegrating and are used by Lauren and her fellow nomadic travelers to reconstellate the roads and highway system of Southern California. I position *Parable* as an engagement with a longer genealogy that links imaginations of emancipation, religion, and Black mobility. Butler developed Earthseed from a combination of an eclectic religious mixture of Euro-Christian and Buddhist belief systems and scientific theories thermodynamics. Earthseed's "destiny," Lauren preaches throughout the novel, is to "take root among the stars" (*Parable of the Sower* 68). Echoing a tradition of Black radicalism, Earthseed connects the earthly limits of Blackness to an intergalactic vision of messianism, and a physical and metaphysical movement that is in excess to, and in critique of, U.S. nationalism. Drawing upon the concepts of social death, and otherworldly epistemologies of Black radicalism, *Parable* reinvigorates the tradition of Black flight and the crossing, conceptualizing Blackness as a practice of perpetual travel since the Middle Passage against, in Hortense Spillers's theorization, a slave's "perceived ... essence of stillness ... an undynamic human state, fixed in time and space."[3] As a twenty-first-century crossing, *Parable* is connected to the forced movement of the Middle Passage that, to borrow from M. Jacqui Alexander, is "never undertaken all at once, and never once and for all."[4] A disparate iteration of Black movement, Lauren's journey stretches from LA's freeways to the stars for a futuristic vision of flight. Reinvigorating the tradition of Black mobility against forced immobility, Lauren's flight transcends the limitations of this world and signals, as Michelle Commander might say, "an escape predicated on imagination and the incessant longing to be free."[5]

Throughout Lauren's flight, the road is a dangerous place but it is also a meeting ground for new devotees of Earthseed whose theory of constant transformation develops from a wandering nomadic journey that, as I study it, builds upon Black feminists' and Esther Belin's Diné call for a pedagogy of the road that refuses colonial appropriations of the landscape. Roads in Butler's novel cultivate spaces for the formation and fracturing of communities as the group travels and moves in desperation out of LA. As Los Angeles burns, tenets of emancipation and the space of the region itself are reimagined. Disparate worlds open onto practices of living in and through disintegration, where death and endings are inevitable and multiple.

Nomadic Crossings: In Octavia Butler's Future, We Will All Be Walking on the Road

As an area built on historical and ongoing Indigenous erasure, Los Angeles is the site of a future that, when imagined through mainstream science fiction genres, is often a world in which nonwhite people hardly exist. Stories about our future, Octavia Butler points outs, showcase "every kind of alien . . . but only one kind of human—white ones."[6] I study *Parable* through the convergence of the science fiction culture of LA and the postapocalyptic road narrative as a reimagination of Black mobility and freedom. Tracing the historicity of the disintegration of modernity's roadway and airspace infrastructures in LA, Butler opens onto a vision of Black radical feminist mobility that dwells in peripeteia, degeneration, senescence, and the breakdown of the material world. Within this breakdown, Butler imagines the life of a multiracial cast of characters that decenters the linear narrative of a messianic road "hero" for a nonteleological story about survival. Building on the previous chapter, I study the relationship between the genre of road travel narratives and the disintegration of capitalist world systems. In *Parable of the Sower*, the infrastructures of automobility are a residue of a bygone era and Lauren's survival in modernity's residual landscapes, and the pathways of Southern California, are connected to a longer history of Black migration as an after-time of automobile travel through walking and space travel. My focus on the road and air travel stitches the overlay of Black migration and mobility, the biblical parable, and Spanish colonial infrastructure layered over Indigenous infrastructure to reimagine the simultaneity of the past, present, and future.

Mobilized by the combination of the road and the car as iconographies of "freedom of activity and movement, to opportunity and success," automobility has predominantly represented futurity in the twentieth century, especially across Southern California.[7] A distinctly "American" genre, road stories have been deployed by white male writers such as Jack Kerouac, John Steinbeck, Jim Harrison, Jonathan Raban, Richard Reeves, and Dayton Duncan, to name a few, as journeys of self-discovery and a search for national identity that unfold as they travel across U.S. highways in their cars.[8] The road journey is "an epic quest, a pilgrimage, a romance, a ritual that helps explain where Americans have been and where they think they might be going."[9] In those stories, roads and cars are exciting spaces of speed, solitude, and new beginnings through which the traveler answers the call for adventure, overcomes conflict, then returns home changed and triumphant. The mobility enabled by cars themselves also shifted the terms of Black exclusion: under Jim Crow, seating for Black Americans was located behind the engine and was dirty, whereas traveling by car symbolized freedom of mobility. While public transportation was a space of Black segregation and degradation, Black travelers saw road trips as a path to self-improvement and self-actualization and used the automobile as a weapon to claim rights and contest racism.[10] Opening up the space of the nation for exploration, the automobile became a symbol of a democratic society, with W. E. B. Du Bois and Booker T. Washington both viewing driving as providing opportunity for physical and social movement. Du Bois loved driving in his car, writing, in his 1932 column in *The Crisis*, that "all over and everywhere the colored people are traveling in their automobiles." For Booker T. Washington, the automobile was essential to gaining economic self-reliance, to leaving the South, and it offered the opportunity to get a job as a chauffeur, truck driver, or taxi driver or start a business.[11] This particular linear narrative arc of the road journey toward resolution and triumph becomes a thing of the past in apocalyptic renderings of the road genre such as Cormac McCarthy's 2006 novel *The Road*, in which a father and son must learn to survive an extinction event in the United States, walking along the interstate, southward, toward the sea in order to survive winter; or, more recently in the postapocalyptic HBO zombie series *The Last of Us* (2023), where an unlikely duo traverses an abandoned and threatening landscape.

Similar to familiar postapocalyptic road narratives, *Parable* is nomadic and restless, and dwells in the mundane life of its protagonists' everyday movements through picaresque tales and episodic adventures. At the same time, Butler's road narrative becomes a space of wandering, disintegration, and entropy for reanimated "road heroes"—different from Kerouac's and McCarthy's nomads and runaways, not yearning for what once was, or for the recuperation of a coherent U.S. nation-state, but calling for total breakdown and transformation. The first half of the novel details the work of preparation Lauren undergoes while living within the "safety" of Robledo, a small multiracial city just twenty miles outside of Los Angeles proper with her Black father Reverend Olamina, Latina stepmother Cory, and four half brothers Keith, Marcus, Gregory, and Bennett. In the 2024 of *Sower*, the United States has colonized Mars and capitalism has exacerbated the divide between the rich and the poor, but we see the world only through the eyes of the destitute. New drugs proliferate and Lauren's "hyperempathy"—a gift, curse, and affliction that enables Lauren to feel others' pain and pleasure—is a byproduct of her late mother's drug addiction. Inside Robledo's walls, armed middle-class residents protect themselves and their property from "the street poor—squatters, winos, junkies, homeless people" living in despair just outside of Robledo. From the beginning of the novel, Lauren knows that soon their walls will fall, and that they must prepare to survive beyond the semi-self-sustaining community. Lauren buries a survival pack in the backyard, looks over her grandparents' old road map and routes, takes stock of their weapons, and studies books on wilderness survival, guns and shooting, basic living, log cabin-building, California native plants and their uses, plant cultivation, livestock raising, soap making, and science fiction novels (50). In many ways the first half of the novel serves as a survival manual for the fall of one's community and neighborhood and the work of study is crucial. When her brother leaves the walled community, he is found murdered; her father never returns home from teaching at the local college; and scavenging people from beyond the walls slowly breach the town and inevitably burn down the community, murdering many and causing others to flee. Lauren escapes and returns to gather her survival pack, also scavenging the ashes of her own home for supplies.

In the second half of the novel Lauren begins a journey northward with her neighbors, gathering companions as they make their way up the coast of California. Fires, water scarcity, riots, earthquake damage, ravaging dogs, drug addiction, company towns, new forms of slavery, and indentured servitude confront the group at every turn. Amid this landscape, a presidential candidate bolstered by the Christian right promises to help "make America great again" (*Parable of the Talents* 21).[12] For Lauren, she either becomes part of Olivar, one of the cities controlled by a big corporation, offering one of the few options open to people in search of safety, or she learns from her grandmother's bookshelves of old science fiction novels about the doomed story of moving into company towns such as Olivar. The hero in those stories, she learns from the novels, will be underpaid and captured. Earthseed is an alternative option and Lauren realizes that to pursue that route she will "have to go outside" (110) and live beyond the walls of Olivar and her home Robledo. Whereas Robledo was "once a rich, green, unwalled little city" (9), according to her father, the Robledo of Lauren's generation is constantly under threat of falling. The "massive" wall, to Lauren, is a "looming presence," like a "crouching animal, perhaps about to spring, more threatening than protective" (5), instilling in her a sense that they are never safe and that she must live in a constant state of preparation and escape.

Against twentieth-century traditional road narratives that romanticized speedy adventures in the automobile, *Parable* offers an alternative temporality to the progressive time of the automobile. The challenge to travel beyond Robledo's wall looms large as the comfort and ease of traveling by car is a relic of a past time. In an October 31, 2026, entry, Lauren gathers her grandparents' old road maps as part of her preparation for the inevitability of her community's collapse. She writes,

> My grandparents once traveled a lot by car. They left us old road maps of just about every county in the state plus several of other parts of the country. The newest of them is 40 years old, but that doesn't matter. The roads will still be there. They'll just be in worse shape than they were back when my parents drove a gas-fueled car over them. (110)

In *Parable*'s future, the infrastructures of automobility—maps, freeways, and cars—serve a temporal narrative function as they are no longer central to Southern California life. What "once" was, is no longer. Lauren marks a temporal dissonance between her relationship with the freeway system and her grandparents living in the latter half of the twentieth century. Her backward glance is necessary, not nostalgic, to planning for the crises to come. While people in the past and her grandparents might have seen the utter breakdown of the freeway system as a dystopian future—in other words, Lauren's present moment—Lauren is proof throughout the novel that change is continual and that survival is possible. Although roads and maps no longer serve the same modality of movement, and the roads are in "bad shape," they are enduring and assist Lauren on her journey northward. In this passage, and throughout the novel, documentation of the highway system is key to figuring out how the group should travel. In many ways, *Parable* is a documentation or a time capsule of escape, moving simultaneously forward, present, and backward, looking for intergenerational contact to prepare for the future, which is entirely fragmented and incomplete.

Lauren's diary entries take on the form of the apocalyptic confessional that reveals, through a retrospective writing practice, a series of revelations about life and death that emphasize an enduring commitment to movement that also draws upon one of the primary genres of African American writing: the autobiographical slave narrative. Although *Parable* is not at first easily recognizable as a slave narrative, Lauren depicts a story of a group's need to run away and out of Southern California. Butler's science fictional text follows in the tradition of Black writers between 1705 and 1901, such as Olaudah Equiano, Frederick Douglass, William Wells Brown, Jarena Lee, Harriet Jacobs, and Amanda Smith, who wrote and imagined freedom through literacy and social and physical mobility. Tropes of reading and writing become central to the novel as Lauren wonders if she can survive outside by teaching people how to read and write, or by reading and writing for others. Throughout the novel, she must write because "there's nothing familiar left to [her] but the writing. God is change. [She] hates God. [She has] to write" (141). In this light, LA's highways system becomes part of a broader narrative that links the centrality of literacy to Black mobility in engagements of emancipation. U.S. Black traveling culture, according to Michelle Commander, explicitly ties mobility to freedom. Freedmen and runaways migrated north and west to places like Los Angeles where slavery was illegal and racism was supposedly less intense.[13] As Gretchen Sorin explains, Black Americans traveled little in the antebellum period and in the decades immediately following emancipation. Rooted in a history of the involuntary journey of Africans across the Middle Passage, Black mobility in the United States reaches back to the Atlantic Crossing. While "freedom of movement has always been a fundamental right" for white Americans, enslaved people were isolated from one another and restricted from moving freely, patrolled by both slave patrollers and urban police forces, subjected to the fugitive slave clause that criminalized enslaved runaways and by Black Codes that controlled and criminalized the mobility of enslaved people at the state level. The freedom of mobility would, enslavers feared, give enslaved people access to learn the landscape that could precipitate methods of escape.[14] In the post-emancipation year of 1863, 90 percent of the U.S. Black Americans lived in the Southern states, and for the first time they had, for all intents and purposes, free choice on their mobility even as their "freedom" remained limited.

During the two Great Migrations, the first taking place between 1910 and 1930 and the second between the 1940s and the 1960s, seven million Black Americans from the South escaped to the Northeast and Midwest and west to California by foot, train, bus, or automobile in an effort to escape Jim Crow laws, sharecropping, and other forms of white supremacist practices.[15] The West, as Quintard Taylor illuminates, was viewed as a place of refuge and economic opportunity for Black Americans in the nineteenth century, a place for migrants to begin anew, even as this dream remained elusive as white settlers created recognizable race-based political, social, and economic restrictions.[16] During World War II, tens of thousands of African Americans came to Los Angeles for employment in the war industry, building airplanes, ships, and other warfare materials. This coincided with, as Kelly Lytle-Hernández described, an intensification of policing in LA's expanding Black belt areas of Watts and Little Tokyo, which became known as Bronzeville for a short time after African Americans moved into the enclave when Japanese and Japanese Americans were dislocated and incarcerated.[17]

Lauren's escape marks the continuation of Black crossings and flights at the turn of the twenty-first century, over a hundred years after Black migrations north and west at the turn of the twentieth century. Instead of escaping through a series of transportation infrastructures such as cars, trains, and buses, Lauren escapes on foot. Butler's emphasis on walking and the freeway presents a temporality of traveling, one in which the speed of the automobile is no longer providing the pathway to Black mobility, progress, and modernity. After Robledo is infiltrated, collapses, and burns down, Lauren loses her family in the destruction and decides to travel as a man for safety. On her journey, she meets and forms a community with a multiracial group of people: Zahra and Harry, a couple; Natividad, her partner Travis, and their son Domingo; Bankole, an older, Frederick Douglass–like man whom she falls in love with and marries; and Allie and Jill. In a journal entry on Monday, August 2, 2027, Lauren carefully describes the first time she walks on the freeway. She walks down to the 118 freeway, turns west, then takes the 23 to the U.S. 101, which will take the group up the California coast toward Oregon. No longer dominated by cars, freeways become main pathways for walkers, even though it is illegal to walk on the freeways in California; "but the law is archaic" (150). Lauren shares: "Everyone who walks walks on the freeways sooner or later. Freeways provide the most direct routes between cities and parts of cities" (157). The emphasis on walking marks an intense slowdown of movement through the landscape that follows in the tradition of Black travel writing and crossings beyond the foundational moment of the Middle Passage. Freeways are transformed into pathways for walkers, but also provide shelter for sex workers and for people peddling food, water, and other supplies to those traveling on and living along the freeway in the open air, shacks, and sheds. A significant moment in the novel, because Lauren had "never walked a freeway before today," Lauren's first time walking on the freeway is simultaneously "fascinating and frightening." Likening what she sees to a "scene" in an old film, Lauren takes on a detached observant point of view that visualizes the people on the freeway as a "street in mid-twentieth century China," filled with "walkers, bicyclers, people carrying, pulling, pushing loads of all kinds." Lauren conjures a frenzied visual image of people and movement as a

> heterogeneous mass—black and white, Asian and Latin, whole families are on the move with babies on backs or perched atop loads in carts, wagons or bicycle baskets, sometimes along with an old or handicapped person. Other old, ill, or handicapped people hobbled along as best they could with the help of sticks or fitter companions. Many were armed with sheathed knives, rifles, and, of course, visible, holstered handguns. The occasional passing cop paid no attention. (157–158)

Lauren depicts a scene of forced migration, and a journey that the old, ill, and handicapped would not make unless necessary for survival because it is also a dangerous space where people are armed for protection and attack. Police are present, but they do not protect the travelers. Seeing the world as a space of disintegration also names a place for the rebuilding of communities within the entropic world, where travel and escape on the road marks the possibilities of losing and creating new communities that defy easy racial alignment and categorization, highlighting the fluidity of rebuilding that harkens back to the political formation of women of color feminists, and practices of making worlds as new ways of being in relation with each other. Lauren's remade field of sociality across LA's disintegrating landscape builds tenuous communities that sometimes must break apart, connecting Los Angeles to otherworldly, speculative, and futurist spaces to emphasize the historicity, rather than the ontology, of race. In this sense, *Parable* counters the ontological turn that situates Blackness and therefore anti-Blackness as monolithic and transhistorical, that at times too soon forecloses cross-racial affiliation for reconfiguring the end of the world. What counts as, or who composes, community in these novels constantly shifts across the freeways to offer new ways of thinking about racial categories, not as separate conglomerations of unique categories, but as existing in a dialectic flow of people.

Lauren depicts the densely populated freeway as a river, transforming the walking travelers into a natural moving body of water to further formulate the tenets of Earthseed. She writes, "We became part of a broad river of people walking west on the freeway. Only a few straggled east against the current—east toward the mountains and the desert. Where were the westward walkers going?" (157). Later in the novel, she muses, "I've come to think that I should be fishing that river even as I follow its current" (200). No longer populated by cars, the freeway becomes a "river of people walking." Describing people as a "river" and "current," their bodies meld with the meandering path of the freeway. Never still, but always moving, the freeway is filled with a current of people that directs and redirects its path. The imagery of the nomadic travelers as a moving body of water ties them to, and transforms, biblical parables about the final judgment. Positioning herself as a fisher in the river of the 101 freeway, Lauren references the biblical figure of Jesus as a fisherman, who tells his apostles in the Gospels, "I will make you fishers of men" (Mark 1:19). In the "Parable of Drawing in the Net" (Matthew 13:47–50) Jesus describes the separation of the righteous (good fish) from the wicked (bad fish) by the angels at the end of the world and the coming Kingdom of God. This account of the final judgment is the last in Matthew 13, which begins with "The Parable of the Sower," or the "Parable of the Soils," a seemingly simple allegorical story that illustrates a spiritual lesson and religious principle by Jesus in the Gospels. The biblical account of the "Parable of the Sower" is an allegory about the Kingdom of God told through a story of a man who sows seeds. Some seeds drop on the path and birds eat them, while other seeds fall onto rocky ground with little soil. These seeds sprout but then are burned by the sun. Other seeds fall in thorn bushes that end up choking the plants, while some seeds fall on rich soil and grow into plants. In the underlying interpretation of the parable, God is the man, and the seeds are His teachings and potential converts. The birds that eat the seeds are Satan, who consumes the "bad seeds," or they are people who hear the message but do not listen to God and are lost. The thorn bushes suffocate and kill God's message. Finally, the seeds in the good soil represent the people of strong faith who can spread God's message. Salvation and regeneration in this biblical sense depends on one's faith in Jesus. Calling her novel a "parable," and ending the novel with the King James Version of the "Parable of the Sower," Butler emphasizes how her own novel might be divulging a secret knowledge. Parables represent Jesus's private teachings to his disciples, after which the disciples would spread His revelations and teachings. Parables, then, are seemingly simple stories that contain within them a concealed "truth" of the immense revelation of God's teachings to realize the Kingdom of God.[18] In this way, parables are performative, creating utterances that give not only information but promises and warnings, making an offering and a demand for faith.[19]

Butler reclaims the freeway in *Parable of the Sower* as a way to connect Lauren's belief system to a longer landscape of the formation of religions in California, and intersects the notion of migration, Black travel, and faith-based systems. Lauren's Earthseed religion, she documents on Sunday, August 15, 2027, "is being born right here on Highway 101—on that portion of 101 that was once El Camino Real the royal highway of California's Spanish past. Now it's a highway, a river of the poor. A river flooding north" (200). Lauren directly links the emergence of Earthseed to a Royal Road that was established as part of a series of expeditions undertaken in the eighteenth century by the Spanish in order to set up missions along the California coast. The Spanish established an aggressive military series of presidios (forts), missions, ports, and settlements along the California coast as part of a global defensive strategy for the Spanish empire. This early infrastructure served frontier institutions in laying claim to Spanish sovereignty in North America. Many parts of the Camino Real grew from ancient Indigenous trails, not newly found routes. Indian tribes guided the Spaniards, and taught them which paths to follow, as the Spaniards moved north along the coast of California.[20] And, over time, these trails grew to be corridors for horses, mules, and wagons that supported an infrastructure of ports, presidios, missions, towns, and ranchos, and then roads and highways for automobiles and now, in Lauren's time, a highway for nomadic travel and the development of Earthseed.[21] Butler's narrative layering of destroyed infrastructures—twentieth-century automobility over Spanish colonial highways that overtake Indigenous footpaths—sutures the transformation of belief systems to practices of mobility to reveal how migration, as M. Jacqui Alexander poses, is "one indication that these cosmological systems are marked by anything but stasis."[22] Black migration and cosmological systems reveal through each other the inevitability of transformation. *Parable*'s cosmology takes readers back to, and intervenes in, the histories of colonial Spanish occupation of California's highway system and Black migration, while also using the roadways to rescale California through a Black radical intergalactic tradition and scientific discourse of entropy that informs the groups' movement up the highway to the cosmos.

Reconstellating Los Angeles and the Universe

Parable of the Sower opens up with Lauren's recurring dream about flight. In the dream, she teaches herself how to fly and levitate. Each time, she improves, "little by little, dream lesson by dream lesson," trusting her ability to fly more and more, but she is still afraid. Unable to control her movements, her body stiffens, she grips the doorway, leans, strains, and slides, "caught between terror and joy," a contradictory mixture of feeling she has throughout the novel (4). As she drifts, a fire springs from nowhere, eats through the wall and comes after her; she grabs at the fire and air, kicking and burning. She wakes when the fire swallows her. She then fades into the second dream: "the part that's ordinary and real"—that happened years ago. The stars brighten the darkness. She is with her stepmother, Corey, a Mexican American woman who runs the neighborhood school. Speaking in Spanish, Corey tells Lauren how she grew up without seeing "so many stars." As they look up at the Milky Way, a night sky filled with stars, taking the wash off the clothesline, Corey explains how the city and its "lights, progress, growth, all those things" kept them from seeing the stars back then, which were, as she was taught by her mother, "windows into heaven" (4–5). While Corey longs for the "blaze" of city lights, Lauren would "rather have the stars," relishing in stargazing and studying the components of the constellations, which initiates her break with her Baptist preacher father's concepts of God and religion.

Home to the first network of freeways, LA is also the site for the material and cultural production of flight in scientific and science fictional exploration of earth and other planets. The setting of much apocalyptic and post-apocalyptic science fiction, Los Angeles is also home to the oldest operating science fiction and fantasy fan club in the world, the Los Angeles Science Fantasy Society (since the 1930s). Los Angeles also played a crucial role in the aerospace industry, boosting its reputation as a city of the future. Aerospace developers and advocates such as John Northrop, Donald Douglas, Amelia Earhart, Howard Hughes, Walt Disney, Wernher von Braun, and Griffith J. Griffith and institutions such as the Jet Propulsion Laboratory boosted the region's aviation industry, which drew two million workers into the city to produce three hundred thousand airplanes in four years to "save the free world." Aiding the war effort while also changing the Southern California landscape and geography, the links between LA and visions of the future influenced futuristic ultramodern architectural design styles in the post–World War II era, marked through space-age designs and symbols of motions such as parabolas, figures of atoms, geometric shapes, boomerangs, and flying saucers. By 1940 more Southern Californians worked at aircraft companies than any other industry, with thirteen thousand industrial workers arriving in Los Angeles every month. By 1965, Los Angeles was home to more than half of the nation's largest aerospace companies, which needed large swaths of land away from urban centers, thus reshaping housing development, suburbs, and freeways. But then, between 1988 and 1993, eight hundred thousand jobs were gone due to a dwindling of Pentagon defense spending.[23] LA's dominance of road- and aerialscapes, and their destruction, are central themes of futurity, dystopia, apocalypse, settler invasion, escape, and outer space that permeate our collective Los Angeles imagination.

By Butler's 2024, humans have begun to colonize outer space because the earth has been so depleted that the best option for human survival is to go to the stars. Perhaps one way to interpret this destiny is through a technological escapism that developed in the Cold War global race of space exploration. While it may seem like Earthseed's destiny is to colonize outer space, Lauren recognizes that the space program is an effort to prove that "we're still a great, forward-looking, powerful nation" (18). Space exploration and the hopes placed upon technology to "save mankind" is limited, is not a sustainable means for transformation, and is a waste of "money . . . when so any people here on earth can't afford water, food, or shelter" (*Parable of the Sower* 15), echoing *Star Trek* fan Dr. Martin Luther King Jr.'s sentiment about the "striking absurdity in committing billions to reach the moon where no people live, while only a fraction of that amount is appropriate to service the densely populated slums."[24] Butler continues, in the tradition of twentieth-century Black radicalism's apocalyptic and their theories of the universe, to imagine social transformation.

In *Parable*, Lauren does not look to outer space for technological advancement, but instead draws upon, and reconfigures, a long legacy of Black radicalism's ideas of intergalactic kinship for political and theological transformation that imagined emancipation as connected to, not conquering or colonizing, the broader universe. While Martin Luther King Jr. articulated Black liberation through a Christian apocalyptic vision that called upon Americans to reject racism and overcome its crises in order to bring about a Kingdom of God, Elijah Muhammad, Louis Farrakhan, and Malcolm X articulated the Black experience through Islam.[25] Through the theology of the Nation of Islam, the Black Power movement found a discourse and strategy that broke with white Christianity. The Nation of Islam's apocalyptic vision of God's imminent destruction of white America was based on the theology of James H. Cone and Albert B. Cleage Jr. in which a non-Christian biblical interpretation aligned God with Black struggle and the coming judgment of white America. In the late 1920s, the Nation of Islam's founder Wallace Fard Muhammad preached a cosmogony that cast Black people as descendants of the Shabazz, a tribe that originated from the moon sixty-six trillion years ago. What we now call earth was once a moon populated by only Black people. Known as "people of the moon," one of them, a "scientist," out of frustration destroyed the people and caused the moon to explode, sending pieces of the moon across the atmosphere and dropping water on the planetary body of what we now call earth. As the only tribe to survive the explosion, the Shabazz lived on the combined continent of what we now call Africa and

Asia, and were the origin point for all races except the white race.[26] According to Wallace Fard Muhammad, Elijah Muhammad, and Malcolm X, the origins of the white man can be found through the story of the antihero devil Yakub. A member of the Meccan branch of Shabazz, the Black scientist Yakub lived sixty-six hundred years ago and sought to breed out Black traits by killing dark babies in order to breed white babies. The evil nature of white people, Malcolm X concluded, was produced through the inhumane conditions of their genesis.[27] In this racial origin story, Allah is imbued with the power to reverse Yakub's experiment, end white domination, remove white people from earth, liberate those faithful to Allah by overcoming Yakub's brood, and thus complete the salvation of Black people.

This strain of Black apocalypticism turns biblical terms into Black retribution against white injustice, where, according to Michael Lieb, the chariot is "no longer simply a means of transport to the other world or a form of liberation in this [world]."[28] The Mother Plane, as a precosmogonic entity in existence before earth, ultimately assumes a regenerative role in which there will be rebirth through the annihilation and cleansing of white domination. This is a central tenet for the Nation of Islam and would deeply impact Black radicalism of the 1960s and 1970s. While Elijah Muhammad's vision does not name a concrete time and place in which this battle will take place, Louis Farrakhan urgently insisted that Armageddon is not a future time, but is the present in which we live.

Butler's work is perhaps in line with Farrakhan's insight that Armageddon is now. She would differ, however, on the messianic strain of Black radicalism and its faith in Allah, or any singular figure, as savior. In her zealousness, Lauren's role as "knower" and "revealer" of Earthseed bears similarity to "prophets" like Elijah Muhammad, Louis Farrakhan, and Malcolm X, who all wanted to change the world. Butler has revealed that she did not like Lauren at first because she was a "power-seeker" and as such should not have power. In an interview, Butler stated:

> Some people know that if they can only find the people responsible for all the chaos and punish them, stop them, kill them, then all will be well again. Hunting for scapegoats is always popular in times of serious trouble. So is hunting for the great leader who will restore prosperity and stability. Some people know that that's the answer. If they could just find the strong, powerful leader that they need, all would be well. And, unhappily for them, they do find such a leader.[29]

The strong powerful leader emerges in relationship to the practice of locating scapegoats and with promises of the restoration of a better world. This is an apocalyptic narrative in the biblical messianic sense, but mob rule, which goes hand in hand with messianism, flashes as figures of danger and ultimately is not the answer. By the time Butler completed *Parable of the Sower*, she came to accept that "power is a tool" that could be used for good or bad, and she came to like Lauren "far too much."[30] Lauren offers a way to imagine another side of modern racism while also formulating a cosmology and religion that precedes and names forces that exceed the modern world.

Butler replaces the messianic figure with transformation itself by fusing the eschatology of the biblical forms with scientific theories of the end of the world, such as the laws of thermodynamics and entropy. All the while, she also refuses the facticity of science and technology. Entropy is understood through the group's movement northward in *Parable*, where the group decides when to stay on the freeway, when to get off, and when to keep moving. The emphasis on movement and dwelling is compounded through the intersection of entropy and the freeway. Lauren introduces the concept of change in terms of thermodynamics—the study of energy, heat, and temperature—in relationship to bodies of matter in her journal entry on Sunday, August 8, 2027. On a Santa Barbara beach, her traveling companion and first convert Travis Charles Douglas asks Lauren to explain Earthseed. She tells him, "I was looking for God. . . . I wasn't looking for mythology or mysticism or magic. I didn't know whether there was a god to find, but I wanted to know. God would have to be a power that could not be defied by anyone or anything." To which Travis responds, "Change. . . . But it's not a god. It's not a person or an intelligence or even a thing. It's just . . . I don't know. An idea." Lauren responds, "It's a truth. . . . Change is ongoing. Everything changes in some way—size, position, composition, frequency, velocity, thinking, whatever. Every living thing, every bit of matter, all the energy in the universe changes in some way. I don't claim that everything changes in every way, but everything changes in some way" (*Sower* 195). Lauren brings the abstract concept of God into their immediate environment, which stands in contrast to a distant aspirational contact with the messianic. By associating "change" with God, Lauren calls on people to enact a form of religious devotion and worship to the idea that everything changes and transforms, placing an even greater emphasis on action guided by careful observation and study. Harry adds to Travis and Lauren's discussion: "God is the second law of thermodynamics," referencing his earlier conversation about Earthseed with Lauren. She replies, "That's an aspect of God. . . . Do you know about the second law?" To which Travis nods, "Entropy, the idea that the natural flow of heat is from something hot to something cool—not the other way—so that the universe itself is cooling down, running down, dissipating its energy" (*Sower* 195). Butler emphasizes change over an orthodox structure of authority that presumes an ordered hierarchical social structure in the service of God. There is something here, too, of Gnosticism's influence. Gnostic writings, according to Elaine Pagels, "reverse the pattern of the New Testament gospels. Instead of telling the history of Jesus biographically from birth to death, gnostic accounts begin where the others end—with stories of the spiritual Christ appearing to his disciples."[31] There is a decentering of Christ as figure and an emphasis on storytelling and scientific knowledge at the end. Inhabiting disintegrating worlds of mundane acts and processes of breakdown, small particles or constituent elements reveal alternative modes of perceiving dissolution, degeneration, and fragmentation across racial lines. For Butler, disintegration is a necessary process for the revelation of alternative cosmologies of Black futurity, as she writes in *Parable of the Sower*: "When civilization fails to serve, it must disintegrate" (89) and so you have to write new ones. Butler's apocalypticism offers a way to understand the critical power of the nondogmatic "truth" that nothing is incontrovertibly fixed.

Butler's laws of thermodynamics and entropy intervenes in the biblical textual production of the apocalyptic, supplanting a devotion to the figuration of God with a devotion to change and turns toward Afrofuturism and science fiction as a challenge to science. Indeed, Butler's oeuvre is a key archive of Afrofuturist writing grappling with Black traditions of messianism, science, the stars, and other worldly planets. Her science fictional *Patternist* series, which includes *Patternmaster* (1976), *Survivor* (1978), *Clay's Ark* (1984), *Mind of My Mind* (1977), and *Wild Seed* (1980), tells a secret history where immortal, telepathic, and shape-shifting characters traverse ancient Egypt into the near and far future world of colonies, mutation, disease, and bioengineering. Her second series, *Xenogenesis*, now called *Lilith's Brood*, includes three books—*Dawn* (1987), *Adulthood Rites* (1988), and *Imago* (1989)—that explore a postnuclear world where humans have been nearly extinguished. An alien race, the Oankali, come to Earth to take remaining survivors, and then return to a more habitable Earth with human-Oankali hybrids. Her popular early novel *Kindred* (1979) presents a time-travel-slave narrative that transports a young Black woman writer, Dana, from Los Angeles, California, in 1976 to a pre–Civil War Maryland plantation where she confronts her Black and white ancestors within a plantation slave economy. Butler has also written a book of short science fiction stories entitled *Bloodchild and Other Stories* (1995), as well as her final book *Fledgling* (2005), a science fiction vampire novel about 53-year-old Shori, a member of the Ina species that survives within a symbiotic relationship with humans: the Ina need human blood to survive and the Ina's venom strengthens human immune systems such that they may live for up to two hundred years. Her *Parable* series includes *Parable of the Sower* (1993) and *Parable of the Talents* (1998). Butler had intended on writing subsequent *Parable* novels (*Parable of the Trickster*, *Parable of the Teacher*, *Parable of Chaos*, and *Parable of Clay*) that would tell the story of life in the colony on the planet Bow, where Earthseed would fulfill its "destiny" to "take root among the stars." Butler never completed these works, however, focusing instead on writing *Fledgling*, her final work before her death on February 24, 2006, in Lake Forest Park, Washington. In 2020 *Parable of the Sower* made the *New York Times* Best Sellers list, fourteen years after her death and thirty-two years after she journaled this affirmation: "I shall be a bestselling writer." At present, Butler has inspired countless writers, podcasts, webinars, small religions, anthologies, an opera, a film adaptation of *Parable of the Sower*, and TV show adaptations of *Fledgling*, *Kindred*, *Wild Seed*, and *Dawn*. Upon her death, Butler left her official archive to the Huntington Library in Pasadena, California, which has become a great resource for fans, writers, and scholars in the exploration of her work and life, and Afrofuturism.[32]

In *Parable of the Sower*, there is a leap from the scientific theory that the earth is going to freeze to imagining a cosmos where specific earthly worlds are imagined in ways that can take us to other planets. Aligning Earthseed with a scientific model of change, entropy, and thermodynamics, Butler follows a long line of writers and intellectuals who invoke the law of entropy as a metaphor for the end of the world. Thomas Pynchon, Samuel Beckett, and Cormac McCarthy have drawn upon doomsday physicists Lord Kelvin, Rudolf Clausius, Ludwig Boltzmann, Hermann von Helmholtz, William Rankine, Josiah Willard Gibbs, Max Planck, and Albert Einstein and their development of entropy and the second law of thermodynamics. American historian Henry Adams, of the prominent political Adams family, outlined in his 1910 *A Letter to American Teachers of History* a theory based on the second law of thermodynamics that predicted the irreversible dissipation of energy that would culminate in the "Heat Death" of the universe. Man, Adams argued, cannot escape this inevitable fate of modernity's decay and disorder.[33] The law of entropy illustrates the steady death of the universe and the irreversible molecular distribution of thermodynamics that produces a disorganized and random state of molecular movement. Entropy is a measure of the dispersal of energy within a system that tends to move toward higher entropy, not a measurement of energy itself. Heat energy becomes more disordered as it is dispersed, and once the molecules are randomly distributed in a uniform way, spontaneous changes in the system will increase entropy, randomness, and disorganization. At the end of the process, the generated energy, because it has equal quantities of energy, cannot be transferred, creating a thermodynamic equilibrium that marks a maximum molecular disorder and greatest molecular homogeneity. Called Heat Death, the Big Chill, or the Big Freeze, this, according to the second law of thermodynamics, is the ultimate fate of the universe.

Butler leaps from the large scale of the universe freezing, to earth, to the West Coast of California, in a scalar shift that connects the group's flight up the highway to the stars, the cosmos, and otherworldly planets. Butler's way of building another world is to literally imagine pathways to other worlds through LA's highways. Science, it seems, cannot totally save the world. What can save it, according to Lauren, is a notion of Earthseed and entropy that perhaps aligns with a universal humanism, or illiberal humanism, that cuts across racial lines for earthly survival. Butler's work echoes the need to conceptualize what Sylvia Wynter has called for in a "universal humanism," or as Kandice Chuh has more recently argued for, an "illiberal humanism," that is a nonidentitarian proposal for a planetary understanding of a notion of the human arrested from bourgeois liberalism.[34] Calling upon entropy, Butler's vision of disintegration disrupts notions of a teleological progress of time where Western modernity is the only goal of change and development. An evolutionary path of the universe that ends in its demise is antithetical to the twentieth century's notion of progress and modernity. Entropy is less forgiving than the regenerative faculties of the biblical sense of apocalypse, as entropy only moves forward toward an irreversible future of disintegration. Human intervention cannot prevent heat death and is utterly irrelevant. Unlike apocalyptic temporality, entropic time refuses any prospect of regeneration or salvation; there is no messianic figure of Christ, or moral or ethical decisions to be made about the future. Entropic time, according to Lois Parkinson Zamora, "invests history with direction, but not with purpose. It is linear and unrepeatable, the future qualitatively different from the past or present, but change is inevitably for the worse."[35] There is only inactive waiting for the moment of equilibrium that will bring about heat death. Entropic time imagines the end of the world as inevitable, just as biblical apocalyptic time, but without the coming of God's Kingdom.

Lauren uses the concept of entropy to describe Earthseed and what she imagines as the inevitable dissolution of the United States, but entropy is an ineffective metaphor for Lauren's philosophy of change. Lauren takes from the law of entropy the notion that everything is always changing and in flux, and that we must somehow measure and account for chaos, but she does not imagine the end as a finality or without purpose. Shifting transformation to the atomic level, to one of vibration and irreversibility in which matter can be irrevocably changed, Butler combines scientific knowledge with biblical urgency. This process of change is connected to a broader planetary and galactic terrain and introduces new states of matter into the universe. It has no definite shape, and no innate structure of "bad" or "good"; it is not discerning, but disintegrates according to the various levels of equilibrium. From entropy, Butler takes the inevitability of disintegration for a theory of change; yet, she does not take science as an ultimate mode of gnosis. Nor does she accept a biblical apocalyptic messianism that awaits the Kingdom of God. When Lauren discusses Earthseed with Travis, he falls into the trap of personifying God, but Lauren is not interested in worshipping a singular figure, and instead shifts the concept of God to change. Lauren contemplates change as Trickster, teacher, Chaos, and Clay, as something wholly mutable, not "punishing or jealous, but infinitely malleable." For Lauren, "there's comfort in realizing that everyone and everything yields to God. There's power in knowing that God can be focused, diverted, shaped by anyone at all. But there's no power in having strength and brains, and yet waiting for God to fix things for you or take revenge for you. . . . God will shape us all every day of our lives. Best to understand that and return the effort: Shape God" (197). Refusing entropic temporality, Lauren ultimately calls for active participation in shaping the regeneration and transformation of the world. Shaping infrastructure in this sense is how Lauren can build the conditions of their own salvation.

Rather than waiting for salvation through the figuration of God or Jesus the Savior, or a fixed figure to worship or the final heat death, God as change becomes an entity that people can shape. Travis asks Lauren, "Why personify change by calling it God? Since change is just an idea, why not call it that? Just say change is important." To which she replies, "Because after a while, it won't be important! . . . People forget ideas. They're more likely to remember God—especially when they're scared or desperate." He follows up by demanding, "Then they're supposed to do what? . . . Read a poem?" Lauren responds, "Or remember a truth or a comfort or a reminder to action. . . . People do that all the time. They reach back to the Bible, the Talmud, the Koran, or some other religious book that helps them deal with the frightening changes that happen in life. . . . God isn't good or evil, doesn't favor you or hate you, and yet God is better partnered than fought. . . . 'God is Trickster, teacher, Chaos, Clay'" (199). Lauren returns Travis to the force of religious writings of the Bible, the Talmud, and the Koran, texts that can serve as sources of change, not just a humanly figuration of God. Lauren's attachment to calling change "God" echoes Sylvia Wynter's desire to "appreciate" and study the "intellectual breakthrough" and power of Euro-Christian beliefs, and how it came to reorganize the world through its powerful "codes" and "genres."[36] Lauren understands the abiding ways in which "God" has become deeply embedded in our cultural-political consciousness, and if Earthseed's followers forget everything else about her teachings, the ideation of "God is change" will remain. In what might seem at first a heretical move, Lauren attempts to transform the dominant meaning of God to one of change, in order to transform the world.

Parable's diary format describes events in Lauren's life and ponderings on Earthseed, and serves as a text to revisit for survival in continuous times of change. Lauren preaches, sometimes dogmatically, that if the tenet of God as change fails and does not help her or the people in her community, then it presents "all the more reason to care for myself and others" (199). Within the law of entropy there is no place for human intervention; yet, for Lauren humans must shape God/Change itself. Within a chaotic and disordered world, with seemingly increasing entropy where harbingers of an eventual heat death loom, Lauren is left with the capacity to make sense of the disorder and chaos through her writings, journal entries, verses, and preaching of Earthseed. A vehicle for Earthseed's revelation, Lauren follows the missive of the apocalypticists' calling to write and unveil "the things which thou has seen, and the things which are, and the things which shall be hereafter . . . and what is past and passing and to come."[37] As a story of survival in the ruins of twentieth-century infrastructures, Butler does not consign her characters or the world to death but asserts the malleability of infrastructure, as something that can be rewritten and repurposed, as an opportunity for endless flight. At the end of the novel, Lauren and her fellow travelers reach Bankole's land in Northern California only to be confronted by death, "bones and ashes" of Bankole's family, and more work (283). While traditional road narratives often end with a homecoming in which the road has healed its protagonists through a neat and tidy character arc, there is no return of a triumphant hero, and no restorative resolution at the end of *Parable of the Sower*. What Lauren is left with at the end of the novel is the work of rebuilding from the ground up.

While *Worlds at the End* begins Chapter 1 with the destruction of the LA River and the region's indigenous oak trees and acorns in Alejandro Morales's *River of Angels*, Butler's *Parable of the Sower* ends with freeways occupied by the foot traffic of displaced people, and the formation of "Acorn," her Earthseed community in Northern California. *Sower*'s sequel, *Parable of the Talents* (1998), continues the development of Earthseed and consists of the journal entries of Lauren and her husband Taylor Franklin Bankole and their daughter Larken Olamina/Asha Vere. President Andrew Steele and his Christian fundamentalist following, "Christian America," are on a crusade to eradicate non-Christian faiths like Earthseed and their Black female leader; slavery has rematerialized; and "dreamasks" permit wearers to virtually escape their dystopian world. At the end of *Talents*, an 81-year-old Lauren dies as the first starship, *Christopher Columbus*, transports settlers from earth to the first human colony in outer space.

For better or worse, there is no "return" to a "normal" life in a postapocalyptic world. Lauren Olamina will likely never return home to the "safety" of her walled community. Butler breaks apart and rebuilds community and worlds, constantly shifting the composition of collectives of people and opening up ways to think across radical coalitions not as conglomerations of unique categories, but as ever-shifting formations for survival. Lauren is left with the knowledge that "no one should travel alone in this world" (285). The same things can be said across all the books I have studied in *Worlds at the End*. People come together and fall apart throughout a series of places in Southern California, the Western hemisphere, and across the universe, offering visions of the world that dwell in movement and dispersal. Karen Tei Yamashita's *Tropic of Orange* ends with Bobby and Rafaela letting go of the lines of the *Tropic* that binds and breaks the various characters. In lê thi diem thúy's *The Gangster We Are All Looking For* the family breaks apart over and over again and is never quite whole. Their stories about surviving in the end of the world operate without their knowing what is on the other side, but the stories offer modes of regeneration at the end of the world. The endings ambiguously open onto a hope that reinvigorates a cultural politics to reimagine our places of dwelling within a burning landscape, and to seize upon fear, pain, anxiety, and loss to imagine more just ways of living in worlds that are falling apart.

THE DARK CENTURY, OR THE CENTURY OF LIGHT

Coda

Across my chapters, I have studied infrastructures of war, militarism, education, waterways, roadways, and airways together to offer a different sense of understanding the materiality of colonization, removal and dispossession, imperialism, and termination, as well as struggles for decolonial mobility and flight. When studied through the apocalyptic literary imagination of Belin, Butler, Morales, Viramontes, and Yamashita, together the building of and breakdown of infrastructure illuminate visions of regeneration and survival in ways that move beyond postmodern nihilism. This sense of regeneration and survival is grounded in a sense of futurity rooted in the creative work of kinship and community; and at times regeneration and survival, as Maile Arvin iterates, are "ugly, uncomfortable, conflicted, and co-opted . . . and are not always straightforwardly 'good.'"[1] Throughout this book, to consider LA and apocalypse together—as the destruction and regeneration of infrastructures, kinship, and community—is at times temporary, ugly, uncomfortable, and conflicted as communities form and break apart across reconstellated geographies of LA. Chapter 1 mapped LA as a palimpsest to move deep down into its subterranean world, up and over its freeways, through its channelized river and aqueducts, and out to its hinterlands in the Owens Valley. Chapter 2 offered an understanding of LA as a militarized archipelagic zone in connection to San Diego, across the Pacific, and through to Vietnam. Chapter 3 reconsidered the infrastructures of termination through the pathways of Diné mobility that stretches from Dinétah, to LA, to Riverside, and to Northern California, and the roads in between. And lastly, Chapter 4 reconstellates LA across the West Coast in a movement to the stars in a reckoning with movements for Black liberation. In this coda I end, through Cynthia Kadohata's 1992 novel *In the Heart of the Valley of Love*, with a meditation on the impossibility of leaving LA.

For a long time, Kadohata's novel has been crucial to my appreciation of, in its protagonist Francie's terms, the contradictory "savage beauty" of LA. Set in 2051–2052, the period in which the U.S. census had projected a nonwhite majority, *In the Heart of the Valley of Love* is a coming-of-age story set in postapocalyptic Los Angeles. The novel is told from the perspective of eighteen-year-old Francie—a Japanese-Chinese-African American orphan who comes to live with her Aunt Annie and Annie's boyfriend Rohn—as she travels across LA and its outskirts via a failing freeway system. *In the Heart* dwells in the unpredictability and decline of Los Angeles for a reimagination of hope. From the outset, Kadohata establishes a deep sense of loss as the condition of life in 2052, and one that our narrator Francie accepts in the aftermath of her parents' death and Rohn's early disappearance in the novel. After his disappearance Auntie Annie spends the rest of the novel searching for Rohn, as Francie continues on with her life, joining the newspaper staff at her community college. Kadohata draws upon her own experience working at a school newspaper when she attended Los Angeles City College in 1974. There, she formed a "comradeship" and community with journalism friends.[2] Similar to Esther Belin's poetic illuminations of infrastructures of education, pedagogical spaces foreclose and open onto different worlds of hope in Francie's world. Francie's construction of LA—better yet, her interaction with and perspective on LA—offers a devotional practice to the politics of place and community-making that contends with the multiracial histories of LA. There, she falls in love with her coworker and peer Mark Trang and builds friendships across a small group of friends—Jewel the managing editor, Bernard the editor, Lucas a Black radical and an ex-gang member—with whom Francie travels across the Los Angeles landscape. Transformation is at the heart of all the texts I study, and *In the Heart* is no different. Kadohata offers visions of an LA that is never static, but changes in large and infinitesimal infrastructural scales daily. All the while, Francie finds conflagration and social collapse frightening, thrilling, and hopeful.

Beginning in medias res, with Francie looking up at a big rig hanging over the edge of a freeway overpass on the outskirts of LA, the novel offers a contradictory understanding of the highway system: as a promise of the "Sunshine System," as broken and looming, as threatening half rainbows. Staring from below with her Aunt Annie and Annie's husband Rohn, along with other spectators, Francie is raptly fixed on the sight of the police, fire trucks, tow trucks, and paramedics gathering in the dark to save the man trapped in the hanging rig, which Francie describes as "a dangling bracelet" (2).

Kadohata reimagines the automobility of LA. Calmly watching this moment of crisis, Francie is "surprised" that there were so many cars behind and in front of Rohn's truck and she shares, "These days people didn't drive much for recreational purposes, so the highways were often empty" (1). She writes on a piece of paper, "The man is going to fall and die" (2), then burns the paper, superstitiously believing that if she writes down her negative thoughts and burns them they will not happen, turning the act of writing into a practice of undoing a catastrophic future outcome. As the drama on the freeway unfolds, she looks at Rohn and Annie and thinks to herself about the world in which they live. Francie believes that you do not want to love people, because they will either die, get arrested, or disappear. This thought is interrupted by the fact that she enjoys seeing her aunt and Rohn happy together, turning a moment of existential crisis into a flash of intimacy. As she is staring at the couple, the freeway overpass is transformed into a theatrical stage when the fireman rescues the truck driver, waves, and bows to the audience below who applauded as though the entertainment had been planned. Freeway systems in Kadohata's novel are described as incomplete, unfinished, and they signal unfulfilled promises of infrastructure and city development; yet, Francie does not mourn their failure. Instead, she perceives them as "concrete rainbows" scattered across the city. When Auntie Annie, Rohn, and Francie snuck up to one of these "abandoned rainbow[s] and leaned over the edge where a road abruptly stopped," it felt to them as though they'd "reached the end of the world" (3). The contrasting image of abandonment, rainbows, and the edge of the world signals Francie's strange narrative perspective throughout the novel. It is one that allows her to see a dilapidated freeway structure as a rainbow at the end of the world and calls to mind the artwork on the cover of my book by LA-based Japanese American artist Rob Sato. As Sato shares in his description of the piece, the *arco iris* (Spanish for "rainbow") is derived from Iris, the Greek messenger goddess who used rainbows as a highway system between gods and humans. The appearance of rainbows in this understanding, and in Christian, Norse, and Japanese traditions, for instance, was not wholly positive or negative, but presented pathways to different dimensions, offering both stability and an imminent unpredictable change, and a system of movement for transformation. According to Sato, "They mean everything is different now. They mean shit is going down."

The highway serves many contradictory functions throughout my *Worlds at the End* and Kadohata's *In the Heart*, expanding exponentially and capriciously. The highway becomes a place that connects Francie to a group of friends and to the violent lives they each lead. Francie and her boyfriend Mark pick up her friend Jewel after she had been beaten by her boyfriend Teddy. In that moment, the freeway offers an ambivalent space of reflection: she hated the freeways but liked them at night because of the way "they were sort of black-green with a hint of blue like water, and the way you moved so softly on them" (64–65). The freeway becomes transformed into a moving body of water that offers a different sensory perception of softness and movement in a moment when the novel is confronting abuse. Toward the end of the novel, Francie drives, opening her windows to frame the city outside the car. Driving through Koreatown, she notices that "the sky was getting light"; she drives through Hollywood, passing two men fighting in front of a taco stand, and "three prostitutes walking confidently down the street"; her fuel light turns on and she realizes that she doesn't "have any gas credits left" and has to take the bus for the remainder of the week. Her descriptions of the mundane through the framing window of her car are cinematically pictured and attentive to the roadway, the people on the sidewalks, and the night sky, reproducing and shifting foundational Hollywood scenes of driving. Driving in this sense offers Francie a sustained moment of connecting to LA and its inhabitants. She casually recalls that smoke bombs were dropped on the freeway that day, forcing her to take surface streets, and she is attentive to the "towering office buildings, down to Highland Avenue, then east on Beverly Boulevard" (172). Riots are so routinized and commonplace that they are pulled into the very infrastructures of the urban landscape in such a way that Francie "didn't think much about them at all." And yet, they "frightened" and "thrilled" her at the same time, because if rich towns fell, she knew change was inevitable. While others plan to flee and leave because "collapse was coming," and LA had for a long time been deteriorating, the dissolution of communities and the city provide openings for new journeys (116). The act of driving in the car offers Francie a space of contemplation as she recalls how Aunt Annie told her when her parents died that "certain people under certain conditions could keep themselves alive for an extra week or month or even longer, in order to finish taking care of the futures of the people they loved. 'It's a type of levitation'" (172), mirroring Viramontes's call for acts of levitation to survive the confines of state violence in *Their Dogs Came with Them*. Moving across the city, Francie constantly feels the specter of death, so much so that it becomes part of her everyday life. Along with that sense of death, Francie ponders how to survive and take care of loved ones through seemingly extraordinary human acts of forcing oneself to survive through flight.

Survival in this sense, and across *Worlds at the End*, is about imagining disparate infrastructures for movement, transformation, mobility, and escape. Kadohata credits her ability to write with her own travels, explaining that in her twenties she rode a Greyhound bus along the West Coast, then down to Nevada, through the Southwest, out to Arkansas, and back to Southern California for thirty days. On this trip around the "stunning American landscape," the "world opened up for [her]" and she "felt like anything was possible."³ A *yonsei* (fourth-generation) Japanese American born to parents who were born in California, Kadohata moved often. When she was two she moved to Georgia, then to Arkansas, Michigan, back to Chicago, and then Los Angeles to attend college at the University of Southern California, where she earned a BA in journalism in 1979. Travel, Kadohata has shared, is a way to make "temporary" communities that interact in unexpected ways and places. Traveling "makes [her] imagination more fertile" and helps her develop stories in ways that staying in one place cannot. Many of her books explore themes of coming of age through the road and travel, including *The Floating World* (1989), *In the Heart of the Valley of Love* (1992), *kira-kira* (2004), and *Weedflower* (2006).⁴

Considering survival, travel, and movement through the literary field emphasizes regeneration as creative work that needs to be actively built, made, and remade in the face of catastrophe. As in Butler's *Parable of the Sower*, change is inevitable in Kadohata's story and LA remains a contradictory space of survival. It is both "surprising and violent" (24), "beautiful and romantic" (27). Even while death exists all around, so does the possibility of love. Francie is able to continue moving on because "there was a whole world to learn about," even as her heart is "empty" because Rohn remains missing (27). Francie does not force herself to reconcile the ambiguous and contradictory feelings about LA and they are allowed to exist simultaneously. This lack of resolution is what allows Francie to imagine the world in infinite ways.

Toward the end of the novel, Francie ponders the cycle of endings and beginnings, through a future backward glance. She wonders if "a hundred years from now, this would be called The Dark Century or The Century of Light. Though others had already declared it the former, [she] hoped it would turn out to be the latter. [She] thought the question might be resolved within a decade" (190). Francie holds out hope that hers would be a time of light, even within darkness, and popular opinion and fears of doom. At the end of the story, Rohn has not been found, but Francie and Annie remain hopeful that he is alive. The city continues to decline, and Francie and her group of friends break apart as they all contemplate leaving the city. In the final scene, Francie and Mark hide in the arroyo, a group of people wound a dog and throw it down the incline as the police are chasing crowds of people firing guns, while off in the distance the dog howls in agony. "My heart broke with every howl," Francie recounts. "Mark did not let go of my hand, and I don't think he slept all night. Los Angeles was the only home either of us had ever known, and maybe this would be the only love we would ever know. For those reasons, I knew I would never leave Los Angeles. I could not" (225). A seemingly sentimental and inappropriate title for such an entropic novel, "in the heart of the valley of love" is an apt way to name the possibilities of hope that dwell in crisis.

Throughout *Worlds at the End*, I have shown how infrastructure presumably operates beyond a certain field of vision; and yet, literature provides a different optic to access worlds that are present but are not easily seen. By thinking of LA through the dialectic of apocalyptic destruction and infrastructural production, I link the relationship between colonial modernity, capitalist accumulation, and legacies of genocidal violence and organized destruction. At the same time, I have studied a set of novels that reveal alternative ways of tracking decolonial infrastructures of mobility, transformation, and worlding. In this sense, I unsettle the presumed permanency and the concreteness of infrastructure as always providing access to clean running water, electricity, and a smooth automobilic life of the highway system. We can read for the breakdown of our world—at times a necessity—in the context of a global pandemic, climate collapse, and war without end as images of extreme drought and flooding proliferate. Recently, images of the breaking of the LA Aqueduct and the conflagration of Southern California's landscape writ over the space of the freeways were published. On March 25, 2023, The *Los Angeles Times* quoted a Los Angeles Department of Water and Power (DWP) inspector's declaration that "We've lost the aqueduct!" as a result of flooding and the region's extreme weather conditions, which threatened to cut off water to four million Angelenos. Accompanying this article were photographs of a flooded highway in Lone Pine, California, and a destroyed section of the aqueduct. Overflow further threatens to expand brine pools in the Owens Lake. Toward the end of 2017, dramatic images of the spread of wildfire covering over fifty acres alongside the 405 freeway near the Getty Center proliferated during the Skirball fire just north of Brentwood, California. Kadohata, along with Belin, Butler, Morales, Viramontes, and Yamashita, offers visions of the persistence of Indigenous, refugee, and migrant life in the dream and nightmare of a concrete empire. Together, they reconfigure infrastructure as a portal into thinking about the inevitability of change and transformation in ways that do not remain in cynicism. We must not stay in a lamentation of decay, disintegration, collapse, and conflagration of modernity, but dwell in moments of apocalyptic clarity that reveal insight into what it might look like to live on in a constant cycle of decolonial formation and deformation.

Notes

INTRODUCTION

1. Franny Choi, "Catastrophe Is Next to Godliness," in *The World Keeps Ending, and the World Goes On* (New York: HarperCollins, 2022), 5.

2. Hortense Spillers, "Mama's Baby, Papa's Maybe: An American Grammar Book," in "Culture and Countermemory: The 'American' Connection," special issue, *Diacritics* 17, no. 2 (Summer 1987): 70; Sylvia Wynter, "1492: A New World View," in *Race, Discourse, and the Origin of the Americas: A New World View*, ed. Vera Lawrence Hyatt and Rex M. Nettelford (Washington, DC: Smithsonian Institution), 5–57. For Sylvia Wynters, the production of the white human and Black other begins in Senegal in the 1440s. Spillers also returns to 1441–1448, before Columbus, when the Portuguese arrived on the shores of West Africa and introduced "Black Africans to the European market of servitude," which marks a key conjuncture of conquest.

3. As Frank Kermode writes, for theologians, "No longer imminent, the End is immanent." This understanding of the End as immanent, as already existing and operating within the "first things," as opposed to imminent, something about to happen, eschews a neat linear teleological interpretation of apocalyptic historical time. Within this temporality of apocalyptic immanence, "eschatology is stretched over the whole of history, the End is present at every moment." Frank Kermode, *The Sense of an Ending: Studies in the Theory of Fiction* (Oxford: Oxford University Press, 1967), 25.

4. Norman Cohn, "How Time Acquired a Consummation," in *Apocalypse Theory and the Ends of the World*, ed. Malcolm Bull (Oxford: Blackwell Publishing, 1995), 21, 27–28. Zoroastrianism condemned the worship of multiple deities of the old Irano-Aryan religion that we now call Hinduism. Advancing the belief that the God Ahura Mazda, the creator and Lord of Wisdom, will bring *asha*, truth and righteousness, Zoroastrianism is the first monotheistic religion. God, Zarathustra preached, would ultimately prevail against evil and establish Paradise.

5. Wayne Cristaudo, "Revolution and the Redeeming of the World: Egen Rosenstock-Huessy's Messianic Reading of History," in *Messianism, Apocalypse and Redemption 20th Century German Thought*, eds. Wayne Cristaudo and Wendy Baker, (Adelaide: ATF Press, 2006), 243–258. Philip Tolliday, "The Power of the Present: Tillich on Messianism, Apocalypse and Redemption," in *Messianism*, 273–292. The ancient literary form of apocalyptic literature was cultivated in a post-exilic Jewish culture and grew out of unfulfilled Jewish prophecies of a messianic kingdom around 167 B.C.E. and the escalating subjugation of Hebrew people under the weight of growing Persian, Greek, and Roman empires. The apocalyptic emerges forcefully in A.D. 81–96, through the Book of Revelation, or in the Apocalypse of John, where the apocalypticist is called upon to describe the end of the world where humankind must wait for God to prevail against the Antichrist and Armageddon to initiate the second coming of Christ, his thousand-year earthly reign, the Last Judgment, and then the appearance of "the holy city, the new Jerusalem" (Revelation 21:2). Christianity's promise of a spectacular end time is not merely a vision of doom but was, for its early reader, the fulfillment of justice and salvation. Within theological apocalypticism, God controls history. The present is a time for the proliferation of evil, and at the end, the final drama of history will unfold and there will arise a divine judgment that will vindicate the good and punish the wicked. The apocalypticist's prophetic account of the End provides a completed historical viewpoint of human history that exceeds the end of time, where the future is already a foregone conclusion. The apocalyptic in this sense is a necessary world-ending catastrophe that is both feared and longed for, because it will usher in a new world. In many ways, it is a genre that gives rise to the hope of regeneration. At the center of this unified history, is the messianic figuration of Jesus Christ, whose presence incorporated fractured notions of time under paganism and Judaism, and symbolized a New Being, and bringer of new things.

6. The apostle John and the apocalypticists Isaiah and Daniel are called upon to describe the evil world and God's promises of retribution that will vindicate those suffering. "And God shall wipe away all tears from their eyes; and there shall be no more death, neither sorrow, nor crying, neither shall there be any more pain: for the former things are passed away. And he that sat on the throne said, 'Behold I make all things anew'" (Revelation 21:4–5).

7. Frank Kermode, *The Sense of an Ending: Studies in the Theory of Fiction* (Oxford: Oxford University Press, 1967). Radical evangelicals such as Billy Sunday, Charles Fuller, and Billy Graham found hope in the chaos of competing ideologies and global war between communism, fascism, and Third World nationalisms; nuclear extinction and mass destruction would bring about the millennium—the thousand-year period of joy and prosperity promised in the Book of Revelation—and would mark an end with a new beginning. God, a young Billy Graham preached, has chosen the United States to help the world in the coming judgment and the second coming of Christ, reinforcing the exceptional position of the United States. Christian apocalypticism, as Frank Kermode argues, is not only the end of history, but the end of historicity.

8. See Elizabeth Castelli, *Martyrdom and Memory: Early Christian Culture Making* (New York: Columbia University Press, 2004), for more on how this worldview becomes part of a contemporary discourse. By the mid-twentieth century, this ancient apocalyptic worldview becomes part of a secular U.S. politics through political, cultural, and economic discourses, writes Mary Dudziak in *Cold War Civil Rights: Race and the Image of American Democracy* (Princeton, NJ: Princeton University Press, 2000), 27. The threat of global nuclear annihilation was so formative to the U.S. state that it formulated the Cold War tactic of brinksmanship (a term first popularized by John Foster Dulles), a new

foreign diplomatic policy and strategy of bluff that sought to push the oppositional sides to the brink of disaster for an expedient outcome. At the beginning of the Cold War, in his 1947 address to Congress, President Truman forewarned the nation that the world was at a precipice. In a break with Truman's long-term European-based diplomacy that supported British colonial interests (1945–1953), the Eisenhower administration (1953–1961) pursued a new confrontational foreign policy of brinksmanship to fight communism on a worldwide scale. It is, as Yehosephat Harkabi describes, "the art of intentionally forcing crises to the brink of hostilities in order to compel the other side to retreat," noted by Richard Ned Lebow in *Between Peace and War: The Nature of International Crisis* (Baltimore: Johns Hopkins University Press, 1981), 71. Nonsecular millennialism becomes enfolded into the secularism of the U.S. nation-state, and the immanence of eschatological time of Christianity gives way to the teleological temporality of Cold War apocalyptic neoliberal governmentality. The Cold War U.S. state, from this vantage, is a state formation that deploys apocalyptic language and specters of the end of the world to resolve its own historical contradictions within its emergent neoliberal capitalist position as "leader of the free world" in a "postcolonial" era. During the Cold War, a masculinist apocalyptic consciousness shaped and was shaped by texts and films such as Ray Bradbury's *Fahrenheit 451* (New York: Ballantine Books, 1953), George Orwell's *Nineteen Eighty-Four* (London: Secker & Warburg, 1949), and Stanley Kubrick's *Dr. Strangelove* (Columbia Pictures, 1964). These stories placed white masculinity as that which is constantly under threat, as worthy vessels for revelation, and as heroic saviors of the world, within neocolonial specters of ever-present threats of war and mass destruction. See Gloria D. Miklowitz's *After the Bomb* (New York: Scholastic, 1985), Pat Frank's *Alas, Babylon* (Philadelphia: J.B. Lippincott, 1959), Jonathan Lethem's *Amnesia Moon* (San Diego: Harcourt Brace, 1995), Aldous Huxley's *Ape and Essence* (New York: Harper, 1948), Kurt Vonnegut's *Cat's Cradle* (New York: Holt, Rinehart and Winston, 1963), Philip K. Dick's *Do Androids Dream of Electric Sheep* (New York: Doubleday, 1968), and H. G. Wells's *The World Set Free* (New York: E. P. Dutton, 1914), along with films such as Roger Corman's *Day the World Ended* (American International Pictures, 1955), Ranald MacDougall's *The World, the Flesh and the Devil* (Metro-Goldwyn-Mayer, 1959), George Pal's *The Time Machine* (Metro-Goldwyn-Mayer, 1960), Ray Milland's *Panic in Year Zero!* (American International Pictures, 1962), Jack Smith's *Damnation Alley* (20th Century Studios, 1977), Lynne Littman's *Testament* (Paramount Pictures, 1983), and Nicholas Meyer's *The Day After* (American Broadcasting Company, 1983). For Francis Fukuyama, the end of the Cold War and the triumph of Western capitalism had pulled the nation back from the brink of catastrophe. Capitalism has prevailed in its struggle against communism and had emerged as the rightful savior for mankind. We had arrived at the "end of history," according to Francis Fukuyama, "The End of History?," *The National Interest*, no. 16 (Summer 1989), 3–18. Toward the close of the Cold War, Fukuyama famously declared, "We may be witnessing . . . the end of history as such: that is, the end point of mankind's ideological evolution and the universalization of Western liberal democracy as the final form of human government." At the time, Fukuyama was unknown beyond the field of Sovietology, but his "end of history" argument proved to be especially prescient in its embrace of the ascendancy of the neoliberal order months before the fall of the Berlin Wall in November 1989, two years before the "official" end of the Cold War on December 26, 1991. Echoing Margaret Thatcher's 1980s political slogan that "There is no alternative" to free-market neoliberalism, and Ronald Reagan's assertion of neoliberalism as the future's only recourse, free-market neoliberalism stood as the endpoint of History for thinkers such as Fukuyama. Forms of liberal capitalism, not communism as Marxists would argue, make up the political-economic structure that will resolve the contradictions of class and enable us to recognize and protect "man's universal right to freedom" (Fukuyama, "The End of History?" 3). By 2003, under George W. Bush's administration, Fukuyama would break ranks with conservative supporters of the Iraq War, calling them "elite-driven policies." The only credible challenge to liberal democracy, Fukuyama later revises, is not U.S. liberal capitalism or socialism, but China's state capitalist model. (www.newstatesman.com /culture/observations/2018/10/francisfukuyama-interview-socialism-ought-come-back). With the presumed death of communism and fascism—the two greatest impediments to capitalism—there is, for Fukuyama, no longer a struggle between opposing systems. Of utmost importance is the "post-historical" U.S./state's ability to fairly distribute and "build up material wealth at an accelerated rate." Those who do not take part in this neoliberal order will "remain stuck in history" (Fukuyama, "The End of History?" 17).

9. Following the signing of the North American Free Trade Agreement (NAFTA) in late 1993, President Bill Clinton proclaimed the arrival of a new economic order that promised resolution to global inequality, environmental protections, and world peace. The trilateral trade pact between the United States, Canada, and Mexico removed tariffs and trade barriers on services, goods, and capital. In response to then-president of Mexico Salinas de Gotarí's signing of NAFTA, and the failure of cultural nationalisms of the 1960s–1970s, came the start of the Zapatista uprising on January 1, 1994. NAFTA ended the 1917 social contract between President Lázaro Cardenas's agricultural policies with the peasant class that promised basic grain subsidies, governmental network for peasant agriculture, and price supports. Agriculture was deregulated, and the Mexican constitution was altered so that communal lands could be privately sold to foreign interests. Mexico's food, seed, and feed markets were open to competition from Canada and the United States, which led to the migration and displacement of peasants who could no longer compete with the mechanized grain exports of the new mechanized market. Patricia Fernández-Kelly and Douglas S. Massey, "Borders for Whom? The Role of NAFTA in Mexico-U.S. Migration," *The Annals of the American Academy of Political and Social Science* 610, no 1 (March 2007): 105.

10. Deborah Cowen, "Following the Infrastructures of Empire: Notes on Cities, Settler Colonialism, and Method," *Urban Geography* 41, no. 4 (2020): 471.

11. Walter Benjamin, "Theses on the Philosophy of History," in *Illuminations,* ed. Hannah Arendt, (New York: Schoken Books, 1968).

12. David Scott, "The Re-Enchantment of Humanism: An Interview with Sylvia Wynter," *Small Axe* 8, no. 120 (2000): 194–195. According to Sylvia Wynter, the millennial Christian Christopher Columbus did not contest the "orthodox theocentric conception of the Christian God," but he also did not want to be beholden to the medieval-aristocratic order, which ultimately allowed him to elevate his position and help build the Spanish empire and his wealth through imperial conquest.

13. Denise Ferreira da Silva, "Toward a Black Feminist Poethics: The Quest(ion) of Blackness Toward the End of the World," *The Black Scholar* 44, no. 2: 88 [my italics].

14. Da Silva, "Toward a Black Feminist Poethics," 90–91.

15. Mike Davis, *Ecology of Fear: Los Angeles and the Imagination of Disaster* (New York: Metropolitan Books, 1998), 276–277. Davis's description of Robert Heinlein's 1952 novella, "The Year of the Jackpot." In his 1998 book Davis finds at least 139 novels and films since 1909 where the destruction of Los Angeles is the central theme.

16. Los Angeles Department of City Planning. 1941. "A Parkway Plan for the City of Los Angeles and the Metropolitan Area." Los Angeles: The Department, May 8. Harry Hanson, *California: A Guide to the Golden State* (New York: Hastings House, 1967), 164, 165.

17. Reyner Banham, *Los Angeles: The Architecture of Four Ecologies* (Berkeley: University of California Press, 2009; originally published 1971), 71–72.

18. Raúl Homero Villa, *Barrio Logos: Space and Place in Urban Chicano Literature and Culture* (Austin: University of Texas Press, 2000), 88.

19. Nikhil Anand, Akhil Gupta, and Hannah Appel, "Introduction: Temporality, Politics, and the Promise of Infrastructure," in *The Promise of Infrastructure*, ed. Nikhil Anand, Akhil Gupta, and Hannah Appel (Durham, NC: Duke University Press, 2018), 3.

20. During the Korean War years (1950–1953), the aircraft industry increased employment by ninety-five thousand jobs, where aircraft was by then diversified into aerospace-electronics-guided missile manufacturing. Edward Soja, *Postmodern Geographies: The Reassertion of Space in Critical Social Theory* (London: Verso, 1989), 196.

21. Kelly Lytle Hernández, *City of Inmates: Conquest, Rebellion, and the Rise of Human Caging in Los Angeles, 1771–1965* (Chapel Hill: University of North Carolina Press, 2017), 10, 15.

22. Mike Davis, "The Case for Letting Malibu Burn," December 4, 2018. https://longreads.com/2018/12/04/the-case-for-letting-malibu-burn/

23. For instance, Joseph Widney, the second president of the University of Southern California, was a booster who authored *Race Life of the Aryan Peoples* (1907), in which LA was ordained as the capital for Aryan supremacy. After six months of walking to Los Angeles, New Englander and writer Charles Lummis arrived in Los Angeles in the 1880s and was part of a cohort of writers, antiquarians, and publicists who promoted the image of Southern California as a dreamland of sunshine and opportunity during the Booster era (1885–1925).

24. Mike Davis, *City of Quartz* (New York: Verso, 1990), 26, 325.

25. Davis, *Ecology of Fear*, 285.

26. Davis, *Ecology of Fear*, 295.

27. Horace McCoy's *They Shoot Horses, Don't They* (London: Arthur Barker, 1935) and Nathanael West's *The Day of the Locust* (New York: New Directions, 1939), through to Kim Stanley Robinson's *Three Californias Trilogy*, which includes *The Wild Shore* (New York: Tom Doherty Associates, 1984), *The Gold Coast* (New York: Tom Doherty Associates, 1988), and *Pacific Edge* (New York: Tom Doherty Associates, 1990).

28. Filmmakers love to destroy Los Angeles through familiar catastrophic tropes. This can be seen in the proliferation of disaster films in recent decades: Roman Polanski's *Chinatown* (Paramount Pictures, 1974), Ridley Scott's *Blade Runner* (Warner Bros., 1982), and James Cameron's *Terminator* (Orion Pictures, 1984), Tim Pope's *The Crow: City of Angels* (Turner Classic Movies, 1996), John Carpenter's *Escape From L.A.* (Paramount Pictures, 1996), Mick Jackson's *Volcano* (20th Century Fox, 1997), Brad Peyton's *San Andreas* (Warner Bros., 2015); James Cameron's *Terminator 2: Judgment Day* (Tri-Star Pictures, 1991), *Terminator 3: Rise of the Machines* (Warner Bros., 2003), *Terminator Salvation* (Warner Bros., 2009); Larry Elikann's *The Great Los Angeles Earthquake* (NBC, 1990), George T. Miller's *Tidal Wave: No Escape* (American Broadcasting Company, 1997), Roland Emmerich's *The Day After Tomorrow* (20th Century Studios, 2004), John Lafia's *10.5* (Hallmark Entertainment, 2004) and *10.5: Apocalypse* (Hallmark Entertainment, 2006), Roland Emmerich's *2012* (Columbia Pictures, 2009); alien attacks in Roland Emmerich's *Independence Day* (20th Century Fox, 1996), The Brothers Strause's *Skyline* (Universal Pictures, 2010), and Jonathan Liebesman's *Battle: Los Angeles* (Sony Pictures, 2011); infections in Duanne Stinnett's *Gangs of the Dead* (Outside Productions, 2006), Ruben Fleischer's *Zombieland* (Sony Pictures, 2009); meteoric catastrophe in Justin Jones's *The Apocalypse* (The Asylum, 2007) and Micho Rutare's *Meteor Apocalypse* (The Asylum, 2009);

and Seth Rogen and Evan Goldberg's satirical comedy *This Is the End* (Sony Pictures, 2013), where the actual apocalypse from the Book of Revelation strikes Hollywood.

29. Sandy Cohen, "Why is it so much fun to destroy Los Angeles?," *Telegram & Gazette*, November 14, 2010, https://www.telegram.com/story/news/local/north/2010/11/15/why-is-it-so-much/51377724007/.

30. Bertolt Brecht, "Hollywood Elegies," translated from the German by Adam Kirsch, *Poetry* Magazine, June 2011 (originally published 1942).

31. See Edward Soja, *Postmodern Geographies: The Reassertion of Space in Critical Social Theory* (London: Verso, 1989); Mike Davis, *Ecology of Fear* and *City of Quartz*; Norman Klein, *History of Forgetting: Los Angeles and the Erasure of Memory* (London: Verso, 1997).

32. See Billy Wilder's *Double Indemnity* (Paramount Pictures, 1944), Howard Hawk's *The Big Sleep* (Warner Bros., 1946), Billy Wilder's *Sunset Boulevard* (Paramount Pictures, 1950), Orson Welles's *Touch of Evil* (Universal Pictures, 1958), Fritz Lang's *The Big Heat* (Columbia Pictures, 1953), André De Toth's *Crime Wave* (Warner Bros., 1953), Jacques Tourneur's *Nightfall* (Columbia Pictures, 1956).

33. Klein, *History of Forgetting*, 30.

34. Women of color feminism is a key formation of critical practice for the theorization of relationality, activist organizing, and cultural work emerging through the insights of Black feminists in the 1970s through the important work of Black feminists such as Toni Cade Bambara, Francis Beal, Angela Davis, and the Combahee River Collective, and through the 1980s with women of color feminist texts such as Gloria Anzaldúa and Cherríe Moraga's seminal edited anthology *This Bridge Called My Back: Writings by Radical Women of Color* (Albany: SUNY Press, 1981). It emerged in this era as a challenge to prevailing notions of identity politics articulated by early- and mid-twentieth-century movements organized around U.S. nationalism, minority cultural nationalism, and second-wave feminism. As a response to the erasures of interlocking differences and oppressions within revolutionary struggle, the emergence of women of color feminism as a methodology sought to constitute a pivotal comparative practice grounded in incommensurability and transnational solidarity.

35. Kimberlé Crenshaw, "Mapping the Margins: Intersectionality, Identity Politics, and Violence against Women of Color," in *Stanford Law Review* 43, no. 6 (July 1991): 1241–1299; Chandra Talpade Mohanty, "Cartographies of Struggle: Third World Women and the Politics of Feminism," in *Feminism without Borders: Decolonizing Theory, Practicing Solidarity* (Durham, NC: Duke University Press, 2003), 43–84; and Roderick Ferguson, "Something Else to Be: *Sula*, The Moynihan Report, and the Negations of Black Lesbian Feminism," in *Aberrations in Black* (Minneapolis: University of Minnesota Press, 2003), 110–137.

36. Chandan Reddy, *Freedom with Violence: Race, Sexuality, and the US State* (Durham, NC: Duke University Press, 2011); Grace Kyungwon Hong, *The Ruptures of American Capital: Women of Color Feminism and the Culture of Immigrant Labor* (Minneapolis: University of Minnesota Press, 2006).

37. Grace Kyungwon Hong and Roderick A. Ferguson, "Introduction," in *Strange Affinities: The Gender and Sexual Politics of Comparative Racialization*, ed. Grace Kyungwon Hong and Roderick A. Ferguson (Durham, NC: Duke University Press, 2011).

38. Hong, *The Ruptures of American Capital*.

39. Jina B. Kim, "Cripping the Welfare Queen: The Radical Potential of Disability Politics," *Social Text* 39, no. 3 (September 2021): 79–101. Lisa Lowe, *The Intimacies of Four Continents* (Durham, NC: Duke University Press, 2015).

40. Audre Lorde, "A Litany for Survival," in *The Collected Poems of Audre Lorde* (W. W. Norton, 1978).

41. Daniel Nemser, *Infrastructures of Race*, 5. Karl Marx, *Capital: A Critique of Political Economy*, Vol. I (New York: Penguin Books, 1976), 874–875.

42. Nikhil Anand, Akhil Gupta, and Hannah Appel, "Introduction: Temporality, Politics, and the Promise of Infrastructure," in *The Promise of Infrastructure*, ed. Nikhil Anand, Akhil Gupta, and Hannah Appel (Durham, NC: Duke University Press, 2018), 4–5.

43. See Patrick Joyce, *The Rule of Freedom: Liberalism and the Modern City* (London: Verso, 2003), and Timothy Mitchell, *Carbon Democracy: Political Power in the Age of Oil* (London: Verso, 2011) for more on infrastructure and liberalism.

44. Arturo Escobar, *Pluriversal Politics: The Real and the Possible* (Durham, NC: Duke University Press, 2020), xvii. The Zapatistas' call for a "world in which many worlds fit" opens up a discourse of the pluriverse, which Walter D. Mignolo and Raymundo Panikkar have taken up to theorize worlding practices that have always disputed notions of single world systems or, in John Law's terms, the powerful imaginary of a "one-world world." Mignolo writes that he first learned of the concept from the Zapatista insurgency, and he cites Franz Hinkelammert, Enrique Dussel, and Raimundo Panikkar as early theorists of the idea that helped Mignolo formulate a pluritopic hermeneutics in *The Darker Side of the Renaissance* (Ann Arbor: University of Michigan Press, 2003; originally published, 1995). Mignolo introduced pluriversality in a series of lectures between 1996 and 1998, and in 2002 he published an essay called "The Zapatistas' Theoretical Revolution: Its Historical, Ethical, and Political Consequences" in *Review (Fernand Braudel Center)* 25, no. 3, Utopian Thinking (2002): 245–275. This essay was then revised for Mignolo's *The Darker Side of Western Modernity* (Durham, NC: Duke University Press, 2011). See also John Law, "What's Wrong with a One-World World?" *Distinktion: Scandinavian Journal of Social Theory* 16, no. 1 (2015): 126–139.

45. Daniel Nemser, *Infrastructures of Race: Concentration and Biopolitics in Colonial Mexico* (Austin: University of Texas Press, 2017), 17. Brian Larkin, "The Politics and Poetics of Infrastructure," *Annual Review of Anthropology* 42 (2013): 327–343.

46. Daniel Nemser's *Infrastructures of Race*, 3. Nemser cites AbdouMaliq Simone, "People as Infrastructure: Intersecting Fragments in Johannesburg," *Public Culture* 16, no. 3 (2004): 407–429; Nikhil Anand, Akhil Gupta, and Hannah Appel, "Introduction: Temporality, Politics, and the Promise of Infrastructure," in *The Promise of Infrastructure*, ed. Nikhil Anand, Akhil Gupta, and Hannah Appel, Durham: Duke University Press, 2018, 3. Also, see Brian Larkin's "The Politics and Poetics of Infrastructure."

47. Nemser, *Infrastructures of Race*, 17. Michael Rubenstein et al. write that "Infrastructure is supposed to go unnoticed when it works"—in "Infrastructuralism: An Introduction," "Infrastructuralism," ed. Michael Rubenstein et al., special issue, *Modern Fiction Studies* 61, no. 4 (2015): 576.

48. Deborah Cowen, "Following the Infrastructures of Empire: Notes on Cities, Settler Colonialism, and Method," *Urban Geography* 41, no. 4 (November 26, 2019): 483.

49. Jina B. Kim, 86.

50. Nikhil Anand et al., "Introduction: Temporality, Politics, and the Promise of Infrastructure," 3, 4–5; Cowen, "Following the Infrastructures of Empire," 483.

51. Joan Didion, *Slouching Towards Bethlehem* (New York: Dell Publishing, 1968), 65.

52. Maile Renee Arvin, *Possessing Polynesians: The Science of Settler Colonial Whiteness in Hawai'i and Oceania* (Durham, NC: Duke University Press, 2019), 20–21.

53. Raymond Williams, *Marxism and Literature* (Oxford: Oxford University Press, 1977).

54. See Mike Davis's *City of Quartz* and Edward W. Soja's *Postmodern Geographies* for more on the ways Los Angeles is imperium and colony.

55. Jean Vengua Gier and Carla Alicia Tejeda, "An Interview with Karen Tei Yamashita," University of California, Berkeley, 1998, https://legacy.chass.ncsu.edu/jouvert/v2i2/YAMASHI.HTM.

56. Raymond Williams, *Marxism and Literature* (Oxford: Oxford University Press, 1977).

57. Frank Kermode, *The Sense of an Ending: Studies in the Theory of Fiction* (Oxford: Oxford University Press, 2000; originally published, 1966), 96–97, 101.

CHAPTER 1

1. Karen Piper, *Left in the Dust: How Race and Politics Created a Human and Environmental Tragedy in L.A.* (New York: Palgrave Macmillan, 2006), 63, 82; Mike Davis, *Ecology of Fear* (New York: Metropolitan Books, 1998), 10; Charles Mulford Robinson, *The City Beautiful: Report to the Municipal Art Commission* (Los Angeles: W. J. Porter, 1909), 71.

2. Daniel Cooper Alarcón, *The Aztec Palimpsest: Mexico in the Modern Imagination* (Tucson: University of Arizona Press, 1997), xvi.

3. Edward Soja, *Postmodern Geographies* (New York: Verso, 1989), 193.

4. See Daniel Nemser, *Infrastructures of Race*; AbdouMaliq Simone, "People as Infrastructure: Intersecting Fragments in Johannesburg," *Public Culture* 16, no. 3 (2004): 407–429; Nikhil Anand, Akhil Gupta, and Hannah Appel, "Introduction: Temporality, Politics, and the Promise of Infrastructure," in *The Promise of Infrastructure*, ed. Nikhil Anand, Akhil Gupta, and Hannah Appel, (Durham: Duke University Press, 2018), 3.

5. Tomás Almaguer, *Racial Fault Lines: The Historical Origins of White Supremacy in California* (Berkeley: University of California Press, 1994), 31. The capitalist replaced the Californio, and Anglo Americans replaced Indian villagers, Mexican landholders, and townspeople. Almaguer illuminates the ways Mexicans occupied a different "group position" from Indian, Black, and Asian immigrants under the new racial hierarchy in the latter half of the nineteenth century. Under the Treaty of Guadalupe Hidalgo of 1848, Mexicans who remained in the "American Southwest" were guaranteed the rights of U.S. citizens. The California State Constitutional Convention of 1849 conceded Mexicans the citizenship rights of "free white persons" in California, and Mexicans were considered part of the "white race."

6. J. Jack Halberstam, *In a Queer Time and Place: Transgender Bodies, Subcultural Lives* (New York: New York University Press, 2005), 9–10; Juana María Rodríguez, *Queer Latinidad: Identity Practices, Discursive Spaces* (New York: New York University Press, 2003), 24.

7. Robert Nichols, *Theft Is Property!: Dispossession and Critical Theory* (Durham, NC: Duke University Press, 2019), 9.

8. Invested in the Mexican American communities he grew up in the surrounding areas of Los Angeles, Alejandro Morales has cemented his position as a leading Chicano novelist through the critical success of *The Brick People* (Houston: Arte Publico Press, 1988), which chronicles the lives of Mexican American workers at the Simons Brickyard at the turn of the twentieth century, and *The Rag Doll Plagues* (Houston: Arte Publico Press, 1992), a story that explores the historical, present, and future of California, the United States, and Mexico, in the face of infectious and catastrophic disaster, moving the reader through three centuries: colonial Mexico; twentieth-century Orange County, California; and a futuristic twenty-first century.

9. Daniel A. Olivas, "An Interview with Alejandro Morales Regarding His New Novel, 'River of Angels,'" *Los Angeles Review of Books*, December 10, 2014, https://lareviewofbooks.org/article/an-interview-with-alejandro-morales-regarding-his-new-novel-river-angels/.

10. Jacques Derrida, "No Apocalypse, Not Now (Full Speed Ahead, Seven Missiles, Seven Missives)," *Diacritics* 14, no. 2, Nuclear Criticism (Summer, 1984), 2–31. For Jacques Derrida the "total and remainderless destruction of the archive" will constitute the final apocalypse, from which nothing new emerges.

11. Saidiya Hartman, *Lose Your Mother: A Journey Along the Atlantic Slave Route* (New York: Farrar, Straus and Giroux, 2007).

12. Kelly Lytle Hernández, *City of Inmates: Conquest, Rebellion, and the Rise of Human Caging in Los Angeles, 1771–1965* (Chapel Hill: University of North Carolina Press, 2017), 16, 21, 28.

13. Daniel Nemser, *Infrastructures of Race: Concentration and Biopolitics in Colonial Mexico* (Austin: University of Texas Press, 2017), 5.

14. Almaguer, *Racial Fault Lines*, 46.

15. For more on the new racial order of migrant populations to Los Angeles in the early years of conquest, see Lytle Hernández, *City of Inmates*, 36. More locally, and in the aftermath of the U.S.-Mexican War, Mexican "Californios" were initially afforded the same rights as the white immigrant population, and were positioned above Indigenous Indian, Asian, and Black immigrant populations in the new racial order. The nation was formulated through the very categories of citizenship for "white male persons," and noncitizenship ("non-whites" and women), which secured rights for white male citizens over and against nonwhites and women. As Lytle Hernández elucidates, anti-Indian and intra-Native violence proliferated, as Mexicans and Anglo Americans often jointly targeted Native peoples in and around Los Angeles.

16. Almaguer, *Racial Fault Lines*, 5.

17. Almaguer, *Racial Fault Lines*, 5.

18. Lytle Hernández, *City of Inmates*, 17.

19. Lytle Hernández, *City of Inmates*, 19. Before the arrival of Mexicans, the Tongva (whom the Spanish called Gabrielinos) lived in *iyáangà* (Yangna), meaning "poison oak place," which constituted one of the largest Tongva villages in the area that is now East Los Angeles.

20. Raúl Homero Villa, *Barrio-Logos: Space and Place in Urban Chicano Literature and Culture* (Austin: University of Texas Press, 2000), 3.

21. Blake Gumprecht, *The Los Angeles River: Its Life, Death, and Possible Rebirth* (Baltimore: Johns Hopkins University Press, 2001), 91. As early as 1810, a Spain-controlled Los Angeles began to claim the rights to the LA River and its water. In 1895, the courts granted Los Angeles "all the waters of the river" under the "pueblo right" right to el Río de Porciúncula, when the Spanish founded Los Angeles in 1781. With this precedence, LA sought to expand its rights to the river's underground basin of water, which would grant the city access to a nearly five hundred square mile area of water. Gumprecht states that the rights to the river are something that continues to confound the courts. In 1968, the Los Angeles County Superior Court judge found that the pueblo right had no traction in Spanish or Mexican law. The justices, though, refuse to reverse a century-old decision for California water laws, which finds that the pueblo right is superior to all other water rights.

22. David Scott, "Introduction: On the Archaeologies of Black Memory," *Small Axe* 12, no. 2 (June 2008): vii. My italics for "sub-terrain."

23. During the 1920s and 1930s, many city boosters and elites still believed that Los Angeles was the Aryan City of the Sun. As Bob Shuler, an Anglo American preacher with a popular radio program, proudly explained, "Los Angeles is the last purely Anglo-Saxon city... in America. It is the only such city not dominated by foreigners. It remains in a class to itself as the one city of the nation in which the white, American, Christian idealism still predominates." Others described Los Angeles as the "nation's white spot." They would continue to do so well into the 1940s and 1950s. But the nation's white spot was also the capital of Mexican America. Although many Mexicans living in Los Angeles seasonally migrated to and from the city in search of work, many others made Los Angeles their permanent home. Lytle Hernández, *City of Inmates*, 146.

24. Piper, *Left in the Dust*, 66–67.

25. Almaguer, *Racial Fault Lines*, 60.

26. Mike Davis notes in *Ecology of Fear* (288–291) that as Native American genocide became universally accepted as a step toward progress, writers explored other genocides. In Pierton W. Dooner's *Last Days of the Republic* (San Francisco: Alta California Publishing House, 1880), the entire ex-slave population perished upon contact with the Chinese. King Wallace's science fiction novel *The Next War* (Washington, DC: Martyn Publishing House, 1892) recreates white fear of Black uprisings and rejoices in the extinction of African Americans. The threat of the yellow horde appears in M. P. Shiel's *The Yellow Danger* (London: Grant Richards, 1898), *The Yellow Wave* (London: Ward Lock, 1905), and *The Dragon* (London: Grant Richards, 1913) as hundreds of millions of Chinese are massacred. Jack London's short story "The Unparalleled Invasion" (in Dale L. Walker, ed., *Curious Fragments* [Port Jefferson, NY: Kenkat Press, 1976; originally published, 1906]) addresses the "Chinese problem" through germ warfare to give way to a recolonization of China by the white race and a democratic American program that brings about peace.

27. Samuel P. Huntington appears to be a fictional character who references the very real Huntington family that amassed a great fortune through real estate, the railroad, shipping, mining, and oil industries.

28. Diana Jean Sandoval Martinez, "Concrete Colonialism: Architecture, Infrastructure, Urbanism, and the American Colonization of the Philippines" (PhD diss., Columbia University, 2017), 3. In her dissertation, Martinez argues that it is not merely concrete's revolutionary durability as a building material, but its transportability (powder, local sand, aggregate, and water) to building infrastructures in its colonies, marking the commodification and expansion of durability itself, transforming the environment at the site of its production and site of use, expanding the industrial capacities of colonies such as India's industrial mills and Manila's cigar factories, redirecting the flow of colonial trade (7–9).

29. Jack Forbes, *Native Americans of California and Nevada* (Happy Camp, CA: Naturegraph Publishers, 1982), 45.

30. Thomas Workman Temple II, "Toypurina the Witch and the Indian Uprising at San Gabriel," *The Masterkey* 32, no 5 (1958): 136–152; reprinted in Edward Castillo, ed., *Native American Perspectives on the Hispanic Colonization of Alta California* (New York: Garland Science, 1992), 326–342; quoted in Steven W. Hackel, "Sources of Rebellion: Indian Testimony and the Mission San Gabriel Uprising of 1785," *Ethnohistory* 50, no. 4 (Fall 2003): 650. The attack and Toypurina's statement were not merely an indictment of the Spaniards and priests but also part of a longer history of preconquest intertribal conflict, and an act of reclaiming lands that were now occupied by Indians relocated to the mission from distant tribes in the San Gabriel Valley. The padres at the San Gabriel Mission lured converting San Gabriel Indians in with food, clothes, and blankets, increasing the population and the amount of livestock needed to sustain that growing population.

Relocated Indian converts not only strained the resources of the area but were forced into farming, which also put pressure on Hapchi-vitam modes of subsistence living, intensifying an antagonistic relationship with San Gabriel Valley tribes. Antipathy arose between tribes as Indian converts living in the mission displaced the Hapchi-vitam.

31. Jean Bosquet, "Lizard People's Catacomb City Hunted," *Los Angeles Times*, January 29, 1934.

32. Nell Irvin Painter, *Standing at Armageddon: A Grassroots History of the Progressive Era* (New York: W.W. Norton, 2008), xiv–xv.

33. Edward Soja, *Postmodern Geographies,* 193; Sharon E. Dean et al., *Weaving a Legacy: Indian Baskets and the People of Owens Valley, California* (Salt Lake City: University of Utah Press, 2004), 27.

34. Donald Worster, *Rivers of Empire: Water, Aridity, and the Growth of the American West* (Oxford: Oxford University Press, 1985), 148–149.

35. The Los Angeles Aqueduct enabled the city to expand its territories; abandon the *acequias*, a "backward" Mexican water system that was perceived to be polluted and ineffective; enable segregation by helping whites to escape the polluted inner city to the suburbs; and end the "Indian problem" in the Owens Valley. In short, "the Los Angeles aqueduct would bring with it a long story of inevitable 'progress'—to meet the needs of the ever-growing white metropolitan populace," according to John Walton, *Western Times and Water Wars: State, Culture, and Rebellion in California* (Berkeley: University of California Press, 1993), 6–7. Theodor Roosevelt's early-twentieth-century Progressive era ideology linked urbanization, "the public good," and imperial expansion to an apocalyptic logic of taking. Often lauded for his conservationist work, Roosevelt (U.S. president from 1901 to 1909) stole and incorporated western regions of the United States into the nation through "conservation" and "land management." Following the Depression of the 1930s and onward, the welfare state expropriated the Owens Valley, managing its economic recovery, resources, and environmental protection. See Theodor Roosevelt, "The Expansion of the White Races," Address at the Celebration of the African Diamond Jubilee of the Methodist Episcopal Church, Washington, DC, January 18, 1909, quoted in Piper, *Left in the Dust*, 31–32.

36. Deepak Narang Sawhney, "Journey beyond the Stars: Los Angeles and Third Worlds," *Unmasking L.A.: Third Worlds and the City*, ed. Deepak Narang Sawhney (New York: Palgrave, 2002), 1.

37. Walton, *Western Times and Water Wars*, 5. Elected Mayor in 1898, Fred Eaton was a key figure in the boom period of Los Angeles who completed negotiations to create the Los Angeles Department of Water and Power (LADWP), and he was the first official to propose an aqueduct from the Owens River to Los Angeles. In the early 1900s William Mulholland, the self-trained lead engineer of the Los Angeles Aqueduct, and J. B. Lippincott, from the U.S. Reclamation Service, went in search of water to support a growing Los Angeles County. Quoted in Piper, *Left in the Dust*, 30. Lippincott and several LADWP agents clandestinely purchased water rights from farmers who believed they were selling their water rights to other farmers and ranchers and that they would benefit the Owens Valley Project, a federal irrigation project. The farmers would come to find out that they had sold their land and water to agents posing as farmers and ranchers, and that the water was being extracted for Los Angeles. The city had strategically purchased lands, forcing property values down, and made it impossible for farmers and ranchers to make a profit. By 1905, Los Angeles commenced "purchasing" land, and therein water rights in order to support its population growth, and would come to own eighty-five percent of the Owens Valley. The conflict between Owens Valley farmers and Los Angeles ulti-

mately was "resolved" by the federal government in 1906 when President Theodore Roosevelt declared, "It is a hundred- or a thousand-fold more important to the state and more valuable to the people as a whole if used by the city than if used by the people of Owens Valley," reflecting Roosevelt's Progressive Party's dictum: "The greatest good for the greatest number."

38. Davis, *Ecology of Fear*, 3.
39. Piper, *Left in the Dust*, 126.
40. Davis, *Ecology of Fear*, 21; Bob Harrington, "Owens Lake: To Dust Bowl and Back?," *Southwest Hydrology*, July/August 2004: 22–23.
41. Elizabeth P. Glixman, "An Interview with Karen Tei Yamashita," *Eclectica Magazine*, October/November 2007, https://www.eclectica.org/v11n4/glixman_yamashita.html.
42. Kandice Chuh, "Of Hemispheres and Other Spheres: Navigating Karen Tei Yamashita's Literary World," in *American Literary History* 18, no. 3 (Fall 2006): 618–637; Claudia Sadowski-Smith, "The U.S.-Mexico Borderlands Write Back: Cross-Cultural Transnationalism in Contemporary U.S. Women of Color Fiction," *Arizona Quarterly* 57, no. 1 (2001): 91–112; Molly Wallace, "Tropics of Globalization: Reading the New North America," *Symplokē* 9 (2001): 145–160; Rachel Adams, "The Ends of America, the Ends of Postmodernism," *Twentieth Century Literature* 53, no. 3 (2007): 248–272; Sherryl Vint, "Orange County: Global Networks in *Tropic of Orange*," *Science Fiction Studies* 39, no. 3 (November 2012): 401–414; Jinqi Ling, *Across Meridians: History and Figuration in Karen Tei Yamashita's Transnational Novels* (Stanford, CA: Stanford University Press, 2012); Stella Oh, "Crossing Borders, Locating Home: Ethical Responsibility in Karen Tei Yamashita's *Tropic of Orange*," in *Transnational Crossroads: Remapping the Americas and the Pacific*, ed. Camilla Fojas and Rudy P. Guevarra Jr. (Lincoln: University of Nebraska Press, 2012); Chiyo Crawford, "From Desert Dust to City Soot: Environmental Justice and Japanese American Internment in Karen Tei Yamashita's *Tropic of Orange*," *MELUS* 38, no. 3 (Fall 2013): 86–106; Julie Sze, "'Not by Politics Alone': Gender and Environmental Justice in Karen Tei Yamashita's *Tropic of Orange*," *Bucknell Review* 44, no. 1 (2000): 29–42; Kara Thompson, "Traffic Stops, Stopping Traffic: Race and Climate Change in the Age of Automobility," *ISLE: Interdisciplinary Studies in Literature and Environment* 24, no. 1 (Winter 2017): 92–112; Elizabeth Ammons, *Brave New Worlds: How Literature Will Save the Planet* (Iowa City: University of Iowa Press, 2010); Xiaojing Zhou, *City of Others: Reimagining Urban Spaces in Asian American Literature* (Seattle: University of Washington Press, 2014); Meagan Meylor, "Los Angeles as Post-National Palimpsest in Karen Tei Yamashita's *Tropic of Orange*," *Watermark* 10:152–160.
43. Glixman, "An Interview with Karen Tei Yamashita."
44. Glixman, "An Interview with Karen Tei Yamashita."
45. Julio Cortázar, *Hopscotch*, trans. Gregory Rabassa (New York: Pantheon, 1966).
46. Glixman, "An Interview with Karen Tei Yamashita."
47. Stephen Cottrell, "Music, Time, and Dance in Orchestral Performance: The Conductor as Shaman," *Twentieth-Century Music* 3, no. 1 (2007): 74.
48. Theodor Adorno, *Introduction to the Sociology of Music*, trans. E. B. Ashton (New York: Continuum, 1989), 104.
49. See Eiichiro Azuma, *Between Two Empires: Race, History, and Transnationalism in Japanese America* (Oxford: Oxford University Press, 2005), 65. Japanese Americans have long been targeted by the U.S. state through anti-Asian legislation that barred Japanese from immigrating with the Johnson-Reed Act of 1924/Immigration Act of 1924, denying naturalization and access to citizenship based on racial categories. Japanese farmers

were seen as threats to white economic security on the West Coast, and in 1913 the Alien Land Law made "the ownership of agricultural land by 'aliens ineligible for citizenship' illegal," also forbidding Japanese immigrants to lease land for more than three years, which as Azuma states produced "a socioeconomic condition that unilaterally favored white landlords." While Japanese Americans were evacuated officially for "defense" purposes, it is significant to understand that they owned and worked on valuable and desirable land. Their evacuation resulted in a severe land-based economic loss for Japanese Americans, as they lost their farmlands to white landowners and agricultural corporations. While the U.S. government claimed that Japanese American farms were tactically located near military bases and main thoroughfares, the farms existed before these bases and highways were developed. Their farms presented threats to white farmers in California. By 1940, 63 percent of Japanese Americans worked in agriculture, and Japanese American–owned and –operated farms were valued at seventy-two million dollars. See Crawford, "From Desert Dust to City Soot," 89–90. According to Jodi Byrd, incarcerated Japanese Americans formed an incarcerated workforce who were seen as improving campground land for future use. Jodi Byrd, *The Transit of Empire* (Minneapolis: University of Minnesota Press, 2011), 185.

50. Gayle K. Sato, "Post-Redress Memory: A Personal Reflection on Manzanar Murakami," *Concentric: Literary and Cultural Studies* 39, no. 2 (September 2013): 127.

51. Piper, *Left in the Dust*, 85–86. Disputes over land usage, and the Paiute's limited access to clean water and sources of food led to intensified conflicts between the white settlers and the Paiute, erupting in the Indian Wars from 1862 to 1865. On July 4, 1862, the U.S. Army moved in to establish Fort Independence, where the army began a methodical process of Paiute starvation, burning Paiute campgrounds, devastating their winter stores, and driving them into the hills. Tricked into the fort with offerings of food, 998 Paiute were "kept" at Fort Independence and then removed to Fort Tejon. Many died of dehydration on the forced journey to Fort Tejon, and once there, they died from starvation and disease, or were shot and killed. Some say that the bodies of escaping Paiute still remain on the bottom of the Owens Lake, crystallized and preserved by the water.

52. Paul Gilroy, *The Black Atlantic: Modernity and Double Consciousness* (New York: Verso, 1993), 337.

53. Carter Mathes, *Imagine the Sound: Experimental African American Literature After Civil Rights* (Minneapolis: University of Minnesota Press, 2015), 3.

54. Alejandro Nava, *In Search of Soul: Hip-Hop, Literature, and Religion* (Oakland: University of California Press, 2017); James Edward Ford III, "When Disaster Strikes: On the Apocalyptic Tone of Hip Hop," *ASAP/Journal* 3, no. 3 (September 2018): 595–622.

55. Fredric Jameson, *Marxism and Form: Twentieth-Century Dialectical Theories of Literature*. (Princeton, NJ: Princeton University Press, 1971), 12–13.

56. Nichols, *Theft is Property!*, 9.

57. Piper, *Left in the Dust*, 133.

58. Thy Phu, "Double Capture: Native Americans in WRA Internment Photography," special issue, *Amerasia Journal* 42, no. 1 (2016): 21–22.

59. Wendi Yamashita, "The Colonial and the Carceral: Building Relationships between Japanese Americans and Indigenous Groups in the Owens Valley," special issue, *Amerasia Journal* 42, no. 1 (2016): 131. Roughly 380 Paiute Indians survived out of the thousand who were dislocated under the forced removal program. Surviving Paiute who returned to the Owens Valley from Fort Tejon between 1864 and 1870 were forced to integrate into white settler land, social, and labor structures. Paiute fertile lands were destroyed and along with them resources for their communal subsistence mode of living and forms of

work. They were hired as agricultural laborers, working in the orchards and small farms that had driven the cattle barons north. Living on public lands or on white homesteads, Paiute labor became central to the region's emerging economic structure.

60. Richard Drinnon, *Keeper of Concentration Camps: Dillon S. Myer and American Racism* (Berkeley: University of California Press, 1987).

61. Walton, *Western Times and Water Wars*, 12–13.

62. Walton, *Western Times and Water Wars*, 14.

63. Julian H. Steward, *Ethnography of the Owens Valley Paiute*, University of California Publications in American Archaeology and Ethnology Vol. 33, September 6, 1933 (Berkeley: University of California Press), 235. Steward speculates that "Paiute" is probably derived from *pa*, meaning "water."

64. Steward, *Ethnography of the Owens Valley Paiute*, 235. U.S. politician and explorer John C. Frémont named the valley "Owens Valley" after his guide and "pioneer" of the West, Richard Leon Owings, better known as "Richard Owens," during his expedition to California in 1845.

65. Julian H. Steward, *Myths of the Owens Valley Paiute*, University of California Publications in American Archaeology and Ethnology Vol. 34, 1934–1936, ed. A.L. Kroeber et al. (Berkeley: University of California Press, 1937), 364.

66. Clarissa Wei, "How the Owens Valley Paiute Made the Desert Bloom," PBS/SoCal, December 15, 2016, https://www.kcet.org/shows/tending-the-wild/how-the-owens-valley-paiute-made-the-desert-bloom.

67. Wei, "Paiute Made the Desert Bloom."

68. Wei, "Paiute Made the Desert Bloom."

69. Walton, *Western Times and Water Wars*, 16; Jane Wehrey, *Voices from This Long Brown Land: Oral Recollections of Owens Valley Lives and Manzanar Pasts* (New York: Palgrave Macmillan, 2006), 1–2.

70. Walton, *Western Times and Water Wars*, 5–6.

71. Wendi Yamashita, "The Colonial and the Carceral," 131; Walton, *Western Times and Water Wars*, 15. The Paiute adhered to common land rights owned by bands and subdivided into plots assigned to families based on subsistence activity, and the production of seeds and tubers along territories extending across the valley between the mountain ranges. Dean et al., *Weaving a Legacy*, 3. Living in semipermanent camps along a reliable water source, the Paiute set up their small villages, with people coming and going, and could be composed of anywhere from twenty to as many as two hundred individuals.

72. Laurie Goering, "In Los Angeles 'Water Colony,' Tribes Fear a Parched Future," *Reuters,* June 4, 2019, https://www.reuters.com/article/us-water-california/in-los-angeles-water-colony-tribes-fear-a-parched-future-idUSKCN1T512S. In 2017, the U.S. Supreme Court maintained the decision to confer California's Agua Caliente tribe groundwater rights below their reservation, setting a precedent for tribal groundwater claims nationally, forcing Los Angeles and other big cities in the West to think differently about their water usage, resources, and extractive practices.

73. In 1987, the U.S. Environmental Protection Agency (EPA) declared that the southern Owens Valley violated the National Ambient Air Quality Standards (NAAQS) for PM-10, and was labelled "the single largest source of fugitive dust in the United States." Given five years to remedy the problem, the Department of Water and Power agreed to implement shallow flooding of the Owens Lake, and in 2001, LA released water from the Los Angeles Aqueduct through a breach into Owens Lake for shallow flooding of over twelve square miles of the lake. See Harrington, "Owens Lake: To Dust Bowl and Back?" 22–23. Brine flies began to appear on the green, red, and orange algae and bacteria growing

in the water; then waterfowl and shorebirds arrived to eat the flies. Having become an avian wetland filled with shorebirds and waders, and the particle air pollution reduced by more than 95 percent in 2018, Owens Lake was hailed as an environmental triumph. Louis Sahagún, "Owens Lake: Former Toxic Dust Bowl Transformed into Environmental Success," *Los Angeles Times*, April 28, 2018, https://www.latimes.com/local/california/la-me-owens-lake-birds-20180425-story.html.

74. Esen Kara, "Rewriting the City as an *Oeuvre* in Karen Tei Yamashita's *Tropic of Orange*," *Interactions* 27, no. 1–2 (Spring 2018): 80.

75. Cristina M. Rodriguez, "'Relentless Geography': Los Angeles' Imagined Cartographies in Karen Tei Yamashita's *Tropic of Orange*," *Asian American Literature: Discourses and Pedagogies* 8 (2017): 124; Edward Soja et al., "Urban Restructuring: An Analysis of Social and Spatial Change in Los Angeles," *Economic Geography* 59, no. 2 (1983): 195; Mike Davis, *City of Quartz* (New York: Verso, 1990), xv.

76. Raúl Homero Villa, *Barrio Logos: Space and Place in Urban Chicano Literature and Culture* (Austin: University of Texas Press, 2000), 116.

77. Jackie T. Cuevas, *Post-Borderlandia: Chicana Literature and Gender Variant Critique* (New Brunswick, NJ: Rutgers University Press, 2018), 75.

78. Cuevas, *Post-Borderlandia*, 75.

79. Cuevas, *Post-Borderlandia*, 68.

80. Paula Moya, "'Remaking Human Being': Loving, Kaleidoscopic Consciousness in Helena María Viramontes's *Their Dogs Came with Them*," in *Theories of the Flesh: Latinx and Latin American Feminisms, Transformation, and Resistance*, eds. Andrea J. Pitts, Mariana Ortega, and José Medina (New York: Oxford University Press, 2020), 144.

81. Moya, "Remaking Human Being," 152.

82. Daniel Olivas, "Interview with Helena María Viramontes," *La Bloga* (blog), April 2, 2007, https://labloga.blogspot.com/2007/04/interview-with-helena-mara-viramontes.html.

83. Moya, "Remaking Human Being," 152.

84. Villa, *Barrio Logos*, 82.

85. Andrew Needham, *Power Lines: Phoenix and the Making of the Modern Southwest* (Princeton, NJ: Princeton University Press, 2014), 2.

86. Alicia Muñoz, "Articulating a Geography of Pain: Metaphor, Memory, and Movement in Helena María Viramontes's *Their Dogs Came with Them*," *MELUS* 38, no. 2 (Summer 2013): 25; Sarah D. Wald, "'Refusing to Halt': Mobility and the Quest for Spatial Justice in Helena María Viramontes's *Their Dogs Came with Them* and Karen Tei Yamashita's *Tropic of Orange*," *Western American Literature*, 48, nos. 1 and 2 (Spring/Summer 2013): 73; Cuevas, *Post-Borderlandia*, 75.

87. Scott Kurashige, *The Shifting Grounds of Race: Black and Japanese Americans in the Making of Multiethnic Los Angeles* (Princeton, NJ: Princeton University Press, 2008), 232–233.

88. Eric Avila, *The Folklore of the Freeway: Race and Revolt in the Modernist City* (Minneapolis: University of Minnesota Press, 2014), 18.

89. Villa, *Barrio Logos*, 71.

90. Muñoz, "Articulating a Geography of Pain," 26.

91. Avila, *The Folklore of the Freeway*, 18.

92. Charles "Chaz" Bojórquez, "Graffiti Is Art: Any Drawn Line That Speaks about Identity, Dignity, and Unity . . . That Line Is Art," in *Chicano and Chicana Art: A Critical Anthology*, eds. Jennifer A. Gonzalez et al. (Durham, NC: Duke University Press, 2019), 117–122.

93. The 38th Street gang (1920s), the Barrio Maravilla (1930s), White Fence (1930s), the Big Hazard, or Hazard Grande (1940s).
94. Bojórquez, "Graffiti Is Art," 118.
95. I owe this insight to Suvad Anthony Natipadab.
96. Marcos Sánchez-Tranquilino, "Space, Power, and Youth Culture: Mexican American Graffiti Murals in East Los Angeles, 1972–1978," in *Chicano and Chicana Art: A Critical Anthology*, eds. Jennifer A. Gonzalez et al. (Durham, NC: Duke University Press, 2019), 278–291; Bojórquez, "Graffiti Is Art," 118.
97. I owe this insight to a conversation with Suvad Anthony Natipadab.
98. Bojórquez, "Graffiti Is Art," 119.
99. Helena María Viramontes, "Scripted Language: Writing Is the Only Way I Know How to Pray" (lecture, Sage Chapel, November 11, 2009).
100. Helena María Viramontes et al., "You Carry the Border with You: Conversation with Helena María Viramontes," in *Conversations with Mexican American Writers: Languages and Literatures in the Borderlands*, ed. Elisabeth Mermann-Jozwiak and Nancy Sullivan Jackson (Jackson: University Press of Mississippi, 2009), 84.
101. According to Theodore Roosevelt, "The awakening of the Orient means very much to all nations of Christendom, commercially no less than politically; and it would be short-sighted statesmanship on our part to refuse to take the necessary steps for securing a proper share to our people of this commercial future." By 1898, Roosevelt had secured Hawaii, Puerto Rico, and the Philippines, and in 1904 he purchased the rights to build the Panama Canal for $1 million, making LA a major port city in the Western Hemisphere. Theodore Roosevelt, "The Administration of the Island Possessions" (address at the Coliseum, Hartford, Connecticut, August 22, 1902), quoted in Theodore Roosevelt, *American Problems* (New York: Charles Scribner's Sons, 1926).

CHAPTER 2

1. Epeli Hau'ofa, "Our Sea of Islands," *The Contemporary Pacific* 6, No. 1 (Spring 1994): 148–161.
2. Édouard Glissant, *Treatise on the Whole-World*, trans. Celia Britton (Liverpool: Liverpool University Press, 2020).
3. Erin Suzuki, *Ocean Passages: Navigating Pacific Islander and Asian American Literatures* (Philadelphia: Temple University Press, 2021), 3–5.
4. Michael Cimino's *The Deer Hunter* (Universal Pictures, 1978), Francis Ford Coppola's *Apocalypse Now* (United Artists, 1979), Oliver Stone's *Platoon* (Orion Pictures, 1986), Stanley Kubrick's *Full Metal Jacket* (Warner Bros., 1987), and Oliver Stone's *Born on the Fourth of July* (Universal Pictures, 1989).
5. Yến Lê Espiritu, *Body Counts: The Vietnam War and Militarized Refuge(es)* (Oakland: University of California Press, 2014), 39.
6. Christina Sharpe, *In the Wake: On Blackness and Being* (Durham, NC: Duke University Press, 2016), 13–14.
7. Lê's novel can be placed alongside the works of Vietnamese and Vietnamese American artists and writers such as Lan Cao, Ocean Vuong, Viet Thanh Nguyen, Eric Nguyen, Monique Truong, Dao Strom, Thi Bui, mai c. doan, and Diana Khoi Nguyen.
8. Rick Berg, "Losing Vietnam: Covering the War in an Age of Technology," in *The Vietnam War and American Culture,* ed. John Carlos Rowe and Rick Berg (New York: Columbia University Press, 1991), 115–116, 117.

9. John Carlos Rowe, "Eyewitness: Documentary Styles in the American Representations of Vietnam," in Rowe and Berg, eds., *The Vietnam War and American Culture*, 197.

10. Viet Thanh Nguyen, *Race and Resistance: Literature and Politics in Asian American*, (Oxford: Oxford University Press, 1997), 618. See films such as Michael Cimino's *The Deer Hunter*, *Apocalypse Now* (1979), *Platoon* (1986), Barry Levinson's *Good Morning, Vietnam* (Touchstone Pictures, 1987), and *Born on the Fourth of July* (1989).

11. Rowe and Berg, "Introduction," *The Vietnam War and American Culture*, 2.

12. See Peter Arnett and Michael Maclear's *The Ten Thousand Day War: Vietnam: 1945–1975* (New York: Avon Books, 1982) and Richard Ellison and Stanley Karnow's *Vietnam: A Television History* (PBS, 1983); Rowe, "Eyewitness: Documentary Styles," in Rowe and Berg, eds., *The Vietnam War and American Culture*, 153.

13. Jodi Melamed tracks through the formation of racial liberalism (1940s–1960s), liberal multiculturalism (1980s–1990s), and neoliberal multiculturalism (2000s) in *Represent and Destroy: Rationalizing Violence in the New Racial Capitalism* (Minneapolis: University of Minnesota Press, 2011), 1. Also see Kathleen Belew, *Bring the War Home: The White Power Movement and Paramilitary America* (Boston: Harvard University Press, 2019).

14. Thuy Linh Nguyen Tu, *Experiments in Skin: Race and Beauty in the Shadows of Vietnam* (Durham, NC: Duke University Press, 2021), 4.

15. Thuy Linh Nguyen Tu, *Experiments in Skin*, 105–106.

16. *Bring the War Home: The White Power Movement and Paramilitary America* (Boston: Harvard University Press, 2019).

17. Louis R. Beam Jr., "Forget? Hell No!," *Essays of a Klansman* (Louis Beam, 1983).

18. See Belew's *Bring the War Home* for a more detailed account. As antisemitism in white nationalism was solidified, so too was the reinforcement of gendered and sexualized roles of white women to uphold purity, save whiteness from annihilation, and protect white masculinity. The post-1970s white supremacist narrative of the Vietnam War as a war that emasculated and threatened white masculinity and marked U.S. governmental abandonment, white supremacists used this narrative to consolidate whiteness, militancy, and masculinity. Returning veterans radicalized the white power movement through the belief that the war was lost because an unethical U.S. government did not allow American soldiers to unleash their force upon the subhuman Vietnamese. In Vietnam, American soldiers contended with death and disease, and when they came home they were derided, unappreciated, and abandoned and their opportunities were inhibited by civil rights. The Vietnam War and its aftermath bemoaned white nationalists, emasculated and threatened white masculinity, and became representative of the breakdown of their world. The specter of continuing the war within the United States proved alluring to veterans, soldiers, and disillusioned white people and offered a way to reclaim white masculinity. The white power movement mobilized through an aesthetics of militarization, camouflage fatigues, military weaponry, and land mines for a never-ending war supported by paramilitary camps that developed from U.S. military experiences crucial to white power activism.

19. Cedric J. Robinson, *Black Movements in America* (New York: Routledge, 1997), 151.

20. Robinson, *Black Movements in America*, 135.

21. Cited in Odd Arne Westad, *The Global Cold War: Third World Interventions and the Making of Our Times* (Boston: Cambridge University Press, 2005), 97.

22. Westad, *The Global Cold War*, 191.

23. Daniel S. Lucks, *Selma to Saigon: The Civil Rights Movement and the Vietnam War* (Frankfort: University Press of Kentucky, 2014), 134.

24. Lucks, *Selma to Saigon*, 136.

25. Martin Luther King Jr., "A Time to Break Silence," in *A Testament of Hope: The Essential Writings and Speeches of Martin Luther King, Jr.*, ed. James Melvin Washington (San Francisco: Harper, 1986), 232–233.

26. According to LAPD Chief William Parker, "This situation is very much like fighting the Viet Cong," as he commanded a paramilitary answer to the uprising. Insurgents also evoked the internationalist connections to the Vietnam War, with some of them pronouncing, "If I've got to die, I ain't dying in Vietnam, I'm going to die here." Gerald Horne, *Fire This Time: The Watts Uprising and the 1960s* (Charlottesville: University Press of Virginia, 1995), 59.

27. See Carol Anderson, "The Histories of African Americans' Anticolonialism During the Cold War," in *The Cold War in the Third World*, ed. Robert J. McMahon (Oxford: Oxford University Press, 2013), 182. Also see Kimberley L. Phillips, *War! What Is It Good For?* (Chapel Hill: The University of North Carolina Press, 2012). Cofounder of SNCC Diane Nash Bevel visited Vietnam in late 1966. Her trip was widely covered by the Black press, as Bevel placed the war within a longer history of U.S. imperialism at home and abroad, stating that the interests at stake in Vietnam are "the same interests that overcame the Indians and led to the enslavement of Negroes." In speaking of Black soldiers and Vietnamese villagers, she invoked: "Negro Americans are going to have to decide whether they want to be murderers of other colored people." During Stokely Carmichael's visit to Cuba in 1967, Carmichael described the Newark, New Jersey, uprising as applying "war tactics of the guerilla for our defense in the cities."

28. Cleveland Sellers interview, May 10, 1989, University of North Carolina, Greensboro.

29. Glenn Omatsu, "The 'Four Prisons' and the Movements of Liberation: Asian American Activism from the 1960s to the 1990s," in *The State of Asian America: Activism and Resistance in the 1990s*, ed. Karen Aguilar-San Juan (Boston: South End Press, 1994), 64.

30. lê thi diem thúy, "Shrapnel Shards on Blue Water," in *The Very Inside: An Anthology of Writing by Asian and Pacific Islander Lesbian and Bisexual Women*, ed. Sharon Lin-Hing (Toronto: Sister Vision Black Women and Women of Color Press, 1994), 2–4.

31. lê thi diém thúy, "Shrapnel Shards on Blue Water."

32. Jutta Gsoels-Lorensen, "lê thi diem thúy's 'The Gangster We Are All Looking For': The Ekphrastic Emigration of a Photograph," *Critique: Studies in Contemporary Fiction* 48, no. 1 (2006): 5.

33. Paul Riceour, *The Rule of Metaphor: Multidisciplinary Studies of the Creation of Meaning in Language* (Toronto: University of Toronto Press, 1975), 24–27.

34. Riceour, *The Rule of Metaphor*, 66, 55.

35. Riceour, *The Rule of Metaphor*, 6, 7, 24, 40–41.

36. Ricoeur, *The Rule of Metaphor*, 5.

37. W.J.T. Mitchell, "Ekphrasis and the Other," in *South Atlantic Quarterly* 91, no. 3 (Summer 1992): 710.

38. Joseph Darda, *The Strange Career of Racial Liberalism*, (Stanford: Stanford University Press, 2022), 13.

39. W.J.T. Mitchell's "Ekphrasis and the Other," 697. Mitchell draws upon Murray Krieger's "The Ekphrastic Principle and the Still Moment of Poetry; or *Laokoon* Revisited," in *The Play and Place of Criticism* (Baltimore: Johns Hopkins University Press, 1967).

40. W.J.T. Mitchell, "Ekphrasis and the Other," 697.

41. W.J.T. Mitchell, "Ekphrasis and the Other," 697.

42. Kandice Chuh, *The Difference Aesthetics Makes: On the Humanities "After Man"* (Durham, NC: Duke University Press, 2019), 68.
43. Nora Alter, "Excessive Pre/Requisites: Vietnam Through the East German Lens," *Cultural Critique* 35 (Winter, 1996–1997): 10.
44. Thuy Linh Nguyen Tu, *Experiments in Skin*, 15.
45. Yến Lê Espiritu, "Thirty Years AfterWARd: The Endings That Are Not Over," *Amerasia Journal* 31, no. 2 (2005): xiii.
46. Jessie Kratz, "Vietnam: The First Television War," *Pieces of History*, National Archives, January 25, 2018, prologue.blogs.archives.gov/2018/01/25/vietnam-the-first-television-war/.
47. In 1964, the Gulf of Tonkin Resolution expanded the war-making power of Lyndon Johnson, who then sent nearly three hundred thousand more troops to fight in Vietnam by the end of 1966. Under Johnson's presidency, "Operation Rolling Thunder" attacked Northern Vietnam by air. The Pentagon Papers includes accounts of the beginning of the Rolling Thunder bombing campaign and "Air War in the North" under "Direct Action: The Johnson Commitments, 1964–1968" in the section on the "Evolution of the War."
48. Trinh T. Minh-Ha, *Women, Native, Other: Writing Postcoloniality and Feminism* (Bloomington: Indiana University Press, 2009), 121.
49. Yến Lê Espiritu, *Body Counts*, 1.
50. Yến Lê Espiritu, *Body Counts*, 2.
51. Evyn Lê Espiritu Gandhi, *Archipelago of Resettlement: Vietnamese Refugee Settlers and Decolonization across Guam and Israel-Palestine* (Oakland: University of California Press, 2022), 2, 11.
52. UNHCR (United Nations High Commissioner for Refugees), "Flight from Indochina," in *The State of the World's Refugees 2000: Fifty Years of Humanitarian Aid*, http://www.unhcr.org3ebf9bad0.html, 86.
53. Yến Lê Espiritu, Lisa Lowe, and Lisa Yoneyama, "Transpacific Entanglements," in *Flashpoints for Asian American Studies*, ed. Cathy Schlund-Vials (New York: Fordham University Press, 2017), 178.
54. Nikhil Singh, *Black Is a Country: Race and the Unfinished Struggle for Democracy* (Cambridge, MA: Harvard University Press, 2004), 8.
55. Jim Miller, "Just Another Day in Paradise," in *Under the Perfect Sun: The San Diego Tourists Never See*, ed. Mike Davis et al. (New York: New Press, 2003), 166.
56. Yến Lê Espiritu, *Body Counts*, 33.
57. Paul Gilroy, "Diaspora and the Detours of Identity," in *Identity and Difference*, ed. Kathryn Woodward (London: Sage Publications, 1997), 327. Also see Paul Gilroy, *The Black Atlantic*; Rinaldo Walcott, "The Black Aquatic," *liquid blackness* 5, no. 1 (April 2021): 64–73; Habiba Ibrahim, *Black Age: Oceanic Lifespans and the Time of Black Life* (New York: NYU Press, 2021); Monique Allewaert, *Ariel's Ecology: Plantations, Personhood, and Colonialism in the American Tropics* (Minneapolis: University of Minnesota, 2013); and Tiffany Lethabo King, *The Black Shoals: Offshore Formations of Black and Native Studies* (Durham, NC: Duke University Press, 2019).
58. Water, according to Viet Thanh Nguyen, functions as a stateless place where "refugee bodies are left to drift and as an extraterritorial space where the UNHCR [United Nations High Commissioner for Refugees] and UNCLOS [United Nations Convention on the Law of the Seas] govern legal agreements between nation-states." Viet Thanh Nguyen, "Refugee Memories and Asian American Critique," *Positions* 20 (2012): 930; Nevzat Soguk, *States and Strangers: Refugees and Displacements of Statecraft* (Minneapolis: University

of Minnesota Press, 1999), 15; Robyn Liu, "Governing Refugees 1919–1945," *Borderlands e-journal* 1, no. 1 (2002), www.borderlands.net.au, 9.

59. Yến Lê Espiritu, "Introduction: Critical Refugee Studies and Asian American Studies," *Amerasia Journal* 47, no. 1 (2021): 3.

60. Brian G. Chen, "Walking and Wandering: Reconsidering Diasporic Subjectivity in T. C. Huo's *Land of Smiles* and Lê Thi Diem Thúy's *The Gangster We Are All Looking For*," *Asian American Literature: Discourses and Pedagogies* 8 (2017): 71.

61. Yến Lê Espiritu, *Body Counts*, 27.

62. Evyn Lê Espiritu Gandhi, *Archipelago of Resettlement: Vietnamese Refugee Settlers and Decolonization across Guam and Israel-Palestine* (Oakland: University of California Press, 2022), 11. Water, according to Evyn Lê Espiritu Gandhi, "is a salient medium and metaphor for diaspora and forced displacement, from the Black Atlantic to the transpacific, from Syrian to Vietnamese boat refugees. . . . The figure of the archipelago, refracted through Vietnamese epistemologies of *nuoc*, reminds us of the entanglements between land and water, Indigenous and refugee; that, indeed, Indigenous peoples can be refugees of settler colonial displacement, and refugees can become settlers on Indigenous lands and waters."

CHAPTER 3

1. Esther Belin, *From the Belly of My Beauty* (Tucson: University of Arizona Press, 1999), 68.

2. Part of the San Juan River's canyon country, the Diné homeland and Navajo creation story is situated within the four sacred directions of four mountains: Hesperus Peak (north), Mount Taylor (south), Blanca Peak (east), and the San Francisco Peaks (west), spanning the places now known as New Mexico, Colorado, Utah, and Arizona.

3. Nicolas G. Rosenthal, *Reimagining Indian Country: Native American Migration and Identity in Twentieth-Century Los Angeles* (Chapel Hill: University of North Carolina Press, 2012), 3. The Bureau of Indian Affairs' (BIA) Branch of Placement and Relocation set up field offices in Chicago; Denver; Salt Lake City; Los Angeles; San Francisco; Oakland; San Jose; Portland, Oregon; Dallas; Oklahoma City; Tulsa; St. Louis; Cincinnati; Cleveland; and Joliet and Waukegan, Illinois. According to the census, in 1940, 27,000 Indians, 8 percent of the Indian population, lived in U.S. cities; the number steadily increased, and by 1980, 807,000 Indians, 53 percent of the Indian population, lived in the city. Mishuana Goeman, *Mark My Words: Native Women Mapping Our Nations* (Minneapolis: University of Minnesota Press, 2013), 91; Ward Churchill, *Kill the Indian, Save the Man: The Genocidal Impact of American Indian Residential Schools* (San Francisco: City Lights, 2004), 13.

4. Ned Blackhawk, "I Can Carry On from Here: The Relocation of American Indians to Los Angeles," *Wicazo Sa Review* 11, no. 2 (Autumn, 1995: 19–20).

5. Joan Didion, *Play It as It Lays* (New York: Farrar, Straus and Giroux, 1970). Paradigmatic LA texts such as *Play It as It Lays* by Joan Didion establishes a detached narrative style through the protagonist Maria's obsession with driving through Southern California's freeway infrastructure.

6. Karen Tongson, *Relocations: Queer Suburban Imaginaries* (New York: NYU Press, 2011), 116. Los Angeles' precipitous growth and economic development was accompanied by toxic waste that necessitated disposal, resulting in the Stringfellow Quarry Waste Pits (also known as the "Acid Pits") in 1956 just a few miles northwest of Riverside's neighborhood of Glen Avon, without much oversight. Located atop Pyrite Canyon, the Acid

Pits were filled with over two hundred hazardous chemicals, including hydrochloric, sulfuric, and nitric acids; trichloroethylene and methylene chloride; lead, nickel, cadmium, chromium, and manganese; volatile compounds (VOCs); and a range of pesticides from the production of the pesticide DDT that had built Riverside's agricultural empire. Most of the hazardous waste runoff came from Los Angeles–based Cold War military and defense industry production of metal, guns, planes, and missiles, from prominent companies such as McDonnell-Douglas, Montrose Chemical, General Electric, Hughes Aircraft, Sunkist Growers, Philco-Ford, Northrop, and Rockwell International.

7. Senator George C. Perkins, July 18, 1901, Sherman Indian School Museum and Archives, 9010 Magnolia Avenue, Riverside, California.

8. Matthew Sakiestewa Gilbert, *Education Beyond the Mesas: Hopi Students at Sherman Institute, 1902–1929* (Lincoln: University of Nebraska Press, 2010), 118.

9. George E. Tinker, "Tracing a Contour of Colonialism: American Indians and the Trajectory of Educational Imperialism," preface to Churchill, *Kill the Indian, Save the Man*, xvii.

10. David Wallace Adams, *Education for Extinction: American Indians and the Boarding School Experience, 1875–1926* (Lawrence: University Press of Kansas, 1995), 23. They learned the "lessons of citizenship," or "civilization," and that the United States was "peopled by men and women who crossed the seas in faith [and that] its foundations [were] laid deep in a divine order," "entrusted with liberty" and with "grave duties: the enlargement of liberty and justice is the victory of the people over the forces of evil." Adams, *Education for Extinction*, 136–149; Michael C. Coleman, *Indian Children at School, 1850–1930* (Jackson: University of Mississippi Press, 1993), 105–112; Horace E. Scudder, *A History of the United States of America* (Philadelphia: J. W. Butler, 1884), qtd. in Churchill, *Kill the Indian, Save the Man*, 27.

11. Beth Piatote, *Domestic Subjects: Gender, Citizenship, and Law in Native American Literature* (New Haven: Yale University Press, 2013), 6.

12. Piatote, *Domestic Subjects*, 173.

13. George E. Tinker, "Tracing a Contour of Colonialism: American Indians and the Trajectory of Educational Imperialism," preface to Churchill, *Kill the Indian, Save the Man*, xv. Officials realized not only that Indian people would have to be separated from their families, but also that their religious lifeways had to be replaced with Christianity through a spiritual transformation of the soul itself. Matthew Sakiestewa Gilbert, *Education Beyond the Mesas*, 118; Margaret Jacobs, *White Mother to a Dark Race: Settler Colonialism, Maternalism, and the Removal of Indigenous Children in the American West and Australia, 1880–1940* (Lincoln: University of Nebraska Press, 2009), 85.

14. Richard Henry Pratt, *Battlefield and Classroom: Four Decades with the American Indian, 1867–1904*, ed. Robert M. Utley (New Haven, CT: Yale University Press, 1964), xiv. In his time commanding Black troops in the U.S. Army, Pratt believed that once Africans were "transplanted . . . from [their] Native habitat and tribal affiliation into a new cultural environment," they adapted to new American customs of speech, dress, and culture, acting less like primitive Africans and more like American citizens. Notably, Pratt also served as an army prison warden at Fort Marion, Florida, succeeding in breaking down "recalcitrant" Native Americans through pioneering techniques of "ideological conversion," reducing his prisoners to an unending state of "psychological incompetence," and innovating "prison industries" that deployed inmates as slave labor to run their facilities and produce profit. Robert G. Hays, *A Race at Bay: New York Times Editorials on "The Indian Problem," 1860–1900* (Carbondale: Southern Illinois University Press, 1997). Churchill, *Kill the Indian, Save the Man*, 14.

15. Richard H. Pratt, "The Advantages of Mingling Indians with Whites," *Proceedings of the National Conference of Charities and Corrections* (1892), 46.

16. Piatote, *Domestic Subjects*, 2–3.

17. Piatote, *Domestic Subjects*, 149.

18. Piatote, *Domestic Subjects*, 52–53.

19. Amanda J. Zink, *Fictions of Western American Domesticity: Indian, Mexican, and Anglo Women in Print Culture, 1850–1950* (Albuquerque: University of New Mexico Press, 2018), 3, 6. In the late-nineteenth to mid-twentieth centuries, writers such as Willa Cather, Edna Ferber, Elinore Cowan Stone, and Evelyn Hunt Raymond created characters who brought "the right ways of living" to the Other women in their western adventures. As historical caricatures of female missionaries, teachers, and reformers living among Indian and Mexican women in the West, Cather's, Ferber's, Stone's, and Raymond's heroines sought to Americanize Indian and Mexican women, by providing them with correct feminine domestic knowledge through Christianity.

20. Piatote, *Domestic Subjects*, 12.

21. Piatote, *Domestic Subjects*, 68, 149.

22. Kevin Pelletier, *Apocalyptic Sentimentalism: Love and Fear in U.S. Antebellum Literature* (Athens: University of Georgia Press, 2015), 2–3, 118. For Harriet Beecher Stowe, "The drama of history comes to an end with Christ's reign on earth, as the righteous of all nations achieve everlasting life and the unregenerate suffer eternal damnation. The surviving black characters who leave America to work as missionaries in Africa do so in order to prepare for and even to set in motion events that will lead to the apocalyptic dénouement of history" (114). Justice for Stowe, Pelletier argues, "is not the worldly justice of liberal citizenship, nor is it being imbued with certain inalienable rights. It is eternal life with God." Within the master narrative of providential history, "the abolition of slavery, the reorganization of the domestic space, the triumph of emotion over reason—these are all secondary concerns within the novel's messianic vision, epiphenomena to the phenomenon of the apocalypse, the event that marks the fulfillment of time and the end of injustice, when all will bear witness to a new heaven and a new earth. For Stowe, justice only becomes possible when it is divinely ordained, with Christ separating the righteous from the unrighteous, the wheat from the chaff" (118). According to James Baldwin, Harriet Beecher Stowe's 1852 *Uncle Tom's Cabin* set a historical precedent for reformist literary writing that remade national identity, stabilized racial meaning and difference by narrating slavery as a moral evil that justified the federal government to engage in civil war against the Southern states.

23. To name a few, see Howard Hawks's *The Big Sleep* (1946), Nicholas Ray's *In a Lonely Place* (1950) adapted from Dorothy B. Hughes's 1947 novel, Billy Wilder's *Sunset Boulevard* (1950), Roman Polanski's *Chinatown* (1974), Ridley Scott's *Blade Runner* (1982) adapted from Philip K. Dick's 1968 novel *Do Androids Dream of Electric Sheep?*, Larry Elikan's *The Great Los Angeles Earthquake* (1990), John Lafia's miniseries *10.5: Apocalypse* (2006), and Seth Rogen and Evan Goldberg's *This Is the End* (2013).

24. Pelletier, *Apocalyptic Sentimentalism*, 9–10. This rhetoric of terror has long been pivotal to Anglo-Protestant settlement in the United States. New England Puritans believed themselves to be chosen by God to manifest a church on earth, and ministers often warned of punishment for any regression. As such, the principal trait of the Puritan sermon, fear of God's retributive wrath, terrified congregants into choosing righteousness over sin to attain everlasting life.

25. Margaret D. Jacobs, *White Mother to a Dark Race*, 77–78.

26. Churchill, *Kill the Indian, Save the Man*, 46.

27. As K. Tsianina Lomawaima notes, "Attempts to teach children English, Christianity, and the moral superiority of a clean life of honest labor were constantly undermined by the so-called bad influences of family and tribe." Sherman students were overworked and corporally punished under an abusive education system that methodically sought to indoctrinate them into a Euro-American way of life through the erasure of, and distance from, their tribe and cultural traditions. Young girls were instructed to discard their tribal notions of womanhood in order to become good Christian wives. K. Tsianina Lomawaima, *They Called It Prairie Light: The Story of Chilocco Indian School* (Lincoln: University of Nebraska Press, 1994), 3.

28. Piatote, *Domestic Subjects*, 13.

29. David Wallace Adams, "Beyond Bleakness: The Brighter Side of Indian Boarding Schools," in *Boarding School Blues: Revisiting American Indian Educational Experiences*, ed. Clifford E. Trafzer et al. (Lincoln: University of Nebraska Press, 2006), 47.

30. Churchill, *Kill the Indian, Save the Man*, 47–48.

31. Jennifer Nez Denetdale, "Representing Changing Woman: A Review Essay on Navajo Women," *American Indian Culture & Research Journal* 25, no. 3, (2001): 1–26; Maureen Trudelle Schwarz, *Molded in the Image of Changing Woman: Navajo Views on the Human Body and Personhood* (Tucson: University of Arizona Press, 1997), 173.

32. Schwarz, *Molded in the Image*, 173–174.

33. Schwarz, *Molded in the Image*, 176, 190–203.

34. Denetdale, "Representing Changing Woman," 8.

35. Denetdale, "Representing Changing Woman," 19. Denetdale here is referencing Bruce Lincoln's *Emerging from the Chrysalis: Studies in Rituals of Women's Initiation* (Cambridge, MA: Harvard University Press, 1981).

36. Zink, *Fictions of Western American Domesticity*, 255.

37. "Introduction: The Indian School on Magnolia Avenue," in *Indian School on Magnolia Avenue: Voices and Images from Sherman Institute*, ed. Clifford E. Trafzer et al. (Corvallis: Oregon State University Press, 2012), 3.

38. Talal Asad argues, "secularism and liberal democracy were centrally involved in *linking* religion to the nation, attaining civil rights for citizens (especially social and political equality), and thus forming the liberal democratic state as a power state." Central to the consolidation of liberal democratic state power was the crystallization of a certain concept of "religion," "a concept of something at once universal, individual, and plural—through which the possibility was increasingly opened up of deploying ritualization (repetition, formalization, tradition) in games of power." Talal Asad, *Secular Translations: Nation-State, Modern Self, and Calculative Reason* (New York: Columbia University Press, 2018), 22, 111.

39. Asad, *Secular Translations*, 103.

40. Shawn Wilson, *Research Is Ceremony: Indigenous Research Methods* (Halifax, Nova Scotia, Canada: Fernwood Publishing, 2008), 60–61.

41. Wilson, *Research Is Ceremony*, 69.

42. Wilson, *Research Is Ceremony*, 87.

43. Alvin M. Josephy Jr., "Kaiparowits: The Ultimate Obscenity," *Audubon* 78, no. 2 (March 1976): 64–90.

44. Andrew Needham, *Power Lines: Phoenix and the Making of the Modern Southwest* (Princeton: Princeton University Press, 2014), 4.

45. Quoted in Needham, *Power Lines*, 8.

46. Needham, *Power Lines*, 9.

47. Needham, *Power Lines*, 15.

48. Connie Jacobs and Esther G. Belin, "From California to the Four Corners: An Urban Navajo Returns Home: An Interview with Esther G. Belin," *Studies in American Indian Literatures*, Series 2, 12, no. 3 (Fall 2000): 8.

49. Simon J. Ortiz, "Towards a National Indian Literature: Cultural Authenticity in Nationalism," *MELUS* 8, no. 2, Ethnic Literature and Cultural Nationalism (Summer 1981): 10.

50. Jacobs and Belin, "From California to the Four Corners," 5.

51. The Tang dynasty lasted from 618 to 907 C.E., with an interregnum between 690 and 705 C.E.

52. Cherríe Moraga and Gloria E. Anzaldúa, *This Bridge Called My Back: Writings by Radical Women of Color* (Albany: SUNY Press, 1981).

53. In the Ethnic Studies department's "Third World Moving Images" course, taught by Loni Ding and Robert Kaputof, Belin found a way to develop her writing.

54. "About," Institute of American Indian Arts, accessed June 25, 2024, https://iaia.edu/about/.

55. Amy Kaplan, "Manifest Domesticity," *American Literature* 70, no. 3, No More Separate Spheres! (September 1998): 582, 591.

56. Kaplan, "Manifest Domesticity," 584, 591, 601. "Transpacific femininities," argues Denise Cruz, positions the Pacific as a "new site" and "thoroughfare" for twentieth-century global expansion through which the empires of the United States, Spain, and Japan competed for domination over Asia and the Pacific Islands. Under U.S. occupation, beginning in 1898, the Philippines and notions of being Filipino or Filipina were profoundly shaped by a gendered U.S. colonial educational system guided by establishing English as the Philippines' national language, and also shaped at the turn of the twentieth century by a new public school and university system that cast the home and homeland as feminine and also put forth claims to a hegemonic masculinist vision of empire. This "benevolent assimilation" by colonial missionary tutelage, according to President William McKinley, would offer the proper education and the indoctrination of American democratic ideology across the archipelago. The formation of the "modern Filipina" by Filipino and Filipina writers, as Cruz demonstrates, was built through the production of the modernizing force of the West, as well as precolonial Filipina femininity as modern and free prior to the coming of European, American, and Japanese empires (Denise Cruz, *Transpacific Femininities: The Making of the Modern Filipina* [Durham, NC: Duke University Press, 2012], 8, 11, 17, 24). Haunani-Kay Trask, Kēhaulani Kauanui, Maile Arvin, and Noelani Goodyear-Kaʻōpua have all also studied the ways that gender politics inflected U.S. nation-making projects in Hawaii. As Arvin points out, when the United States annexed Hawaii in 1808 to establish a coaling station for the U.S. Navy during the Spanish-American War in the Philippines, Hawaii, along with the Philippines, Cuba, and Puerto Rico, became one of the United States's "new possessions" (Maile Renee Arvin, *Possessing Polynesians: The Science of Settler Colonial Whiteness in Hawaiʻi and Oceania* [Durham, NC: Duke University Press, 2019], 16–17; J. Kēhaulani Kauanui, *Paradoxes of Hawaiian Sovereignty: Land, Sex, and the Colonial Politics of State Nationalism* [Durham, NC: Duke University Press, 2018], 116, 136–137). For Trask, Americanization created a world of "economic ghettoization" where Hawaiian women and men were forced into a semiskilled labor force through the loss of their land base, political, and economic power. The colonial *haole* world that replaced the Hawaiian world educated men for an American political system that contained women into the space of the home, working low-paying service jobs. Christian colonial conceptions of marriage after 1820, Kauanui points

out, instigated a normative patriarchal heterosexual marriage system that subordinated Hawaiian women under a redefined Hawaiian masculinity organized through a logic of property and ownership of land, and control over women and children. This notion of "possession," according to Arvin, of Indigenous women, was crucial to settler heteropatriarchy (Arvin, *Possessing Polynesians*, 16–17). At the same time, these anti-imperial feminists crucially demonstrate how possession and its multiple imperial epistemological, supernatural, legal, scientific, and political forms are never finished or complete, with Hawaiian and Indigenous women and femininity becoming crucial to imagining movements for land and sovereignty. Women's leadership, writes Noelani Goodyear-Kaʻōpua (*A Nation Rising: Hawaiian Movements for Life, Land, and Sovereignty* [Durham, NC: Duke University Press, 2014]), "was like the water in which we swam." Indeed, 1955—just a year before the Indian Relocation Act of 1956—was a pivotal year for U.S. Cold War relations in which the landmark Bandung conference in Indonesia, wherein African and Asian nations assembled to proclaim their alignment or nonalignment with the United States and the Soviet Union, also commemorates the inauguration of the Filipina feminist movement (Cruz, *Transpacific Femininities*, 28).

57. Gerald Vizenor, *Wordarrows: Indians and Whites in the New Fur Trade* (Minneapolis: University of Minnesota Press, 1978), 17.

58. Goeman, *Mark My Words*, 88–89.

59. Jacobs and Belin, "From California to the Four Corners," 7.

60. Piatote, *Domestic Subjects*, 6.

CHAPTER 4

1. Octavia E Butler Papers (OEB) 3221 (San Marino, CA: The Huntington Library).

2. Octavia E. Butler, "Reading Group Guide: A Conversation with Octavia E. Butler," in *Parable of the Talents* (New York: Warner Books, 1998), 409–417, 415–416.

3. Hortense Spillers, "Mama's Baby, Papa's Maybe: An American Grammar Book," in "Culture and Countermemory: The 'American' Connection," special issue, *Diacritics* 17, no. 2 (Summer 1987): 78.

4. M. Jacqui Alexander, *Pedagogies of Crossing: Meditations on Feminism, Sexual Politics, Memory, and the Sacred* (Durham, NC: Duke University Press, 2005), 290.

5. Michelle D. Commander, *Afro-Atlantic Flight: Speculative Returns and the Black Fantastic*, (Durham, NC: Duke University Press, 2017), 7.

6. Beal, Frances M., "Black Scholar Interview with Octavia Butler: Black Women and the Science Fiction Genre," *Black Scholar* 17, no. 2 (1986): 17.

7. Fishwick, Marshall, and Ray B. Browne, eds. *Icons of Popular Culture* (Bowling Green, OH: Bowling Greene State University Popular Press, 1970).

8. See Jack Kerouac's *On the Road* (New York: Viking, 1957), John Steinbeck's *Travels with Charley* (New York: Penguin, 1962), Jim Harrison's *A Good Day to Die* (New York: Simon and Schuster, 1973), Jonathan Raban's *Old Glory* (London: William Collins, 1981), Richard Reeves's *American Journey* (New York: Simon & Schuster, 1982), and Dayton Duncan's *Out West* (Lincoln: University of Nebraska Press, 2000).

9. Ronald Primeau, *Romance of the Road: The Literature of the American Highway*, Bowling Green, OH: Bowling Green State University Popular Press, 1996.

10. Gretchen Sorin, *Driving While Black: African American Travel and the Road to Civil Rights* (New York: Liveright, 2020), 15, 17. In their own cars, Black travelers could not be asked to sit in the back or to enter through the back door of the bus. The automo-

bile renegotiated the social behavior and encounters between Black and white motorists within the white spaces of the United States. Black motorists were able to move quickly and more freely throughout the landscape.

11. Sorin, *Driving While Black*, 36, 37, 39.
12. Butler, *Parable of the Talents*, 21.
13. Commander, *Afro-Atlantic Flight*, 9.
14. Sorin, *Driving While Black*, 1–5.
15. Sorin, *Driving While Black*, 11.
16. Quintard Taylor, *In Search of the Racial Frontier: African Americans in the American West 1528–1990* (New York: W.W. Norton, 1998), 81.
17. Kelly Lytle Hernández, *City of Inmates: Conquest, Rebellion, and the Rise of Human Caging in Los Angeles, 1771–1965* (Chapel Hill: University of North Carolina Press, 2017).
18. According to the New Testament's Gospel of Mark, Jesus said to his disciples, "To you has been given the secret of the kingdom of God, but for those outside everything is said in parables; so that they may indeed see but not perceive, and may indeed hear but not understand; lest they should turn again, and be forgiven." Matthew, too, relates that when Jesus spoke in public, he spoke only in parables; when his disciples asked the reason, he replied, "To you it has been given to know the secrets [*mysteria*; literally, "mysteries"] of the kingdom of heaven, but to them it has not been given."
19. For more on this turn in parable studies, see Craig L. Blomberg, *Interpreting the Parables*, 2nd ed. (Downers Grove, IL: IVP Academic, 2012), 155.
20. Joseph P. Sánchez, *El Camino Real de California: From Ancient Pathways to Modern Byways* (Albuquerque: University of New Mexico Press, 2019), 107, 145.
21. Sánchez, *El Camino Real de California*, 154–155.
22. Alexander, *Pedagogies of Crossing*, 292.
23. Wade Graham, "Blueprinting the Regional City: The Urban and Environmental Legacies of the Air Industry in Southern California," in *Blue Sky Metropolis: The Aerospace Century in Southern California*, ed. Peter J. Westwick (Berkeley: University of California Press, 2012), 247–274.
24. Paul Gilroy, *Against Race: Imagining Political Culture beyond the Color Line* (Cambridge, MA: The Belknap Press of Harvard University Press, 2000), 346.
25. David Bobbitt and Harold Mixon, "Prophecy and Apocalypse in the Rhetoric of Martin Luther King, Jr.," *Journal of Communication and Religion* 17, no. 1 (March 1994): 27, 30, 32. His speech "I Have a Dream" invokes a historical narrative of the United States's sacred journey from a foundation of a promised land as inscribed in the documents of the Declaration of Independence, to the failure of the promise in the present, and moves through to the future, a cosmic vision, in which the promise will be fulfilled (David Bobbitt and Harold Mixon, "Prophecy and Apocalypse in the Rhetoric of Martin Luther King, Jr.," *Journal of Communication and Religion* 17, no. 1 [1994]: 32–35). In Martin Luther King Jr.'s secular prophetic rhetoric, King interpreted the civil rights movement through biblical genres that imagined transformation and redemption through struggle (Bobbitt and Mixon, "Prophecy and Apocalypse," 27, 30). Acting as the apocalypticist, King assumes the status of prophet to reveal the predetermined future millennium. In this vision, the United States is preordained to fulfill its promise of providing "all men—yes, black men as well as white men . . . the unalienable rights of life, liberty, and the pursuit of happiness" (Bobbitt and Mixon, "Prophecy and Apocalypse," 32). And his "dream . . . was of the sure and certain coming of equality and brotherhood" (1). King's hope is not placed, however, in white America, but in God. This is the preordained cosmic order of things, and the state's teleological time is supplanted by a sacred eschatological temporal-

ity. King claims the democratic promise of the U.S. state wherein the future of racial equality has always been present since the founding of the U.S. nation: "I have a dream that one day this nation will rise up and live out the true meaning of its creed: 'We hold these truths to be self-evident; that all men are created equal'" ("Prophecy and Apocalypse," Bobbit and Mixon quote King's "I Have a Dream" speech from R.F. Reid's *Three Centuries of American Rhetorical Discourse* [Prospect Heights, IL: Waveland, 1988], 723–726). His "dream that one day every valley shall be exalted, every hill and mountain shall be made low, the rough places will be made plain and the crooked places will be made straight, and the glory of the Lord shall be revealed, and all flesh shall see it together" (R.F. Reid's *Three Centuries of American Rhetorical Discourse*, 725–726.) King's vision of racial harmony evokes a future in which racial crises have been resolved and the founding of the destiny of the United States has been fulfilled (Bobbit and Mixon, "Prophecy and Apocalypse," 35). Speaking on the impending new world, King declares, "We've got some difficult days ahead. But it doesn't matter with me now. Because I've been to the mountaintop. . . . I just want to do God's will. And He's allowed me to go up to the mountaintop. And I've looked over. And I've seen the promised land. I may not get there with you. But I want you to know tonight, that we, as a people, will get to the promised land. And I'm happy tonight. I'm not worried about anything. I'm not fearing any man. Mine eyes have seen the glory of the coming of the Lord" (Bobbit and Mixon quote King's speech from J.M. Washington, *A Testament of Hope: The Essential Writings of Martin Luther King, Jr.* [San Francisco: Harper & Row, 1986], 286).

26. Marjorie Corbman, "The Creation of the Devil and the End of the White Man's Rule: The Theological Influence of the Nation of Islam on Early Black Theology," *Religions* 11, no. 6 (2020): 1.

27. Michael Lieb, *Children of Ezekiel: Aliens, UFOs, the Crisis of Race, and the Advent of End Time* (Durham, NC: Duke University Press, 1998), 141–142. Cone, Cleage, and Malcolm X drew upon these stories to describe the "white devil," and his "beastly behavior," where the progression of light skin was accompanied by more wickedness and corruption (Corbman, "The Creation of the Devil," 6). This is how one might account, according to the Nation of Islam, for the indefensible and depraved behaviors of lynching, genocide, and the detonation of atomic bombs.

28. Lieb, *Children of Ezekiel*, 149. Within the Nation of Islam's anti-Christian eschatology, Elijah Muhammad and Louis Farrakhan connected the biblical account of Ezekiel's purifying destruction of Jerusalem to the appearance of UFOs as a harbinger of the Day of Judgment. Painting an apocalyptic vision that binds Black people to an earth destroyed by weapons of mass destruction, Elijah Muhammad's 1965 *Message to the Blackman in America* invokes Ezekiel's *Visio Dei*, or "Inaugural vision," a momentous moment of revelation in Hebrew scripture in which Ezekiel is envisioned as a divine warrior riding in on a battle chariot drawn by four living creatures, with a wheel beside each creature; some note that these hold the spirit of four angels protecting the holiness of God. The wheels, moving in any direction, represent God's divine providence and omnipotence. Within the Nation of Islam, Ezekiel's wheel comes to play a central role in the Nation's struggle against their enemies. A combination of Islam and Afrocentric cosmology, the Nation of Islam found in the Mother Plane or Mother Wheel, or unidentified flying object (UFO), a weapon of mass destruction built by the "good" scientist Allah, an apocalyptic machine of import that would serve as the vehicle through which the Nation would struggle against members of the white race, Christianity, or Judaism. For the Nation, these enemies must be countered through the Mother Plane that will bring about destruction and salvation by annihilating their enemies and bringing about Armageddon.

29. "A Conversation with Octavia E. Butler," in Octavia E. Butler, *Parable of the Talents* (New York: Warner Books, 1998), 412.
30. Butler, "A Conversation with Octavia E. Butler," 410.
31. Elaine Pagels, *The Gnostic Gospels* (New York: Random House, 1979), 15.
32. See the podcast "Octavia's Parables"; the webinar "Octavia Tried to Tell Us," led by Tananarive Due and Monica A. Coleman; religions such as Earthseed and the Terasem movement; anthologies such as *Octavia's Brood: Science Fiction Stories from Social Justice Movements*, ed. Adrienne Maree Brown and Walidah Imarisha (Chico, CA: AK Press, 2015); and Toshi Reagon and Bernice Johnson Reagon's opera *Parable of the Sower*. A24 has acquired the rights to *Parable of the Sower* to develop the novel into a film; currently, Sonya Winton-Odamtten and Jonathan I. Kidd of *Lovecraft Country* are slated to write the pilot, and Issa Rae and J. J. Abrams are attached to executive-produce a TV adaptation of *Fledgling*; MacArthur Genius Award–winner and *Watchmen* consultant Branden Jacobs-Jenkins has been tapped to write and executive produce an FX pilot based on *Kindred*; Amazon is developing a TV series based on *Wild Seed*, cowritten by Nnedi Okorafor and Wanuri Kahiu; Amazon is also developing a series based on *Dawn*, with Ava Duvernay attached to direct.
33. Keith R. Burich, "Henry Adams, the Second Law of Thermodynamics, and the Course of History," *Journal of the History of Ideas* 48, no. 3 (July–September 1987): 467.
34. David Scott and Sylvia Wynter, "The Re-Enchantment of Humanism: An Interview with Sylvia Wynter," *Small Axe* 8 (September 2000): 119–207; Kandice Chuh, *The Difference Aesthetics Makes: On the Humanities "After Man"* (Durham, NC: Duke University Press, 2019).
35. Lois Parkinson Zamora, *Writing the Apocalypse: Historical Vision in Contemporary U.S. and Latin American Fiction* (Cambridge: Cambridge University Press, 1989), 59.
36. Scott and Wynter, "The Re-Enchantment of Humanism," 121.
37. Revelation 1:19.

CODA

1. Maile Renee Arvin, *Possessing Polynesians: The Science of Settler Colonial Whiteness in Hawai'i and Oceania* (Durham, NC: Duke University Press, 2019), 22.
2. Hsiu-chuan Lee and Cynthia Kadohata, "Interview with Cynthia Kadohata," *MELUS* 32, no. 2, Thresholds, Secrets, and Knowledge (Summer, 2007): 172.
3. Cynthiakadohata.com
4. Lee and Kadohata, "Interview with Cynthia Kadohata," 166–167, 171. Unlike Kadohata, who grew up in a small Japanese American community, her parents were born and raised in some of the largest Japanese communities in the United States. Kadohata's mother and grandmother were both born in Southern California and moved to Hawaii in the 1930s. After her grandfather drowned in Hawaii, the family moved to Chicago, where Kadohata was born on July 2, 1956. Her father's side of the family moved from Japan in the 1920s to Southern California, where they worked as tenant farmers. A few decades later, during World War II, he and his family were incarcerated at the Poston Internment Camp in Yuma, Arizona, on the Colorado River Indian Reservation over the protestations of the Tribal Council. After attending graduate school at the University of Pittsburgh and Columbia University, where she sold her first story to *The New Yorker* and then got an agent, she returned to Los Angeles in 1990.

Bibliography

Adams, David Wallace. "Beyond Bleakness: The Brighter Side of Indian Boarding Schools." In *Boarding School Blues: Revisiting American Indian Educational Experiences*, edited by Clifford E. Trafzer, Jean A. Keller, and Lorene Sisquoc, 35–64. Lincoln: University of Nebraska Press, 2006.

———. *Education for Extinction: American Indians and the Boarding School Experience, 1875–1926*. Lawrence: University Press of Kansas, 1995.

Adams, Rachel. "The Ends of America, the Ends of Postmodernism." *Twentieth Century Literature* 53, no. 3 (2007): 248–272.

Adorno, Theodor. *Introduction to the Sociology of Music*. Translated by E. B. Ashton. New York: Continuum, 1989.

Alarcón, Daniel Cooper. *The Aztec Palimpsest: Mexico in the Modern Imagination*. Tucson: University of Arizona Press, 1997.

Alexander, M. Jacqui. *Pedagogies of Crossing: Meditations on Feminism, Sexual Politics, Memory, and the Sacred*. Durham, NC: Duke University Press, 2005.

Allewaert, Monique. *Ariel's Ecology: Plantations, Personhood, and Colonialism in the American Tropics*. Minneapolis: University of Minnesota Press, 2013.

Almaguer, Tomás. *Racial Fault Lines: The Historical Origins of White Supremacy in California*. Berkeley: University of California Press, 1994.

Alter, Nora. "Excessive Pre/Requisites: Vietnam Through the East German Lens," *Cultural Critique*, no. 35 (Winter, 1996–1997): 39–79.

Ammons, Elizabeth. *Brave New Worlds: How Literature Will Save the Planet*. Iowa City: University of Iowa Press, 2010.

Anand, Nikhil, Akhil Gupta, and Hannah Appel. *The Promise of Infrastructure*. Durham, NC: Duke University Press, 2018.

Anderson, Carol. "The Histories of African Americans' Anticolonialism During the Cold War." In *The Cold War in the Third World*, edited by Robert J. McMahon, 178–191. Oxford: Oxford University Press, 2013.

Anzaldúa, Gloria, and Cherríe Moraga. *This Bridge Called My Back: Writings by Radical Women of Color.* Albany: SUNY Press, 1981.
Arnett, Peter, and Michael Maclear. *The Ten Thousand Day War: Vietnam: 1945—1975.* New York: Avon Books, 1982.
Arvin, Maile Renee. *Possessing Polynesians: The Science of Settler Colonial Whiteness in Hawai'i and Oceania.* Durham, NC: Duke University Press, 2019.
Asad, Talal. *Secular Translations: Nation-State, Modern Self, and Calculative Reason.* New York: Columbia University Press, 2018.
Avila, Eric. *The Folklore of the Freeway: Race and Revolt in the Modernist City.* Minneapolis: University of Minnesota Press, 2014.
Azuma, Eiichiro. *Between Two Empires: Race, History, and Transnationalism in Japanese America.* Oxford: Oxford University Press, 2005.
Banham, Reyner. *Los Angeles: The Architecture of Four Ecologies.* Berkeley: University of California Press, 2009 (originally published 1971).
Beam, Louis R., Jr. "Forget? Hell No!," *Essays of a Klansman* (Louis Beam, 1983).
Beal, Frances M. "Black Scholar Interview with Octavia Butler: Black Women and the Science Fiction Genre." *Black Scholar* 17, no. 2 (1986): 14–18.
Belew, Kathleen. *Bring the War Home: The White Power Movement and Paramilitary America.* Boston: Harvard University Press, 2019.
Belin, Esther. *From the Belly of My Beauty.* Tucson: University of Arizona Press, 1999.
———. *Of Cartography.* Tucson: University of Arizona Press, 2017.
Benjamin, Walter. "Theses on the Philosophy of History." In *Illuminations*, edited by Hannah Arendt and translated by Harry Zohn, 253–264. New York: Schoken Books, 1968.
Berg, Rick. "Losing Vietnam: Covering the War in an Age of Technology." In *The Vietnam War and American Culture*, edited by Rick Berg and John Carlos Rowe, 115–147. New York: Columbia University Press, 1991.
Berg, Rick, and John Carlos Rowe, "Introduction." In *The Vietnam War and American Culture*, 1–17. New York: Columbia University Press, 1991.
Blackhawk, Ned. "I Can Carry On from Here: The Relocation of American Indians to Los Angeles." *Wicazo Sa Review* 11, no. 2 (Autumn, 1995): 16–30.
Blomberg, Craig L. *Interpreting the Parables,* 2nd ed. Downers Grove, IVP Academic, 2012.
Bobbitt, David, and Harold Mixon. "Prophecy and Apocalypse in the Rhetoric of Martin Luther King, Jr." *Journal of Communication and Religion* 17, no. 1 (1994): 27–38.
Bojórquez, Charles "Chaz." "Graffiti Is Art: Any Drawn Line that Speaks about Identity, Dignity, and Unity . . . That Line Is Art." In *Chicano and Chicana Art: A Critical Anthology*, edited by Jennifer A. Gonzalez, C. Ondine Chavoya, Chon Noriega, and Terezita Romo. Durham, NC: Duke University Press, 2019.
Bosquet, Jean. "Lizard People's Catacomb City Hunted." *Los Angeles Times*, January 29, 1934.
Bradbury, Ray. *Fahrenheit 451.* New York: Ballantine Books, 1953.
Brecht, Bertolt. "Hollywood Elegies." Translated from the German by Adam Kirsch. *Poetry* Magazine, June 2011 (originally published 1942).
Brothers Strause, The. *Skyline.* Universal City, CA: Universal Pictures, 2010.
Brown, Adrienne Maree, and Walidah Imarisha, eds. *Octavia's Brood: Science Fiction Stories from Social Justice Movements.* Chico, CA: AK Press, 2015.
Burich, Keith R. "Henry Adams, the Second Law of Thermodynamics, and the Course of History." *Journal of the History of Ideas* 48, no. 3 (July–September 1987): 467–482.
Butler, Octavia E. *Parable of the Sower.* New York: Warner Books, 1993.

———. *Parable of the Talents*. New York: Warner Books, 1998.
———. "Reading Group Guide: A Conversation with Octavia E. Butler." In *Parable of the Talents*, 409–417. New York: Warner Books, 1998.
Byrd, Jodi. *The Transit of Empire*. Minnesota: University of Minnesota Press, 2011.
Cameron, James. *Terminator*. Los Angeles: Orion Pictures, 1984.
———. *Terminator 2: Judgment Day*. Culver City, CA: TriStar Pictures, 1991.
———. *Terminator 3: Rise of the Machines*. Burbank, CA: Warner Bros., 2003.
———. *Terminator Salvation*. Burbank, CA: Warner Bros., 2009.
Carpenter. John. *Escape from L.A.* Los Angeles: Paramount Pictures, 1996.
Castelli, Elizabeth. *Martyrdom and Memory: Early Christian Culture Making*. New York: Columbia University Press, 2004.
Castillo, Edward, ed. *Native American Perspectives on the Hispanic Colonization of Alta California* (New York: Garland Science, 1992).
Chen, Brian G. "Walking and Wandering: Reconsidering Diasporic Subjectivity in T.C. Huo's *Land of Smiles* and Lê Thi Diem Thúy's *The Gangster We Are All Looking For*." *Asian American Literature: Discourses and Pedagogies* 8 (2017): 62–80.
Choi, Franny. "Catastrophe Is Next to Godliness." In *The World Keeps Ending, and the World Goes On*. New York: HarperCollins, 2022.
Chuh, Kandice. *The Difference Aesthetics Makes: On the Humanities "After Man."* Durham, NC: Duke University Press, 2019.
———. "Of Hemispheres and Other Spheres: Navigating Karen Tei Yamashita's Literary World." *American Literary History* 18, no. 3 (Fall 2006): 618–637.
Churchill, Ward. *Kill the Indian, Save the Man: The Genocidal Impact of American Indian Residential Schools*. San Francisco: City Lights, 2004.
Cimino, Michael. *The Deer Hunter*. University City, CA: Universal Pictures, 1978.
Cohen, Sandy. "Why Is It So Much Fun to Destroy Los Angeles?" *Telegram & Gazette*, November. 14, 2010. https://www.telegram.com/story/news/local/north/2010/11/15/why-is-it-so-much/51377724007/.
Cohn, Norman. "How Time Acquired a Consummation." In *Apocalypse Theory and the Ends of the World*, edited by Malcolm Bull, 21–37. Oxford: Blackwell Publishing, 1995.
Coleman, Michael C. *Indian Children at School, 1850–1930*. Jackson: University of Mississippi Press, 1993.
Commander, Michelle D. *Afro-Atlantic Flight: Speculative Returns and the Black Fantastic*. Durham, NC: Duke University Press, 2017.
Coppola, Francis Ford. *Apocalypse Now*. Beverly Hills, CA: United Artists, 1979.
Corbman, Marjorie. "The Creation of the Devil and the End of the White Man's Rule: The Theological Influence of the Nation of Islam on Early Black Theology." *Religions* 11, no. 6 (2020): 305.
Corman, Roger. *Day the World Ended*. Los Angeles: American International Pictures, 1955.
Cortázar, Julio. *Hopscotch*. Translated by Gregory Rabassa. New York: Pantheon Books, 1966.
Cottrell, Stephen. "Music, Time, and Dance in Orchestral Performance: The Conductor as Shaman." *Twentieth-Century Music* 3, no. 1 (2007): 73–96.
Cowen, Deborah. "Following the Infrastructures of Empire: Notes on Cities, Settler Colonialism, and Method." *Urban Geography* 41, no. 4 (2019): 469–486.
Crawford, Chiyo. "From Desert Dust to City Soot: Environmental Justice and Japanese American Internment in Karen Tei Yamashita's *Tropic of Orange*." *MELUS* 38, no. 3 (Fall 2013): 86–106.

Crenshaw, Kimberlé. "Mapping the Margins: Intersectionality, Identity Politics, and Violence against Women of Color." *Stanford Law Review* 43, no. 6 (July 1991): 1241–1299.
Cristaudo, Wayne. "Revolution and the Redeeming of the World: Egen Rosenstock-Huessy's Messianic Reading of History." In *Messianism, Apocalypse and Redemption 20th Century German Thought,* edited by Wayne Cristaudo and Wendy Baker, 243–258. Adelaide: ATF Press, 2006.
Cristaudo, Wayne and Wendy Baker, eds. *Messianism, Apocalypse and Redemption 20th Century German Thought,* 273–292. Adelaide: ATF Press, 2006.
Cruz, Denise. *Transpacific Femininities: The Making of the Modern Filipina.* Durham, NC: Duke University Press, 2012.
Cuevas, Jackie T. *Post-Borderlandia: Chicana Literature and Gender Variant Critique.* New Brunswick, NJ: Rutgers University Press, 2018.
Darda, Joseph. *The Strange Career of Racial Liberalism,* Stanford, CA: Stanford University Press, 2022.
Davis, Mike. "The Case for Letting Malibu Burn," December 4, 2018. https://longreads.com/2018/12/04/the-case-for-letting-malibu-burn/.
———. *City of Quartz.* New York: Verso, 1990.
———. *Ecology of Fear: Los Angeles and the Imagination of Disaster.* New York: Metropolitan Books, 1998.
Davis, Mike, Kelly Mayhew, and Jim Miller, eds. *Under the Perfect Sun: The San Diego Tourists Never See.* New York: New Press, 2003.
Dean, Sharon E., Peggy S. Ratcheson, Judith W. Finger, Ellen F. Daus, and Craig D. Bates. *Weaving a Legacy: Indian Baskets and the People of Owens Valley, California.* Salt Lake City: University of Utah Press, 2004.
Denetdale, Jennifer Nez. "Representing Changing Woman: A Review Essay on Navajo Women." *American Indian Culture & Research Journal* 25, no. 3 (2001): 1–26.
Derrida, Jacques. "No Apocalypse, Not Now (Full Speed Ahead, Seven Missiles, Seven Missives)." *Diacritics* 14, no. 2, Nuclear Criticism (Summer, 1984): 2–31.
De Toth, André. *Crime Wave.* Burbank, CA: Warner Bros., 1953.
Dick, Philip K. *Do Androids Dream of Electric Sheep?* New York: Doubleday, 1968.
Didion, Joan. *After Henry: Essays.* New York: Simon and Schuster, 1992.
———. *Play It As It Lays.* New York: Farrar, Straus and Giroux, 1970.
———. *Slouching Towards Bethlehem.* New York: Dell Publishing, 1968.
Dooner, Pierton W. *The Last Days of the Republic.* San Francisco: Alta California Publishing House, 1880.
Drinnon, Richard. *Keeper of Concentration Camps: Dillon S. Myer and American Racism.* Berkeley: University of California Press, 1987.
Dudziak, Mary. *Cold War Civil Rights: Race and the Image of American Democracy.* Princeton, NJ: Princeton University Press, 2000.
Due, Tananarive, and Monica A. Coleman. "Octavia Tried to Tell Us." Webinar. https://octaviatried.com/.
Duncan, Dayton. *Out West.* Lincoln: University of Nebraska Press, 2000.
Elikann, Larry. *The Great Los Angeles Earthquake.* New York: NBC, 1990.
Ellison, Richard, and Stanley Karnow. *Vietnam: A Television History.* Arlington, VA: PBS, 1983.
Emmerich, Roland. *The Day After Tomorrow.* Los Angeles: 20th Century Studios, 2004.
———. *Independence Day.* Los Angeles: 20th Century Fox, 1996.
———. *2012.* Los Angeles: Columbia Pictures, 2009.

Escobar, Arturo. *Pluriversal Politics: The Real and the Possible.* Durham, NC: Duke University Press, 2020.
Espiritu, Yến Lê. *Body Counts; The Vietnam War and Militarized Refuge(es).* Oakland: University of California Press, 2014.
———. "Introduction: Critical Refugee Studies and Asian American Studies." *Amerasia Journal* 47, no. 1 (2021): 2–7.
———. "Thirty Years AfterWARd: The Endings That Are Not Over." *Amerasia Journal* 31, no. 2 (2005): xiii–xxiii.
Espiritu, Yến Lê, Lisa Lowe, and Lisa Yoneyama. "Transpacific Entanglements," in *Flashpoints for Asian American Studies*, edited by Cathy Schlund-Vials, 175–189. New York: Fordham University Press, 2017.
Ferguson, Roderick. "Something Else to Be: *Sula*, The Moynihan Report, and the Negations of Black Lesbian Feminism." In *Aberrations in Black*, 110–137. Minneapolis: University of Minnesota Press, 2003.
Fernández-Kelly, Patricia, and Douglas S. Massey. "Borders for Whom? The Role of NAFTA in Mexico-U.S. Migration." *The Annals of the American Academy of Political and Social Science* 610, no. 1 (March 2007): 98–118.
Ferreira da Silva, Denise. "Toward a Black Feminist Poethics: The Quest(ion) of Blackness Toward the End of the World." *The Black Scholar* 44, no. 2 (2014): 81–97.
Fishwick, Marshall, and Ray B. Browne, eds. *Icons of Popular Culture.* Bowling Green, OH: Bowling Greene State University Popular Press, 1970.
Fleischer, Ruben. *Zombieland.* Culver City, CA: Sony Pictures, 2009.
Forbes, Jack. *Native Americans of California and Nevada.* Happy Camp, CA: Naturegraph Publishers, 1982.
Ford, James Edward, III. "When Disaster Strikes: On the Apocalyptic Tone of Hip Hop." *ASAP/Journal* 3, no. 3 (2018): 595–622.
Frank, Pat. *Alas, Babylon.* Philadelphia: J.B. Lippincott, 1959.
Fukuyama, Francis. "The End of History?" *The National Interest*, no. 16 (Summer 1989), 3–18.
Gandhi, Evyn Lê Espiritu. *Archipelago of Resettlement: Vietnamese Refugee Settlers and Decolonization across Guam and Israel-Palestine.* Oakland: University of California Press, 2022.
Gier, Jean Vengua, and Carla Alicia Tejeda. "An Interview with Karen Tei Yamashita." University of California, Berkeley, 1998. https://legacy.chass.ncsu.edu/jouvert/v2i2/YAMASHI.HTM.
Gilbert, Matthew Sakiestewa. *Education Beyond the Mesas: Hopi Students at Sherman Institute, 1902–1929.* Lincoln: University of Nebraska Press, 2010.
Gilroy, Paul. *Against Race: Imagining Political Culture beyond the Color Line.* Cambridge, MA: The Belknap Press of Harvard University Press, 2000.
———. *The Black Atlantic: Modernity and Double Consciousness.* New York: Verso, 1993.
———. "Diaspora and the Detours of Identity." In *Identity and Difference*, edited by Kathryn Woodward, 299–329. London: Sage Publications, 1997.
Glissant, Édouard. *Treatise on the Whole-World.* Translated by Celia Britton. Liverpool: Liverpool University Press, 2020.
Glixman, Elizabeth P. "An Interview with Karen Tei Yamashita." *Eclectica Magazine*, October/November 2007. https://www.eclectica.org/v11n4/glixman_yamashita.html.
Goeman, Mishuana. *Mark My Words: Native Women Mapping Our Nations.* Minneapolis: University of Minnesota Press, 2013.

Goering, Laurie. "In Los Angeles 'Water Colony', Tribes Fear a Parched Future." *Reuters*, June 4, 2019. https://www.reuters.com/article/us-water-california/in-los-angeles-water-colony-tribes-fear-a-parched-future-idUSKCN1T512S.
Goodyear-Ka'ōpua, Noelani. *A Nation Rising: Hawaiian Movements for Life, Land, and Sovereignty*. Durham, NC: Duke University Press, 2014.
Graham, Wade. "Blueprinting the Regional City: The Urban and Environmental Legacies of the Air Industry in Southern California." In *Blue Sky Metropolis: The Aerospace Century in Southern California*, edited by Peter J. Westwick, 247–274. Berkeley: University of California Press, 2012.
Gsoels-Lorensen, Jutta. "lê thi diem thúy's 'The Gangster We Are All Looking For': The Ekphrastic Emigration of a Photograph." *Critique: Studies in Contemporary Fiction* 48, no. 1 (2006): 3–18.
Gumprecht, Blake. *The Los Angeles River: Its Life, Death, and Possible Rebirth*. Baltimore: Johns Hopkins University Press, 2001.
Hackel, Steven W. "Sources of Rebellion: Indian Testimony and the Mission San Gabriel Uprising of 1785." *Ethnohistory* 50: 4 (Fall 2003): 643–669.
Halberstam, J. Jack. *In a Queer Time and Place: Transgender Bodies, Subcultural Lives*. New York: New York University Press, 2005.
Hanson, Harry. *California: A Guide to the Golden State*. New York: Hastings House, 1967.
Harrington, Bob. "Owens Lake: To Dust Bowl and Back?" *Southwest Hydrology*, July/August 2004: 22–23.
Harrison, Jim. *A Good Day to Die*. New York: Simon and Schuster, 1973.
Hartman, Saidiya. *Lose Your Mother: A Journey Along the Atlantic Slave Route*. New York: Farrar, Straus and Giroux, 2007.
Hau'ofa, Epeli. "Our Sea of Islands." *The Contemporary Pacific* 6, no. 1 (Spring 1994): 148–161.
Hawk, Howard. *The Big Sleep*. Burbank, CA: Warner Bros., 1946.
Hays, Robert G. *A Race at Bay: New York Times Editorials on "The Indian Problem," 1860–1900*. Carbondale: Southern Illinois University Press, 1997.
Hong, Grace. *The Ruptures of American Capital: Women of Color Feminism and the Culture of Immigrant Labor*. Minneapolis: University of Minnesota Press, 2006.
Hong, Grace Kyungwon, and Roderick A. Ferguson. *Strange Affinities: The Gender and Sexual Politics of Comparative Racialization*. Durham, NC: Duke University Press, 2011.
Horne, Gerald. *Fire This Time: The Watts Uprising and the 1960s*. Charlottesville: University Press of Virginia, 1995.
Huxley, Aldous. *Ape and Essence*. New York: Harper, 1948.
Ibrahim, Habiba. *Black Age: Oceanic Lifespans and the Time of Black Life*. New York: NYU Press, 2021.
Jackson, Mick. *Volcano*. Los Angeles: 20th Century Fox, 1997.
Jacobs, Connie, and Esther G. Belin. "From California to the Four Corners: An Urban Navajo Returns Home: An Interview with Esther G. Belin." *Studies in American Indian Literatures*, Series 2, 12, no. 3 (Fall 2000): 1–13.
Jacobs, Margaret D. *White Mother to a Dark Race: Settler Colonialism, Maternalism, and the Removal of Indigenous Children in the American West and Australia, 1880–1940*. Lincoln: University of Nebraska Press, 2009.
Jameson, Fredric. *Marxism and Form: Twentieth-Century Dialectical Theories of Literature*. Princeton, NJ: Princeton University Press, 1971.
Jones, Justin. *The Apocalypse*. Burbank, CA: The Asylum, 2007.
Josephy, Alvin M., Jr. "Kaiparowits: The Ultimate Obscenity." *Audubon* 78 (March 1976): 64–90.

Joyce, Patrick. *The Rule of Freedom: Liberalism and the Modern City*. London: Verso, 2003.
Kadohata, Cynthia. *In the Heart of the Valley of Love*. Berkeley: University of California Press, 1992.
Kaplan, Amy. "Manifest Domesticity." *American Literature* 70, no. 3, No More Separate Spheres! (September 1998): 581–606.
Kara, Esen. "Rewriting the City as an *Oeuvre* in Karen Tei Yamashita's *Tropic of Orange*." *Interactions* 27, no. 1–2 (Spring 2018): 75–89.
Kauanui, J. Kēhaulani. *Paradoxes of Hawaiian Sovereignty: Land, Sex, and the Colonial Politics of State Nationalism*. Durham, NC: Duke University Press, 2018.
Kermode, Frank. *The Sense of an Ending: Studies in the Theory of Fiction*. Oxford: Oxford University Press, 1967.
Kerouac, Jack. *On the Road*. New York: Viking, 1957.
Kim, Jina B. "Cripping the Welfare Queen: The Radical Potential of Disability Politics." *Social Text* 39, no. 3 (September 2021): 79–101.
King, Martin Luther, Jr. "A Time to Break Silence (1967)." In *A Testament of Hope: The Essential Writings and Speeches of Martin Luther King, Jr.*, edited by James Melvin Washington, 232–233. San Francisco: Harper, 1986.
King, Tiffany Lethabo. *The Black Shoals: Offshore Formations of Black and Native Studies*. Durham, NC: Duke University Press, 2019.
Klein, Naomi. "Dancing the World into Being: A Conversation with Idle No More's Leanne Simpson." *Yes! Magazine*, March 5, 2013. https://www.yesmagazine.org/social-justice/2013/03/06/dancing-the-world-into-being-a-conversation-with-idle-no-more-leanne-simpson.
Klein, Norman. *History of Forgetting: Los Angeles and the Erasure of Memory*. London: Verso, 1997.
Kratz, Jessie. "Vietnam: the First Television War." *Pieces of History*. National Archives, January 25, 2018. prologue.blogs.archives.gov/2018/01/25/vietnam-the-first-television-war/.
Krieger, Murray. "The Ekphrastic Principle and the Still Moment of Poetry; or *Laokoon* Revisited." In *The Play and Place of Criticism*. Baltimore: Johns Hopkins University Press, 1967.
Kubrick, Stanley. *Dr. Strangelove*. Columbia Pictures, 1964.
———. *Full Metal Jacket*. Burbank, CA: Warner Bros., 1987.
Kurashige, Scott. *The Shifting Grounds of Race: Black and Japanese Americans in the Making of Multiethnic Los Angeles*. Princeton, NJ: Princeton University Press, 2008.
Lafia, John. *10.5*. Los Angeles: Hallmark Entertainment, 2004.
———. *10.5: Apocalypse*. Los Angeles: Hallmark Entertainment, 2006.
Lang, Fritz. *The Big Heat*. Culver City, CA: Columbia Pictures, 1953.
Larkin, Brian. "The Politics and Poetics of Infrastructure." *Annual Review of Anthropology* 42 (2013): 327–343.
Law, John. "What's Wrong with a One-World World?" *Distinktion: Scandinavian Journal of Social Theory* 16, no. 1 (2015): 126–139.
Lebow, Richard Ned. *Between Peace and War: The Nature of International Crisis*. Baltimore: Johns Hopkins University Press, 1981.
Lee, Hsiu-chuan, and Cynthia Kadohata. "Interview with Cynthia Kadohata," *MELUS* 32, no. 2, Thresholds, Secrets, and Knowledge (Summer, 2007): 165–186.
Lethem, Jonathan. *Amnesia Moon*. San Diego: Harcourt Brace, 1995.
lê thi diem thúy. *The Gangster We Are All Looking For*. New York: Anchor Books, 2003.
———. "Shrapnel Shards on Blue Water." In *The Very Inside: An Anthology of Writing by*

Asian and Pacific Islander Lesbian and Bisexual Women, edited by Sharon Lin-Hing, 2–4. Toronto: Sister Vision Black Women and Women of Color Press, 1994.
Levinson, Barry. *Good Morning, Vietnam*. Burbank, CA: Touchstone Pictures, 1987.
Lieb, Michael. *Children of Ezekiel: Aliens, UFOs, the Crisis of Race, and the Advent of End Time*. Durham, NC: Duke University Press, 1998.
Liebesman, Jonathan. *Battle: Los Angeles*. Culver City, CA: Sony Pictures, 2011.
Lincoln, Bruce. *Emerging from the Chrysalis: Studies in Rituals of Women's Initiation*. Cambridge, MA: Harvard University Press, 1981.
Ling, Jinqi. *Across Meridians: History and Figuration in Karen Tei Yamashita's Transnational Novels*. Stanford, CA: Stanford University Press, 2012.
Littman, Lynne. *Testament*. Los Angeles: Paramount Pictures, 1983.
Liu, Robyn. "Governing Refugees 1919–1945." *Borderlands e-journal* 1, no. 1 (2002). www.borderlands.net.au.
Lomawaima, K. Tsianina. *They Called It Prairie Light The Story of the Chilocco Indian School*. Lincoln: University of Nebraska Press, 1994.
London, Jack. "The Unparalleled Invasion." In *Curious Fragments*, edited by Dale L. Walker. Port Jefferson, NY: Kenkat Press, 1976 (originally published 1906).
Lorde, Audre. "A Litany for Survival." In *The Collected Poems of Audre Lorde*. New York: W. W. Norton, 1978.
Los Angeles Department of City Planning. "A Parkway Plan for the City of Los Angeles and the Metropolitan Area." Los Angeles: Department of City Planning, 1941.
Lowe, Lisa. *The Intimacies of Four Continents*. Durham, NC: Duke University Press, 2015.
Lucks, Daniel S. *Selma to Saigon: The Civil Rights Movement and the Vietnam War*. Frankfort: University Press of Kentucky, 2014.
Lytle Hernández, Kelly. *City of Inmates: Conquest, Rebellion, and the Rise of Human Caging in Los Angeles, 1771–1965*. Chapel Hill: University of North Carolina Press, 2017.
MacDougall, Ranald. *The World, the Flesh and the Devil*. Beverly Hills, CA: Metro-Goldwyn-Mayer, 1959.
Martinez, Diana Jean Sandoval. "Concrete Colonialism: Architecture, Infrastructure, Urbanism, and the American Colonization of the Philippines." PhD diss, Columbia University, 2017.
Marx, Karl. *Capital: A Critique of Political Economy*. Vol. I. New York: Penguin Books, 1976.
Mathes, Carter. *Imagine the Sound: Experimental African American Literature After Civil Rights*. Minneapolis: University of Minnesota Press, 2015.
McCoy, Horace. *They Shoot Horses, Don't They*. London: Arthur Barker, 1935.
Melamed, Jodi. *Represent and Destroy: Rationalizing Violence in the New Racial Capitalism*. Minneapolis: University of Minnesota Press, 2011.
Meyer, Nicholas. *The Day After*. New York: American Broadcasting Company, 1983.
Meylor, Meagan. "Los Angeles as Post-National Palimpsest in Karen Tei Yamashita's *Tropic of Orange*." *Watermark* 10:152–160.
Mignolo, Walter D. *The Darker Side of the Renaissance*. Ann Arbor: University of Michigan Press, 2003 (originally published 1995).
Miklowitz, Gloria D. *After the Bomb*. New York: Scholastic, 1985.
Milland, Ray. *Panic in Year Zero!* Los Angeles: American International Pictures, 1962.
Miller, George T. *Tidal Wave: No Escape*. New York: American Broadcasting Company, 1997.
Miller, Jim. "Just Another Day in Paradise?" In *Under the Perfect Sun: The San Diego Tourists Never See*, edited by Mike Davis, Kelly Mayhew, and Jim Miller, 159–261. New York: New Press, 2003.

Mitchell, Timothy. *Carbon Democracy: Political Power in the Age of Oil*. London: Verso, 2011.
Mitchell, W.J.T. "Ekphrasis and the Other." *South Atlantic Quarterly* 91, no. 3 (Summer 1992): 695–719.
Mohanty, Chandra Talpade. "Cartographies of Struggle: Third World Women and the Politics of Feminism." In *Feminism without Borders: Decolonizing Theory, Practicing Solidarity*, 43–84. Durham, NC: Duke University Press, 2003.
Momaday, N. Scott, *House Made of Dawn*. New York: Harper and Row, 1968.
Morales, Alejandro. *The Brick People*. Houston: Arte Publico Press, 1988.
———. *The Rag Doll Plagues*. Houston: Arte Publico Press, 1992.
Moya, Paula. "'Remaking Human Being': Loving, Kaleidoscopic Consciousness in Helena María Viramontes's *Their Dogs Came with Them*." In *Theories of the Flesh: Latinx and Latin American Feminisms, Transformation, and Resistance*, edited by Andrea J. Pitts, Mariana Ortega, and José Medina, 135–156. New York: Oxford University Press, 2020.
Muñoz, Alicia. "Articulating a Geography of Pain: Metaphor, Memory, and Movement in Helena María Viramontes's *Their Dogs Came with Them*." *MELUS* 38, no. 2 (Summer 2013): 24–38.
Nava, Alejandro. *In Search of Soul: Hip-Hop, Literature, and Religion*. Oakland: University of California Press, 2017.
Needham, Andrew. *Power Lines: Phoenix and the Making of the Modern Southwest*. Princeton, NJ: Princeton University Press, 2014.
Nemser, Daniel. *Infrastructures of Race: Concentration and Biopolitics in Colonial Mexico*. Austin: University of Texas Press, 2017.
Nguyen, Viet Thanh. *Race and Resistance: Literature and Politics in Asian American*. Oxford: Oxford University Press, 1997.
———. "Refugee Memories and Asian American Critique." *Positions* 20 (2012): 911–942.
———. *The Sympathizer*. New York: Grove Press, 2015.
Nichols, Robert. *Theft Is Property!: Dispossession and Critical Theory*. Durham, NC: Duke University Press, 2019.
Octavia E Butler Papers (OEB) 3221. San Marino, CA: The Huntington Library.
Oh, Stella. "Crossing Borders, Locating Home: Ethical Responsibility in Karen Tei Yamashita's *Tropic of Orange*." In *Transnational Crossroads: Remapping the Americas and the Pacific*, edited by Camilla Fojas and Rudy P. Guevarra Jr. Lincoln: University of Nebraska Press, 2012.
Okanagan Traditional, "The Beginning and the End of the World."
Olivas, Daniel. "An Interview with Alejandro Morales Regarding His New Novel, 'River of Angels.'" *Los Angeles Review of Books*, December 10, 2014. https://lareviewofbooks.org/article/an-interview-with-alejandro-morales-regarding-his-new-novel-river-angels/.
———. "Interview with Helena María Viramontes." *La Bloga* (blog), April 2, 2007.
Omatsu, Glenn. "The 'Four Prisons' and the Movements of Liberation: Asian American Activism from the 1960s to the 1990s." In *The State of Asian America: Activism and Resistance in the 1990s*, edited by Karen Aguilar-San Juan. Boston: South End Press, 1994.
Ortiz, Simon J. "Towards a National Indian Literature: Cultural Authenticity in Nationalism." *MELUS* 8, no. 2, Ethnic Literature and Cultural Nationalism (Summer, 1981): 7–12.
Orwell, George. *Nineteen Eighty-Four*. London: Secker & Warburg, 1949.

Pagels, Elaine. *The Gnostic Gospels*. New York: Random House, 1979.
Painter, Nell Irvin. *Standing at Armageddon: A Grassroots History of the Progressive Era*. New York: W. W. Norton, 2008.
Pal, George. *The Time Machine*. Beverly Hills, CA: Metro-Goldwyn-Mayer, 1960.
Pelletier, Kevin. *Apocalyptic Sentimentalism: Love and Fear in U.S. Antebellum Literature*. Athens: University of Georgia Press, 2015.
Perkins, Senator George C. Sherman Indian School Museum and Archives. Riverside, California, July 18, 1901.
Peyton, Brad. *San Andreas*. Burbank, CA: Warner Bros., 2015.
Phillips, Kimberley L. *War! What Is It Good For?* Chapel Hill: The University of North Carolina Press, 2012.
Phu, Thy. "Double Capture: Native Americans in WRA Internment Photography." Special issue, *Amerasia Journal* 42, no. 1 (2016): 16–40.
Piatote, Beth. *Domestic Subjects: Gender, Citizenship, and Law in Native American Literature*. New Haven, CT: Yale University Press, 2013.
Piper, Karen. *Left in the Dust: How Race and Politics Created a Human and Environmental Tragedy in L.A.* New York: Palgrave MacMillan, 2006.
Polanski, Roman. *Chinatown*. Los Angeles: Paramount Pictures, 1974.
Pope, Tim. *The Crow: City of Angels*. Atlanta, GA: Turner Classic Movies, 1996.
Pratt, Richard Henry. "The Advantages of Mingling Indians with Whites." Proceedings of the National Conference of Charities and Corrections, 1892.
———. *Battlefield and Classroom: Four Decades with the American Indian, 1867–1904*, edited by Robert M. Utley. New Haven, CT: Yale University Press, 1964.
Primeau, Ronald. *Romance of the Road: The Literature of the American Highway*. Bowling Green, OH: Bowling Green State University Popular Press, 1996.
Raban, Jonathan. *Old Glory*. London: William Collins, 1981.
Reagon, Toshi, and Bernice Johnson Reagon. *Parable of the Sower*. Rock opera, 2020.
Reddy, Chandan. *Freedom with Violence: Race, Sexuality, and the US State*. Durham, NC: Duke University Press, 2011.
Reeves, Richard. *American Journey*. New York: Simon & Schuster, 1982.
Reid, R.F. *Three Centuries of American Rhetorical Discourse*. Prospect Heights, IL: Waveland, 1988.
Riceour, Paul. *The Rule of Metaphor: Multidisciplinary Studies of the Creation of Meaning in Language*. Toronto: University of Toronto Press, 1975.
Robinson, Cedric J. *Black Movements in America*. New York: Routledge, 1997.
Robinson, Charles Mulford. *The City Beautiful: Report to the Municipal Art Commission*. Los Angeles: W. J. Porter, 1909.
Robinson, Kim Stanley. *The Gold Coast*. New York: Tom Doherty Associates, 1988.
———. *Pacific Edge*. New York: Tom Doherty Associates, 1990.
———. *The Wild Shore*. New York: Tom Doherty Associates, 1984.
Rodriguez, Cristina M. "'Relentless Geography': Los Angeles' Imagined Cartographies in Karen Tei Yamashita's *Tropic of Orange*." *Asian American Literature: Discourses and Pedagogies* 8 (2017): 104–130.
Rodríguez, Juana María. *Queer Latinidad: Identity Practices, Discursive Spaces*. New York: New York University Press, 2003.
Rogen, Seth, and Evan Goldberg. *This is the End*. Culver City, CA: Sony Pictures, 2013.
Roosevelt, Theodore. "The Administration of the Island Possessions." Address at the Coliseum, Hartford, Connecticut, August 22, 1902.
———. *American Problems*. New York: Charles Scribner's Sons, 1926.

———. "The Expansion of the White Races." Address at the Celebration of the African Diamond Jubilee of the Methodist Episcopal Church, Washington, DC, January 18, 1909.

Rosenthal, Nicolas G. *Reimagining Indian Country: Native American Migration and Identity in Twentieth-Century Los Angeles*. Chapel Hill: University of North Carolina Press, 2012.

Rowe, John Carlos. "Eyewitness: Documentary Styles in the American Representations of Vietnam." In *The Vietnam War and American Culture*, edited by John Carlos Rowe and Rick Berg, 148–174. New York: Columbia University Press, 1989.

Rubenstein, Michael, Bruce Robbins, and Sophia Beal. "Infrastructuralism: An Introduction." Special issue, *Modern Fiction Studies* 61, no. 4 (2015): 576–585.

Rutare, Micho. *Meteor Apocalypse*. Burbank, CA: The Asylum, 2009.

Sadowski-Smith, Claudia. "The U.S.-Mexico Borderlands Write Back: Cross-Cultural Transnationalism in Contemporary U.S. Women of Color Fiction." *Arizona Quarterly* 57, no. 1 (2001): 91–112.

Sahagún, Louis. "Owens Lake: Former Toxic Dust Bowl Transformed into Environmental Success." *Los Angeles Times*, April 28, 2018. https://www.latimes.com/local/california/la-me-owens-lake-birds-20180425-story.html.

Sánchez, Joseph P. *El Camino Real de California: From Ancient Pathways to Modern Byways*. Albuquerque: University of New Mexico Press, 2019.

Sánchez-Tranquilino, Marcos. "Space, Power, and Youth Culture: Mexican American Graffiti Murals in East Los Angeles, 1972–1978." In *Chicano and Chicana Art: A Critical Anthology*, edited by Jennifer A. Gonzalez, C. Ondine Chavoya, Chon Noriega, and Terezita Romo, 278–291. Durham, NC: Duke University Press, 2019.

Sato, Gayle K. "Post-Redress Memory: A Personal Reflection on Manzanar Murakami." *Concentric: Literary and Cultural Studies* 39, no. 2 (September 2013): 119–135.

Sawhney, Deepak Narang. "Journey beyond the Stars: Los Angeles and Third Worlds." In *Unmasking L.A.: Third Worlds and the City*, edited by Deepak Narang Sawhney, 1–20. New York: Palgrave, 2002.

Schwarz, Maureen Trudelle. *Molded in the Image of Changing Woman: Navajo Views on the Human Body and Personhood*. Tucson: University of Arizona Press, 1997.

Scott, David. "Introduction: On the Archaeologies of Black Memory," *Small Axe* 12, no. 2 (June 2008): v–xvi.

———. "The Re-Enchantment of Humanism: An Interview with Sylvia Wynter." *Small Axe* 8, no. 120 (2000): 173–211.

Scott, David, and Sylvia Wynter. "The Re-Enchantment of Humanism: An Interview with Sylvia Wynter." *Small Axe* 8 (September 2000): 119–207.

Scott, Ridley. *Blade Runner*. Burbank, CA: Warner Bros., 1982.

Scudder, Horace E. *A History of the United States of America*. Philadelphia: J. W. Butler, 1884.

Sellers, Cleveland. Interview, May 10, 1989, University of North Carolina, Greensboro.

Sharpe, Christina. *In the Wake: On Blackness and Being*. Durham, NC: Duke University Press, 2016.

Shiel, M. P. *The Dragon*. London: Grant Richards, 1913.

———. *The Yellow Danger*. London: Grant Richards, 1898.

———. *The Yellow Wave*. London: Ward Lock, 1905.

Silko, Leslie Marmon. *Ceremony*. New York: Penguin Books, 1977.

Simone, AbdouMaliq. "People as Infrastructure: Intersecting Fragments in Johannesburg." *Public Culture* 16, no. 3 (2004): 407–429.

Singh, Nikhil. *Black Is a Country: Race and the Unfinished Struggle for Democracy.* Cambridge, MA: Harvard University Press, 2004.
Smith, Jack. *Damnation Alley.* Los Angeles: 20th Century Studios, 1977.
Soguk, Nevzat. *States and Strangers: Refugees and Displacements of Statecraft.* Minneapolis: University of Minnesota Press, 1999.
Soja, Edward. *Postmodern Geographies: The Reassertion of Space in Critical Social Theory.* London: Verso, 1989.
Soja, Edward, Rebecca Morales, and Goetz Wolff. "Urban Restructuring: An Analysis of Social and Spatial Change in Los Angeles." *Economic Geography* 59, no. 2 (1983): 195–230.
Sorin, Gretchen. *Driving While Black: African American Travel and the Road to Civil Rights.* New York: Liveright, 2020.
Spillers, Hortense. "Mama's Baby, Papa's Maybe: An American Grammar Book." In "Culture and Countermemory: The 'American' Connection." Special issue, *Diacritics* 17, no. 2 (Summer 1987): 64–81.
Steinbeck, John. *Travels with Charley.* New York: Penguin, 1962.
Stephens, Michelle. "Just in Time: Managing Fear and Anxiety at the End of the World." *History of the Present: A Journal of Critical History* 12, no. 1 (April 2022): 60–79.
Steward, Julian H. *Ethnography of the Owens Valley Paiute.* In University of California Publications in American Archaeology and Ethnology Vol. 33 (September 6, 1933), 233–336. Berkeley University of California Press.
———. *Myths of the Owens Valley Paiute.* In University of California Publications in American Archaeology and Ethnology Vol. 34 (1934–1936), edited by A. L. Kroeber, R. H. Lowie, and R. L. Olson, 355–440. Berkeley: University of California Press, 1937.
Stinnett, Duanne. *Gangs of the Dead.* Naples, FL: Outside Productions, 2006.
Stone, Oliver. *Born on the Fourth of July.* Universal City: Universal Pictures, 1989.
———. *Platoon.* Los Angeles: Orion Pictures, 1986.
Suzuki, Erin. *Ocean Passages: Navigating Pacific Islander and Asian American Literatures.* Philadelphia: Temple University Press, 2021.
Sze, Julie. "'Not by Politics Alone': Gender and Environmental Justice in Karen Tei Yamashita's *Tropic of Orange.*" *Bucknell Review* 44, no. 1 (2000): 29–42.
Taylor, Quintard. *In Search of the Racial Frontier: African Americans in the American West 1528–1990.* New York: W. W. Norton, 1998.
Temple, Thomas Workman, II. "Toypurina the Witch and the Indian Uprising at San Gabriel." *The Masterkey* 32, no. 5 (1958): 136–52.
Thompson, Kara. "Traffic Stops, Stopping Traffic: Race and Climate Change in the Age of Automobility." *ISLE: Interdisciplinary Studies in Literature and Environment* 24, no. 1 (Winter 2017): 92–112.
Tinker, George E. "Tracing a Contour of Colonialism: American Indians and the Trajectory of Educational Imperialism." Preface to Ward Churchill, *Kill the Indian, Save the Man: The Genocidal Impact of American Indian Residential Schools.* San Francisco: City Lights, 2004.
Tolliday, Philip. "The Power of the Present: Tillich on Messianism, Apocalypse and Redemption." In *Messianism, Apocalypse and Redemption 20th Century German Thought,* edited by Wayne Cristaudo and Wendy Baker, 273–292. Adelaide: ATF Press, 2006.
Tongson, Karen. *Relocations: Queer Suburban Imaginaries.* New York: NYU Press, 2011.
Tourneur, Jacques. *Nightfall.* Los Angeles: Columbia Pictures, 1956.

Trafzer, Clifford E., Jean A. Keller, and Lorene Sisquoc, eds. *Boarding School Blues: Revisiting American Indian Educational Experiences*. Lincoln: University of Nebraska Press, 2006.

Trinh T. Minh-Ha. *Women, Native, Other: Writing Postcoloniality and Feminism*. Bloomington: Indiana University Press, 2009.

Tu, Thuy Linh Nguyen. *Experiments in Skin: Race and Beauty in the Shadows of Vietnam*. Durham, NC: Duke University Press, 2021.

UNHCR (United Nations High Commissioner for Refugees). "Flight from Indochina." In *The State of the World's Refugees 2000: Fifty Years of Humanitarian Aid*. http:www.unhcr.org3ebf9bad0.html.

Villa, Raúl Homero. *Barrio Logos: Space and Place in Urban Chicano Literature and Culture*. Austin: University of Texas Press, 2000.

Vint, Sherryl. "Orange County: Global Networks in *Tropic of Orange*." *Science Fiction Studies* 39, no. 3 (November 2012): 401–414.

Viramontes, Helena María. "Scripted Language: Writing Is the Only Way I Know How to Pray." Lecture, Sage Chapel, November 11, 2009.

———. *Their Dogs Came with Them*. New York: Washington Square Press, 2007.

Viramontes, Helena María, Elisabeth Mermann-Jozwiak, and Nancy Sullivan. "You Carry the Border with You: Conversation with Helena María Viramontes." In *Conversations with Mexican American Writers: Languages and Literatures in the Borderlands*, edited by Elisabeth Mermann-Jozwiak and Nancy Sullivan, 79–94. Jackson: University Press of Mississippi, 2009.

Vizenor, Gerald. *Wordarrows: Indians and Whites in the New Fur Trade*. Minneapolis: University of Minnesota Press, 1978.

Vonnegut, Kurt. *Cat's Cradle*. New York: Holt, Rinehart and Winston, 1963.

Walcott, Rinaldo. "The Black Aquatic." *liquid blackness* 5, no. 1 (April 2021): 64–73.

Wald, Sarah D. "'Refusing to Halt': Mobility and the Quest for Spatial Justice in Helena María Viramontes's *Their Dogs Came with Them* and Karen Tei Yamashita's *Tropic of Orange*." *Western American Literature* 48, nos. 1 and 2 (Spring/Summer 2013): 70–89.

Wallace, King. *The Next War*. Washington, DC: Martyn Publishing House, 1892.

Wallace, Molly. "Tropics of Globalization: Reading the New North America." *Symploke* 9 (2001): 145–60.

Walton, John. *Western Times and Water Wars: State, Culture, and Rebellion in California*. Berkeley: University of California Press, 1993.

Washington, J.M. *A Testament of Hope: The Essential Writings of Martin Luther King, Jr.* San Francisco: Harper & Row, 1986.

Wehrey, Jane. *Voices from This Long Brown Land: Oral Recollections of Owens Valley Lives and Manzanar Pasts*. New York: Palgrave Macmillan, 2006.

Wei, Clarissa. "How the Owens Valley Paiute Made the Desert Bloom." PBS/SoCal, December 15, 2016. https://www.kcet.org/shows/tending-the-wild/how-the-owens-valley-paiute-made-the-desert-bloom.

Welles, Orson. *Touch of Evil*. Universal City, CA: Universal Pictures, 1958.

Wells, H. G. *The World Set Free*. New York: E. P. Dutton, 1914.

West, Nathanael. *The Day of the Locust*. New York: New Directions, 1939.

Westad, Odd Arne. *The Global Cold War: Third World Interventions and the Making of Our Times*. Boston: Cambridge University Press, 2005.

Wilder, Billy. *Double Indemnity*. Los Angeles: Paramount Pictures, 1944.

———. *Sunset Boulevard*. Los Angeles: Paramount Pictures, 1950.

Williams, Raymond. *Marxism and Literature*. Oxford: Oxford University Press, 1977.
Wilson, Shawn. *Research Is Ceremony: Indigenous Research Methods*. Halifax, Nova Scotia, Canada: Fernwood Publishing, 2008.
Worster, Donald. *Rivers of Empire: Water, Aridity, and the Growth of the American West*. Oxford: Oxford University Press, 1985.
Wynter, Sylvia. "1492: A New World View." in *Race, Discourse, and the Origin of the Americas: A New World View*, edited by Vera Lawrence Hyatt and Rex M. Nettelford, 5–57. Washington, DC: Smithsonian Press, 1995.
Wynter, Sylvia, and Katherine McKittrick. "Unparalleled Catastrophe for Our Species? Or, to Give Humanness a Different Future: Conversations." In *Sylvia Wynter: On Being Human as Praxis*, edited by Katherine McKittrick, 9–73. Durham, NC: Duke University Press, 2014.
Yamashita, Karen Tei. *Tropic of Orange*. Minneapolis, MN: Coffee House Press, 1997.
Yamashita, Wendi. "The Colonial and the Carceral: Building Relationships between Japanese Americans and Indigenous Groups in the Owens Valley." Special issue, *Amerasia Journal* 42, no. 1 (2016): 121–138.
Zamora, Lois Parkinson. *Writing the Apocalypse: Historical Vision in Contemporary U.S. and Latin American Fiction*. Cambridge: Cambridge University Press, 1989.
Zhou, Xiaojing. *City of Others: Reimagining Urban Spaces in Asian American Literature*. Seattle: University of Washington Press, 2014.
Zink, Amanda J. *Fictions of Western American Domesticity: Indian, Mexican, and Anglo Women in Print Culture, 1850–1950*. Albuquerque: University of New Mexico Press, 2018.

Index

Adams, Ansel, 45
Adams, David Wallace: on Indian boarding schools, 175n10; on outing programs, 109. *See also* Indian boarding schools
Adams, Henry, 143
adaptability, 37, 102, 111, 113, 118
Adorno, Theodor: on the conductor as imago, 43. *See also* conductor; music
aerospace: and Los Angeles, 8, 138–39. *See also* flight
Afrofuturism, 142–43. *See also* Butler, Octavia E.
Alarcón, Daniel Cooper: on the palimpsest, 22
Alexander, M. Jacqui: on the Middle Passage, 129; on migration, 137
Allan, Paula Gunn, 125
Almaguer, Tomás: on Mexicans' "group position," 162n5; on non-elite Mexicans and Indians, 31
Alter, Nora: on the Vietnam War, 80. *See also* Vietnam
American Indian Movement (AIM), 74
Anzaldúa, Gloria, 160n34
apocalypse, 1–6, 10, 14–16, 21; Biblical, 18, 144; Black apocalypticism, 139–40; and gender, 156n8; and regeneration, 3; and temporality, 6, 125, 144, 155n3; and transformation, 2, 13; and transition, 18; as unveiling, 2; and Vietnam, 69, 77–78; and writing, 1–3. *See also* doomsday
archipelagic thinking/imagination, 68–70, 73–76, 80. *See also* lê thi diem thúy
archive: and apocalypse, 163n10; of Octavia Butler, 127, 143; and capitalism, 33; and destruction, 27; elision from, 41; infrastructure as (and vice versa), 25, 27
Arvin, Maile, 124; on regeneration, 15, 149; on settler colonial whiteness in Hawaii, 178n56
Asad, Talal: on ritualization, 111–12, 177n27
assimilation, 18, 99–100, 104–5, 125; "benevolent," 178n56; and gender, 106–10; as redemption, 104. *See also* Indian boarding schools
Atlantic Ocean: and Black cultural production, 90

Bacock, Alan: on tribal water rights, 50
Baldwin, James: on *Uncle Tom's Cabin*, 176
Bambara, Toni Cade, 160n34
Banham, Reyner: on Los Angeles's freeway networks, 7. *See also* freeways
Beal, Francis, 160n34

Beam, Louis: memory (and white supremacy) of, 73. See also memory; white supremacy
Beckett, Samuel, 143
Belew, Kathleen: on post-Vietnam white nationalism, 73, 171n18. See also white supremacy; Vietnam
Belin, Esther, 6, 12–13, 15, 96, 99–125, 149–50, 154; "Atmospheric Correction," 102; childhood of, 99–100; *From the Belly of My Beauty*, 17, 101, 114, 117, 124; on the Indian boarding school system, 15–18; "In the Cycle of the Whirl," 99, 101, 117–23; and language, 118–20, 124; *Of Cartography*, 17, 101–2, 114, 124; and "the whirl," 101–2, 111; writing forms of, 117; and the UC Berkeley Ethnic Studies department, 121–23, 178n53
Berg, Rick: on Vietnam and the U.S. culture industry, 71. See also Vietnam
Bevel, Diane Nash: visit to Vietnam, 172n27. See also Vietnam
Biblical apocalypse, 18, 144. See also Revelation, book of
Blackhawk, Ned: on the portrayal of American Indians, 101
Black Panthers, 55, 74–75. See also race
Bojórquez, Charles "Chaz": on Mexican American gangs, 60; on Mexican American graffiti, 62. See also graffiti
breathing: the air of Los Angeles, 114; the air of war, 83; underwater, 38
Brecht, Bertolt: on Los Angeles, 10. See also Los Angeles
Brown, William Wells, 133
Bureau of Indian Affairs, 48, 100, 103, 174n3
Bush, George W., 156n8
Butler, Octavia E., 6, 12–13, 15, 149, 154; adaptations of the works of, 143, 182n32; *Bloodchild and Other Stories*, 142; childhood of, 127; and "disintegration," 127–37, 142, 144; *Fledgling*, 142–43, 182n32; *Kindred*, 142–43; *Parable* series, 142, 146; *Parable of the Sower*, 18, 125, 127–47, 153, 182n32; *Patternist* series, 142; on race and science fiction, 130; research of, 15; *Xenogenesis* series, 142

Camp Pendleton, 69–70, 88–89. See also military; refugees; San Diego

Cardenas, Lázaro, 158n9
Carlisle Indian Industrial School, 105. See also Indian boarding schools
Carmichael, Stokely: on the Newark uprising, 172n27
catastrophe: clarity of, 1; multiplicity of, 2, 4; temporality of, 128; weather of, 15
Cather, Willa: and Western American domesticity, 176n19. See also domesticity
ceremony, 112–13. See also "Euro-American Womanhood Ceremony" (Belin)
change: as continual, 133, 141, 144; devotion to, 142; and entropy, 143; excuse for, 1; God as, 128, 133, 141–42, 145–46; inevitability of, 152–54; of name, 31–32; qualitative neutrality of, 144. See also transformation
Chen, Brian G.: on water in lê's *The Gangster We Are All Looking For*, 91. See also *Gangster We Are All Looking For, The* (lê); water
Chicano Power, 55–56
children: death of, 81–84, 93–94, 140; and labor, 108–9; removal of Indian, 105. See also family
Choi, Franny: on catastrophe, 1. See also catastrophe
Chuh, Kandice, 78
civil rights movement, 73–75, 127, 180n25. See also race
Cleage, Albert B., Jr., 139, 181n27
Clinton, Bill, 158n9. See also North American Free Trade Agreement (NAFTA)
Cold War: and brinksmanship, 156n8; and the visual, 70–80, 81, 84
Columbus, Christopher, 158n12; and the beginning of the end, 1–2
Combahee River Collective, 160n34
Commander, Michelle: on U.S. Black traveling culture, 133. See also mobility: Black
communities, 149; destruction of, 6, 17, 22, 88, 153; in *In the Heart of the Valley of Love* (Kadohata), 150, 152; in *Parable of the Sower* (Butler), 135–36, 146; temporary, 153
concrete: colonialism, 164n28; entombment within, 35–36; vs. freedom (of the river), 33; rainbows (freeways), 150–51; seawall, 89. See also Los Angeles Aqueduct

conductor: as shaman, 43–44, 51–52. *See also* freeways; music; *Tropic of Orange* (Yamashita)
Cone, James H., 139, 181n27
Congress of Racial Equality (CORE), 74
continuation, 1–2; and change, 133, 141, 144
conversion: religious, 29, 164n30; ideological, 175n14. *See also* Indian boarding schools
Coppola, Francis Ford: *Apocalypse Now*, 69, 73. *See also* film; Hollywood; Vietnam
Cortázar, Julio: *Hopscotch*, 42
Cottrell, Stephen: on the figure of the conductor, 43. *See also* conductor
Counter Intelligence Program (COINTELPRO), 74
Cowen, Deborah, 4; on infrastructure, 13. *See also* infrastructure
Crenshaw, Kimberle, 11
Cruz, Denise, 124; on transpacific femininities, 178n56
Cuevas, Jackie T.: on *Their Dogs Came with Them*, 55–56. *See also* *Their Dogs Came with Them* (Viramontes)

Davis, Angela, 160n34
Davis, Mike, 10–11; on literature featuring genocides, 164n23; on literature featuring Los Angeles's destruction, 10, 158n15; on Los Angeles, 11; on Los Angeles roads and freeways, 7
death: of children, 81–84, 93–94, 140; of a parent, 127, 150; non-combatant, 81–82; premature, 14, 62–63; social, 129; of the universe, 143–44; and water, 81–84, 87, 93–94, 167n51, 182n4. *See also* mourning
Denetdale, Jennifer Nez: on the Kinaaldá ritual, 110. *See also* Kinaaldá (ceremony)
Derrida, Jacques: on the archive, 27, 163n10. *See also* archive
destruction: and the archive, 27; of communities, 6, 17, 22, 88, 153; and democracy, 72; and growth, 82–83; as "investment," 33; and Los Angeles, 10, 14–15, 107, 158n15; and perfection, 2; and realignment, 85; and regeneration, 4–5, 15, 18–19, 22, 140, 149; and the sea, 87; and transformation, 2
Didion, Joan: on the death of Los Angeles, 15; on driving in Los Angeles, 7, 15, 174n5; *Play It as It Lays*, 174n5

Dinétah, 6, 16, 18, 99–101, 109, 114–15, 149, 174n2
dislocation, 4, 9, 15, 24, 32, 44, 48, 56–59, 63, 68, 84, 93, 134, 167n59. *See also* refugees
Disney, Walt, 138. *See also* flight
dogs: becoming, 63; weaponized, 58, 63; wounded, 153. *See also* *Their Dogs Came with Them* (Viramontes)
domesticity: apocalyptic, 114, 125; and gender, 106–10, 124, 177n27, 178n56; and progress, 108
doom: doomsday, 1–2, 18–19, 143; and Los Angeles, 4–6. *See also* apocalypse
Douglas, Donald, 138. *See also* flight
Douglass, Frederick, 133
drought, 6, 40, 64, 154. *See also* floods; water
Du Bois, W. E. B.: on driving, 130–31. *See also* mobility: Black
Dudziak, Mary, 156n8
Dulles, John Foster: and "brinksmanship," 156n8. *See also* Cold War
Duncan, Dayton, 130

Earhart, Amelia, 138. *See also* flight
earthquakes, 57, 62, 132; and Los Angeles, 3, 6, 10, 14, 40
Eaton, Fred: and the LADWP, 165n37. *See also* Los Angeles; water
education: and class, 122; and gender, 106, 108–9; and incarceration, 127; Indian, 111, 113. *See also* Indian boarding schools
Eisenhower, Dwight D., 156n8
ekphrasis, 17, 70, 78, 96. *See also* lê thi diem thúy
endlessness: of ceremony, 113; of refugee worldmaking, 70–71, 87; of warfare, 80–81, 83–84, 92
end of the world, 1–3, 5–6, 12, 15, 18, 21, 32, 72, 74, 94, 135–36, 141, 143–44, 147, 156n5, 156n8. *See also* apocalypse
entropy, 18, 128, 141, 143–44, 153
Environmental Protection Agency (EPA), 168n73. *See also* pollution
Equiano, Olaudah, 133
erasure, 25–27; and "beginnings," 40; and memorialization, 47–48; Native, 44–45, 88, 107, 120–24, 129, 177n27; Vietnamese, 72
Escobar, Arturo: on Los Angeles, 13. *See also* Los Angeles

Espiritu, Yến Lê: on Vietnamese refugees, 86, 90; on the Vietnam War, 80. *See also* refugees; Vietnam
"Euro-American Womanhood Ceremony" (Belin), 106–12. *See also From the Belly of My Beauty* (Belin)
extinction: cultural, 16
extraction, resource, 9, 17, 28, 100–102, 114–15, 165n35
eyes: crying, 58, 156n6; of the destitute, 131; lizard, 38; (famously) sad, 78; Zapata, 27

failure: for Butler, 127; for and Los Angeles, 4–5, 14; of Southern California, 104; of state governance, 6; of U.S. imperialism, 69; and visibility, 13
family, 79; broken, 147; and education, 111; excision from, 93; and photography, 77–79, 84–86, 92–93; and war, 105; and water, 67–68, 90–91. *See also* children; kinship
Farrakhan, Louis, 139–40, 181n28
fatalism, 3
Ferber, Edna: and Western American domesticity, 176n19. *See also* domesticity
Ferguson, Roderick, 11
Ferreira da Silva, Denise: on Black emancipation and temporality, 5
film: disaster (and Los Angeles), 6, 159n28. *See also* Hollywood
fires: and Los Angeles, 6, 10, 15, 40, 154
Fixico, Donald, 101
flight, 137–39. *See also* levitation; space
floods, 3, 10, 30, 33, 48–49, 137, 154, 168n73; abatement of, 22; Biblical, 120; of tears, 58. *See also* drought; water
Four Corners region, 100, 102, 124; Four Corners Generating Station, 114–15
Francisco, Nia, 125
freedom: and the automobile, 130–31, 133, 179n10; Cold War narratives of, 69; and literacy, 133; of the river, 33; and sociality, 79
freeways, 6–7, 9, 17–18, 22–23, 128–29, 150–52; and car accidents, 42, 51; and community-destruction, 6, 17, 22, 88, 153; conducting the, 42–44; and connection, 151; disintegration of, 129–33; and displacement, 58–59; and literary function of, 14; and migration, 128; as palimpsest, 51, 56–57; as pathways to other worlds, 144; reclamation of (by Butler), 137; and record-keeping, 24, 27; and reflection, 151–52; as river, 136–37; and segregation, 14, 54, 58–59; as site of struggle, 51; and spatial control, 54; and temporality, 59; as water, 152. *See also* mobility; roads
From the Belly of My Beauty (Belin), 17, 101, 114, 117, 124; "Directional Memory," 114; "Euro-American Womanhood Ceremony," 106–12; "In the Cycle of the Whirl," 99, 101, 117–23; "Night Travel," 114. *See also* Belin, Esther
Fukuyama, Francis: on the end of history, 156n8; on History, 3. *See also* history

Gandhi, Evyn Lê Espiritu, 69; on water, 174n62. *See also* water
Gangster We Are All Looking For, The (lê), 17, 67–96, 147, 170n7. *See also* lê thi diem thúy
gender: and apocalypse, 156n8; and domesticity, 106–10, 124, 177n27, 178n56; and education, 106, 108–9; and labor, 27–28, 30–31, 106–7; and Manifest Destiny, 35; and morality, 107; and progress, 108; and road trips, 112; and safety, 134; and white futurity, 34; and white supremacy, 171n18
gentrification, 6; as *gentefication*, 4
Gilroy, Paul, 46; on the ocean, 90
Glissant, Édouard: on archipelagic thinking, 68–69
Gnosticism, 141–42
God: as change, 128, 133, 141–42, 145–46; and history, 156n5; personification of, 144–45; as savior, 104; wrath of, 107–8, 176n24. *See also* messianism
Goeman, Mishuana: on U.S. global expansion and Native people, 124
Goldwater, Barry: on resource extraction from Native lands, 115. *See also* extraction, resource
good: vs. evil, 3, 136; refugee, 85–86
Goodyear-Ka'ōpua, Noelani, 124; on settler colonial whiteness in Hawaii, 178n56
graffiti, 60–62; and boundaries, 61; and reclamation, 60–61
Graham, Billy, 156n7
Grant, Ulysses S.: and Native "assimilation," 104. *See also* assimilation

Griffith, Griffith J., 138. *See also* flight
guerilla warfare, 75, 172n27
Gulf of Tonkin Resolution, 173n47
Gumprecht, Blake: on rights to the Los Angeles River, 163n21. *See also* Los Angeles River; water

Halberstam, Jack: on queer subjects, 25
Hall, Harwood: and the Sherman Institute, 103–4. *See also* Sherman Institute
Harjo, Joy, 125
Harkabi, Yehosephat: on brinksmanship, 156n8
Harrison, Jim, 130
Hartman, Saidiya: on the archive, 27. *See also* archive
healing, 113–14
history, 3; Chicano, 32; end of, 156n8; end of the drama of, 176n22; God and, 156n5
Hollywood, 8, 11, 67; driving through, 152; and the portrayal of Vietnam, 69–73, 80–81. *See also* film
home: for Dinétah, 114; returning, 101, 122–25, 146
Hong, Grace, 11–12
hope: in chaos, 156n7; in crisis, 153; endings and, 147; in God, 180n25; of permanence, 61–62; reimagination of, 150
Hughes, Howard, 138. *See also* flight
Huntington, Henry, 39. *See also* Los Angeles Aqueduct

incarceration, 29; and education, 127; and graffiti, 60; Japanese, 4, 6, 24, 40, 44–48, 100, 182n4; and Los Angeles, 4, 6, 9; Native, 102–3, 105, 125
Indian boarding schools, 6, 8, 15–18, 96, 103, 105–6, 121, 175n10, 177n27. *See also* erasure: Native; Sherman Institute
Indian New Deal, 105
Indian Relocation Act, 99–100, 178n56
Indian Reorganization Act, 105
Indian Wars, 167n51
infrastructure: as archive (and vice versa), 25, 27; of automobility, 132–33; becoming, 36; and domination, 13, 47; as fluid, 154; invisible operations of, 13; as method of inquiry, 3; military, 67–96, 149; as palimpsest, 3, 13, 21–64, 149; people as, 23; postapocalyptic, 127–47; race as, 30; as relational, 12–14; of resettlement, 67–96; of separation, 93; as site of contestation, 6; as taken for granted, 14; of termination, 18, 99–125; and transformation, 13–14
Institute of American Indian Arts (IAIA), 102, 113, 123
intersectionality, 11
In the Heart of the Valley of Love (Kadohata), 18, 150–54. *See also* Kadohata, Cynthia

Jacobs, Harriet, 133
Jacobs, Margaret: on the weaponization of kinship, 105. *See also* kinship
Jameson, Fredric: on the modern Western symphony, 46
Japanese: incarceration, 4, 6, 24, 40, 44, 46–48, 100; legislation against, 166n49. *See also* Manzanar Concentration Camp
Jim Crow, 130, 134. *See also* segregation
Johnson, Lyndon: and the Vietnam War, 173n47. *See also* Vietnam
Joyce, Patrick: on infrastructure, 13. *See also* infrastructure

Kadohata, Cynthia, 6, 12–13, 15; childhood of, 153, 182n4; *In the Heart of the Valley of Love*, 18, 150–54; *The Floating World*, 153; *kira-kira*, 153; and traveling, 152–53; *Weedflower*, 153
Kaplan, Amy: on U.S. foreign policy and civilizing projects, 124
Kauanui, J. Kēhaulani, 124; on settler colonial whiteness in Hawaii, 178n56
Kermode, Frank: on crisis, 19; on the End (for theologians), 155n3; on the end of historicity, 156n7
Kerouac, Jack, 130–31
Kim, Jina B.: on infrastructure, 13. *See also* infrastructure
Kinaaldá (ceremony), 109–11. *See also* Dinétah
King, Martin Luther, Jr.: "I Have a Dream" speech, 180n25; on space-program spending, 139; on the Vietnam War, 75
King, Rodney, 11
kinship, 149; intergalactic, 139; and Vietnam, 70, 79–86; weaponization of, 105–6, 117, 175n13. *See also* family
Kinunway, Lionel: on ceremony, 113. *See also* ceremony

Klein, Norman: on Los Angeles, 11. *See also* Los Angeles
Kubrick, Stanley: *Full Metal Jacket*, 72–73. *See also* film; Vietnam

labor: Black (during WWII), 134; child, 108–9; communal, 50; exploitation, 29–30, 88, 108–9, 175n14; and gender, 27–28, 30–31, 106–7; and race, 35; repetition of, 111
Lange, Dorothea, 45
language: ambiguity of, 87; and connection, 119; of the enemy, 117–20; feeling, 118; figurative, 70–71, 76–79, 82–85, 89, 91, 93–95; games, 77; and memory, 82; as obscuring, 76; silencing of, 99, 121–22; and stasis, 77–78
Last of Us, The (Mazin, Druckmann), 131
Law, John, 161n44
Lee, Jarena, 133
Léon-Portilla, Miguel: on freeway-building (as another moment of conquest), 58
lê thi diem thúy, 6, 12–13, 15; childhood of, 71; figurative language of, 70–71, 76–79, 82–85, 89, 91, 93–95; *The Gangster We Are All Looking For*, 17, 67–96, 147, 170n7; "Shrapnel Shards on Blue Water," 76; on Vietnam, 76
levitation: and survival, 26, 63–64, 152. *See also* flight; *Their Dogs Came with Them* (Viramontes)
Lieb, Michael: on Black retribution against white injustice, 140. *See also* race
Liebesman, Jonathan: on the enjoyment of Los Angeles's destruction, 10
Lippincott, J. B., 165n37. *See also* Los Angeles Aqueduct
Lomawaima, K. Tsianina: on Indian boarding schools, 177n27. *See also* Indian boarding schools
looting, 51
Lorde, Audre, 12
Los Angeles: and aerospace, 8, 138–39; as alienating, 101; and apocalypse, 10; as awesome/astonishing, 114; and destruction, 10, 14–15, 107, 158n15; and disaster, 5–6, 40; and doomsday, 4–6; and driving, 7, 15; as ever-changing, 150; and fires, 6, 10, 15, 40, 154; freeways, 6–7, 9, 17–18, 22–23, 128–29, 138; and "the good life," 10; as imperial metropole, 64, 68; and incarceration, 4, 6, 9; as living city, 44; and Mexican Americans, 164; and the military, 8–9, 17, 69–70, 149; and noir, 10–11, 14, 40, 107; as port city, 170n101; and racial uprisings, 4, 10–11, 14–15, 40; and resource extraction, 9; savage beauty of, 150, 153; and science fiction, 138; and segregation, 4, 40, 165n35; and toxic waste, 174n6; as urban Indian capital of the U.S., 100; and white supremacy, 10, 159n23, 164n23
Los Angeles Aqueduct, 6–8, 17, 22–24, 38–40, 44, 49–50, 59, 154, 165n35. *See also* concrete
Los Angeles Department of Water and Power (LADWP), 165n37, 168n73. *See also* water
Los Angeles River, 6–8, 17, 21–39, 53, 59, 163n21; kindness of, 37; as living river, 28–30, 39; and pollution, 22, 35; and segregation, 32; suppression of, 34–35
Lummis, Charles: on Southern California, 159n23
Lytle Hernández, Kelly: on Los Angeles and Anglo settler society, 9, 163n15; on policing in LA's Black belt areas, 134

Malcolm X, 139–40, 181n27
Manifest Destiny, 10, 34–35, 108, 115, 123–24
Manzanar Concentration Camp, 6, 24, 44, 46–48. *See also* Japanese: incarceration
Martinez, Diana Jean Sandoval: on concrete colonialism, 164n28. *See also* concrete
Marx, Karl, 12
matrilineality: in Belin's "In the Cycle of the Whirl," 117–23; in Morales's *River of Angels*, 36–37. *See also* motherhood; *River of Angels* (Morales)
McCarthy, Cormac, 143; *The Road*, 131
McKinley, William: on "benevolent assimilation," 178n56; and U.S. imperial domination, 92
memorialization, 44–48; and erasure, 47–48. *See also* memory
memory: "Directional Memory" (Belin), 114; in *The Gangster We Are All Looking For* (lê), 95–96; haptic, 118; and language, 82; and objects, 57; in "Study on the Road to Los Angeles" (Belin), 116; and war, 73. *See also* memorialization

messianism, 104, 106, 108, 129–30, 140–42, 144, 156n5, 176n22. See also God
Meyer, Dillon S., 48. See also Bureau of Indian Affairs; War Relocation Authority
Middle Passage, 18, 129, 133, 135
Mignolo, Walter: on the pluriverse, 161n44
military: and San Diego, 8, 17, 64, 69–71, 88, 149. See also Camp Pendleton
Miller, Frank: and the Sherman Institute, 104. See also Sherman Institute
Minh-Ha, Trinh T.: on *The Gangster We Are All Looking For*, 84. See also *Gangster We Are All Looking For, The* (lê)
miscegenation, 34–36, 73
Mississippi Democratic Freedom Party, 74
Mitchell, W.J.T.: on ekphrasis, 78. See also ekphrasis
mobility, 18; Black, 129–47, 179n10; criminalized, 133–34; decolonial/Native, 112–125, 149; immobility of termination, 102–12; social, 133. See also running; walking
Mohanty, Chandra Talpade, 11
Momaday, N. Scott: *House Made of Dawn*, 101
Moraga, Cherríe, 12, 160n34
Morales, Alejandro, 6, 12–13, 15, 149, 154, 162n8; *The Brick People*, 162n8; *The Rag Doll Plagues*, 162n8; *River of Angels*, 17, 22–39, 41, 53, 56, 64, 146
motherhood, 117–23; and race, 107. See also matrilineality
mourning, 31, 58, 123; birth and, 83. See also death
Moya, Paula: on *Their Dogs Came with Them*, 56–57. See also *Their Dogs Came with Them* (Viramontes)
Muhammad, Elijah, 139–40, 181n28
Muhammad, Wallace Fard: cosmogony of, 139–40
Mulholland, William, 39, 50, 165n37. See also Los Angeles Aqueduct
music, 8, 44–46, 56, 60, 111; and sociality, 44; and temporality, 45–46. See also conductor; song; sound
Myer, Dillon: on relocation, 100

name: change/loss of, 31–32; hardening of, 62; sound of one's, 85; summoning by, 103; as tree, 84
napalm, 81–82, 86, 92, 94–95. See also Vietnam

National Association for the Advancement of Colored People (NAACP), 74–75. See also race
National Liberation Front (NLF), 75
Nation of Islam, 74; apocalyptic vision of, 139–40, 181n28
Natipadab, Suvad Anthony, 170n95, 170n97
Needham, Andrew: on the beginning of "urban time," 58; on the Termination era and resource extraction, 115
Nemser, Daniel: on infrastructure, 12; on infrastructure scholarship, 13; on race, 30
neoliberalism: and Christian millenarianism, 3
Nguyen, Patricia, 69
Nguyen, Viet Thanh: on American movies (and the rest of the world), 67; on Hollywood and Vietnam, 72; on water and refugees, 173n58. See also Hollywood; refugees; Vietnam
Nichols, Robert: on recursion, 26, 46
North American Free Trade Agreement (NAFTA), 3, 40, 158n9
Northrop, John, 138. See also flight

Of Cartography (Belin), 17, 101–2, 114, 124; "Atmospheric Correction," 102; "Study on the Road to Los Angeles," 114–17. See also Belin, Esther
Ortiz, Simon J.: on Indigenous use of colonialist languages, 119. See also language: of the enemy
Otis, Harrison Gray, 39. See also Los Angeles Aqueduct
Owens Valley, 6, 17, 22, 24, 38–40, 44, 46–49, 115, 165n35, 165n37, 167n59; Lake, 39–40, 154; as palimpsest, 48; and pollution, 168n73; poisoning of, 40. See also Paiute; water

Pagels, Elaine: on Gnostic writing, 142. See also Gnosticism
Paiute, 6, 17, 22, 24, 40, 47–50, 167n51, 167n59, 168n71; creation story of, 49–50; diet of, 49–50; and memorialization, 47; and sovereignty, 48; and water, 49–50, 115, 168n63. See also Owens Valley
palimpsest: Los Angeles's infrastructure as, 3, 13, 21–64, 149; Los Angeles River as, 33; Owens Valley as, 48; and temporality, 61–62

Panama Canal, 170n101
Panikkar, Raymundo: on the pluriverse, 161n44
Parable of the Sower (Butler), 18, 125, 127–47, 153, 182n32. *See also* Butler, Octavia E.
parables, 180n18; and the truth, 136–37
paradise, 2; Southern California as, 104, 159n23
Parker, William: on the Watts Uprising, 172n26
passing: gendered, 134; racial, 30–31
paternalism, 105–8; federal, 105, 111, 108, 110–11
pedagogy of the road, 112–23. *See also* Belin, Esther; mobility
Pelletier, Kevin: on justice for Stowe, 176n22; on the genealogy of sentimentalism, 107. *See also* sentimentalism, apocalyptic
Pendleton, Camp. *See* Camp Pendleton
Perkins, Senator George C.: on the Sherman Institute, 104. *See also* Sherman Institute
Philp, Kenneth R., 101
photography: photojournalism, 43–44, 48, 70–81; and spatiality, 79; and temporality, 27, 78–79
Phu, Thy: on the War Relocation Authority, 47
Piatote, Beth: on Indian wars and Indian families, 105
pluriversality, 161n44
Polanski, Roman: *Chinatown*, 40
pollution: of Los Angeles (smog), 103, 114; of the Los Angeles River, 22, 35; of the Owens Valley, 40, 168n73; and space, 115; of Vietnam, 80
Pratt, Captain Richard Henry: assimilation philosophy of, 105; on Black troops, 175n14. *See also* assimilation; Indian boarding schools
progress: Biblical notion of, 104; and domesticity, 108; fear and, 5; freeways as symbol of, 59; and gender, 108; and spatiality, 5; and temporality, 8, 11, 102
Puerto Rican Socialist Party, 74
Pynchon, Thomas, 143

Raban, Jonathan, 130
race: and citizenship, 166n49; as infrastructure, 30; and labor, 35; and mobility, 129–47; and motherhood, 107; racial order, 163n15; racial uprisings, 4, 10–11, 14–15, 40; and science fiction, 130; and the Vietnam War, 75. *See also* Black Panthers; civil rights movement; Jim Crow; National Association for the Advancement of Colored People (NAACP)
rainbows, 150–51
Raymond, Evelyn Hunt: and Western American domesticity, 176n19. *See also* domesticity
Reagan, Ronald, 156n8
record-keeping: and infrastructure, 24–25; and the Los Angeles River, 33
recursion, 26, 46
Reddy, Chandan, 11
Reeves, Richard, 130
refugees: "good," 85–86; as heterogenous, 90; and Indigenous people, 174n62; and sociality, 91, 96; and water, 173n58; and worldmaking, 67–96. *See also Gangster We Are All Looking For, The* (lê); Vietnam
regeneration: apocalypse and, 3; as creative work, 153; and destruction, 4–5, 15, 18–19, 22, 140, 149; and the jungle, 80; settler narratives of, 7; and urban Indian spaces, 125; and women of color feminism, 109–13
relationality, 6–7, 11–14; and infrastructure, 12–14; and metaphor, 77–78; and women of color feminism, 11–12, 160n34
repetition: in "Euro-American Womanhood Ceremony," 109; in *The Gangster We Are All Looking For*, 85, 95; of labor, 111. *See also From the Belly of My Beauty* (Belin); *Gangster We Are All Looking For, The* (lê)
resource extraction, 9, 17, 28, 100–102, 114–15, 165n35
return: of the disappeared, 38; home, 101, 122–25, 146; lack of (to "normal" life), 146
Revelation, book of, 1–3, 108, 156nn5–7. *See also* Biblical apocalypse
Riceour, Paul, 77
ritualization, 111–12, 177n27
River of Angels (Morales), 17, 22–39, 41, 53, 56, 64, 146. *See also* Morales, Alejandro

roads: disintegrating, 129–33; Indigenous, 8–9, 137. See also freeways; mobility
Rodriguez Cabrillo, Juan, 9
Rodriguez, Juana María: on queer subjects, 25
Rogers, Michael: on giving back in Native American culture, 39
Roosevelt, Theodore: on the "awakening of the Orient," 170n101; on the conflict between Los Angeles and Owens Valley, 165n37; and the logic of taking, 165n35; on urbanization and Native Americans, 39
running: and womanhood, 109–11. See also mobility; walking

Salinas de Gortari, Carlos, 158n9. See also North American Free Trade Agreement (NAFTA)
San Diego, 6, 77, 79, 86, 90–96; and the military, 8, 17, 64, 69–71, 88, 149; and resettlement, 67, 69–70, 88–89; and segregation, 89. See also Camp Pendleton; *Gangster We Are All Looking For, The* (lê)
Sato, Gayle K.: on Yamashita's *Tropic of Orange*, 45. See also *Tropic of Orange* (Yamashita)
Sato, Rob: on *arco iris*, 151
savagery: as trope/stereotype, 31, 39, 104, 107–8, 124
Scott, David: on the archive, 33. See also archive
segregation: and freeways, 14, 54, 58–59; and Los Angeles, 4, 40, 165n35; and public transportation, 32, 130; and San Diego, 89. See also Jim Crow; race
sentimentalism, apocalyptic, 106–8, 110, 176n22
Sherman, Moses, 39. See also Los Angeles Aqueduct
Sherman Institute, 6, 96, 99, 102–4, 106, 108–9, 123, 177n27; cemetery, 123. See also Indian boarding schools
Shuler, Bob: on Los Angeles as Anglo-Saxon city, 164n23
silencing: via irony, 123; of language/voice, 99, 121–22
Silko, Leslie Marmon, 124; *Ceremony*, 101

Simpson, Leanne: on regeneration, 15
Smith, Amanda, 133
sociality, 4, 135; and freedom, 79; and music, 44; and refugees, 91, 96; of the train, 12; and Vietnam, 70
song: salt songs, 123–24; silencing of, 99; as story, 84. See also music; sound
Sorin, Gretchen: on Black American travel post-Emancipation, 133. See also mobility: Black
sound, 43–46; and Black fugitive resistance, 46; playing with, 85. See also music; song
Southern Christian Leadership Conference (SCLC), 74
sovereignty: Indigenous claims of, 9, 47–48, 88–90, 100, 113–14, 120, 125, 17n56; and the sea, 87
space: and the Cold War, 139; and colonization, 131, 139; travel, 8, 130–31, 139. See also flight; *Parable of the Sower* (Butler)
spatiality: and photography, 79; and progress, 5
Steinbeck, John, 130
Steward, Julian H.: on the Paiute and water, 168n63. See also Paiute; water
Stone, Elinore Cowan: and Western American domesticity, 176n19. See also domesticity
Stowe, Harriet Beecher: on justice, 176n22
Student Nonviolent Coordinating Committee (SNCC), 74–75, 172n27
"Study on the Road to Los Angeles" (Belin), 114–17. See also *Of Cartography* (Belin)
Suri, Jeremi: on global rebellions, 75
survival, 149; Black feminist, 127–47; and familial reimagination, 90; under genocidal policies, 99–125; and levitation, 26, 63–64, 152; literary, 12; and prayer, 118; refugee, 77–78, 85, 95–96; and voice, 89
Suzuki, Erin, 69
synesthesia, 84

Tapahonso, Luci, 125
Taylor, Quintard: on the West for nineteenth-century Black Americans, 134

temporality: antediluvian, 120; apocalyptic, 6, 125, 144, 155n3; the beginning and the end, 1–2; and Black emancipation, 5; capitalist, 5, 116; of catastrophe, 128; of cyclical, 37, 46; desert time, 116; entropic time, 144–45; eschatological, 180n25; and the freeways, 59; and gang graffiti, 61–62; and infrastructures of automobility, 132–33; of lê's *The Gangster We Are All Looking For*, 89–90; and liberalism's racial order, 14; linear, 5–6, 8, 15–16, 116; and music, 45–46; and photographs, 27, 78–79; and progress, 8, 11, 102; and the residual, 15; settlement, 90; and simultaneity, 130; stopped time, 87; and typography, 116; urban time, 58; and Vietnam, 72; of war, 83–84; and water, 86 within, 45, 47; and the freeway, 24, 43–44, 51–52, 54, 56; and hypertextuality, 41–43; and temporality, 44–47. *See also* Yamashita, Karen Tei

Truman, Harry S., 156n8

truth: change as, 128; and parables, 136–37

Tu, Thuy Linh Nguyen: on post-war Vietnam, 80; on Vietnam War photography, 72–73. *See also* photography; Vietnam

termination: infrastructure of, 18, 99–125; immobility of, 102–12

Thatcher, Margaret, 156n8

theft: of land, 44, 48; of water, 17, 22, 38–40, 48, 115, 163n21, 165n37

Their Dogs Came with Them (Viramontes), 17, 22–26, 54–64, 152; character count of, 56; and the freeway, 24. *See also* Viramontes, Helena María

Third World radicalism, 74–75, 121–22

Tinker, George E.: on Indian boarding school's weaponization of kinship, 105

Tongson, Karen: on Riverside, California, 104

Tongva, 8–9, 16–17, 23, 31, 36, 163n19; cosmology, 29–30; and the Los Angeles River, 21

Toypurina, 36, 164n30

transformation: and apocalypse, 2, 13; and Black imagination, 137; Changing Woman (Diné), 110; through destruction, 2; disappearance as, 103; of East Los Angeles, 57; and infrastructure, 13–14; in *In the Heart of the Valley of Love* (Kadohata), 150; of landscape, 48–49; and lê's figurative language, 89; linear logic of, 128; music and, 44; and the sea, 94; and Yamashita's *Tropic of Orange*, 41. *See also* change

Trask, Haunani-Kay, 124; on settler colonial whiteness in Hawaii, 178n56

Treaty of Guadalupe Hidalgo, 162n5

Tropic of Orange (Yamashita), 1–4, 17, 22–26, 40–54, 56–57, 62, 64, 147; absences

UC Berkeley Ethnic Studies department, 102, 113, 120–23. *See also* erasure: Native

unhoused, the: claiming the right to the city (in Yamashita's *Tropic of Orange*), 51; and the freeways (in Butler's *Parable of the Sower*), 135; and the state (in Yamashita's *Tropic of Orange*), 45, 47, 52–53

university, the. *See* UC Berkeley Ethnic Studies department

urban blight, 59–60

urban Indian, 99–103, 109, 112–14, 122, 125. *See also* Belin, Esther

urbanization, 39

Urban League, 75

Ut, Nick: and the "Napalm Girl," photograph, 81. *See also* photography; Vietnam

victims: American Indians seen as, 101, 105; Vietnamese seen as, 86, 96

Vietnam, 67–96, 173n47; and anticolonialism, 73–76; and apocalypse, 69, 77–78; as artful, 76–77; and Black soldiers, 75; Hollywood's portrayal of, 69–73, 80–81; and kinship, 70, 79–86; and napalm, 81–82, 86, 92, 94–95; as photograph, 77–79; post-war ecology of, 80; and sociality, 70; and temporality, 72; Vietnamese Revolution, 75

Villa, Raúl Homero: on the legacy of Los Angeles's freeway construction, 59; on Los Angeles and Chicano history, 32; on Viramontes's political commitments, 54

Viramontes, Helena María, 6, 12–13, 15, 149, 154; on her commitment to writing, 62; on the impetus for writing *Their Dogs*, 63; political commitments of, 54; *Their Dogs Came with Them*, 17, 22–26, 54–64, 152

visuality: and the Chinese language, 119; and the Cold War, 70–80, 81, 84. *See also* photography
Vizenor, Gerald, 124
voice: collective, 122; of the river, 28–30; silencing of, 99, 121–22; strength of, 110; and survival, 89; "touch" of the, 85; and vision, 84; of Yamashita's characters, 43
von Braun, Wernher, 138. *See also* flight

walking: on the freeway, 131, 134–35, 146. *See also* mobility; running
Walton, John: on the Los Angeles Aqueduct, 165n35. *See also* Los Angeles Aqueduct
Wang, Wei, 119–20
war: and "comfort," 91–92; and family, 105; waving one's penis as a gesture of, 52; as without end (or beginning), 80–81, 83–84, 92, 154. *See also* Vietnam
War Relocation Authority, 47–48
Washington, Booker T.: on driving, 130–31. *See also* mobility: Black
water, 70–71; and citizenship/belonging, 90; and connectivity, 67–68, 87; and death, 81–84, 87, 93–94, 167n51, 182n4; and family, 67–68, 90–91; freeways as, 151; and homeland, 87; and Paiute life, 49–50, 115, 168n63; and refugees, 173n58, 174n62; and the relocation of the Sherman Institute, 103–4; rights, 50, 163n21, 165n37, 168n72; and temporality, 86; theft of, 17, 22, 38–40, 48, 115, 163n21, 165n37; in Wang's "Apricot-Grain Cottage," 120. *See also* drought; floods

Watts Rebellion, 14–15, 172n26
weaponization: of dogs, 58, 63; of kinship, 105–6, 117
Westad, Odd: on Vietnam and a new Left, 75
white flight, 32
white supremacy, 34–35; and Los Angeles, 10, 159n23, 164n23; and the Vietnam War, 72–74, 170n18
Williams, Harry: on water and life, 49. *See also* water
Williams, Raymond: on the residual, 15
Wilson, Shawn: on ceremony, 113. *See also* ceremony
women of color feminism, 11–14, 25, 64, 109–13, 120, 135, 160n34
Workman, Boyle: on Los Angeles real estate development, 39
Wynter, Sylvia, 5; on Columbus, 158n12; on the human, 155n2. *See also* Columbus, Christopher

Yamashita, Karen Tei, 6, 12–13, 15, 149, 154; character-creation of, 43; childhood of, 40; on fiction, 16; *Tropic of Orange*, 1–4, 17, 22–26, 40–54, 56–57, 62, 64, 147
Yellow Peril, 10, 88, 164n26
Young Lords, 74

Zamora, Lois Parkinson: on entropic time, 144. *See also* entropy; temporality
Zink, Amanda: on the portrayal of Indigenous women, 111; on race and motherhood, 107
Zoroastrianism, 2, 155n4

Pacharee Sudhinaraset is Assistant Professor of English at New York University.

www.ingramcontent.com/pod-product-compliance
Lightning Source LLC
Chambersburg PA
CBHW061254230426
43665CB00027B/2946